Critical Acclaim for
TRUE BLUE: The Oxford Boat Race Mutiny

"The constitutional struggles, cultural misunderstandings and unrelenting pressure make this much more than a story about sportsmen'
Sunday Times

'A gripping story of intrigue and counter-intrigue amid heightened emotions'
Daily Telegraph

'Fascinating . . . It is all completely compulsive stuff'
Sunday Telegraph

'A brilliant and compelling account'
Donald Macdonald, *Guardian*

'Stirring stuff . . . High drama, no adjectives spared, the last laugh and the last crushing word to the forces of loyalty and light . . . Great stuff'
Observer

'A revealing account . . . a gripping read'
Mail on Sunday

'The ultimate inside story . . . You don't have to be a wetbob to enjoy this amazing tale of mutiny on the river'
Harry Carpenter

'*True Blue* is a real page-turner, the story of a fantastic fight-back against all the odds. Nervous readers may need a tranquiliser for the last four chapters'
John Bertrand

Also by Daniel Topolski

MUZUNGU: ONE MAN'S AFRICA
TRAVELS WITH MY FATHER: SOUTH AMERICA
BOAT RACE: THE OXFORD REVIVAL

Also by Patrick Robinson

BORN TO WIN (with John Bertrand)
CLASSIC LINES
DECADE OF CHAMPIONS
THE GOLDEN POST

DANIEL TOPOLSKI
WITH PATRICK ROBINSON

TRUE BLUE

THE OXFORD BOAT RACE MUTINY

BANTAM BOOKS
TORONTO · NEW YORK · LONDON · SYDNEY · AUCKLAND

TRUE BLUE:
THE OXFORD BOAT RACE MUTINY
A BANTAM BOOK : 0 553 50539 4

Originally published in Great Britain by Doubleday,
a division of Transworld Publishers Ltd

PRINTING HISTORY
Doubleday edition published 1989
Bantam Books edition published 1990
Bantam edition reprinted 1990
Bantam edition reprinted 1995
Bantam edition reissued 1996

Bantam Books are published by Transworld Publishers Ltd,
61–63 Uxbridge Road, Ealing, London W5 5SA,
in Australia by Transworld Publishers (Australia) Pty Ltd,
15–25 Helles Avenue, Moorebank, NSW 2170,
and in New Zealand by Transworld Publishers (NZ) Ltd,
3 William Pickering Drive, Albany, Auckland.

Printed and bound in Great Britain by
Cox & Wyman Ltd, Reading, Berkshire.

In memory of 'Jumbo', the truest Blue of all

PHOTOGRAPHIC ACKNOWLEDGEMENTS

The Publishers have made every attempt to contact the owners of the photographs and cartoons appearing in this book. In the few instances where they have been unsuccessful they invite the copyright holders to contact them direct.

Photographs:
Donald Macdonald and family: *by kind permission of the Guardian*
Clark training with Oriel College: *by kind permission of Times Newspapers Ltd*
Cadoux-Hudson, Clark, Clay, Fish, Gish, Gleeson, Hull, Huntingdon, Leach, Penny, Ridgewell, Screaton, Stewart, Ward: *by kind permission of Richard Burnell*
Lobbenberg and Stewart: *by kind permission of Times Newspapers Ltd*
Trials clash: *by kind permission of Times Newspapers Ltd*
Gleeson at stroke: *by kind permission of the Daily Telegraph*
The finish: *London Express News and Feature Services*
Other photographs courtesy of Donald Macdonald

Cartoons:
Mel Calman: *copyright Mel Calman*
Rex Audley: *reproduced by kind permission of the Sunday Telegraph*
Mark Boxer: *reproduced by kind permission of the Tatler*
Ben Swains: *reproduced by kind permission of the Daily Telegraph*
George Gale: *reproduced by kind permission of the Daily Telegraph*

CONTENTS

FOREWORD
THE BOAT RACE

With the possible exception of an Olympic marathon, or a World Boxing Championship, the race between the Dark and Light Blues represents the most brutal, harsh and uncompromising struggle in all of sport. They call it simply the Boat Race, and the oarsmen of England's two great universities have rowed the Race on the London Tideway almost every year since 1836. In general the only acceptable excuse ever advanced for a postponement has been a world war. It has remained essentially unchanged since it was first rowed on the River Thames in 1829, just fourteen years after the Battle of Waterloo, in the reign of King George IV.

The Duke of Wellington was Prime Minister when the oarsmen of Oxford University first raced the oarsmen of Cambridge University. This was an England devoid of compassion; an England in which eight-year-old children worked in factories, in which a poor man could still be hanged for stealing a sheep; an England which still condoned the slave trade. Much was expected of England's sportsmen and standards were pretty brutal. The Heavyweight Boxing Champion James (Deaf) Burke, around this time fought ninety-nine rounds at St Albans, in a bareknuckle bout which lasted well over three hours and caused the death of his opponent Simon Byrne.

In character the Boat Race has never changed. It remains today the same murderous test which had the riverside crowds up and roaring in their thousands back in the 1830s – among them the Heavyweight Champion himself, the son of a Thames waterman. Now 150 million people around the world watch the race on television every year.

It is a four-and-a-quarter mile marathon – three times longer than a regular modern Olympic summer course. The route is invariably windswept and cold, the waters rough and dangerous, with a fast tide bearing the oarsmen often into 'sinking water'. A far cry from the six-lane still-water courses of the international regatta circuit. It is rowed at the back end of winter on the surging spring tide in late March on a Saturday, on the wide urban River Thames between Putney and Mortlake, the stretch to the west of the city, which divides the counties of Surrey and Middlesex.

It is one of the world's great endurance tests, and it takes its participants to the brink of total collapse and sometimes beyond. Old oarsmen once believed it could knock five years off a man's life just to have taken part. It demands courage, strength, skill, superb fitness and dedication. A fit athletic oarsman with two or three years of solid training experience behind him requires a further intensive seven months of hard preparation, all through the worst weeks of the English winter. Ambulances are waiting at the finish.

The race demands a near fanatical willpower and contempt for the opposition. But perhaps above all it demands team spirit and a selflessness that recognizes no barrier. The Boat Race is a pure throwback to the old bareknuckle days of sport.

It represents the ultimate challenge to the hard, quiet gladiators of world rowing, one of the few Olympic events in which there is still no possibility of any monetary reward whatsoever. Those who seek the grim, private glory of participation in the Boat Race have been called The Last Amateurs. They are men whose pride it is to absorb the self-imposed punishment of the race. They are men who may sometimes dread the forthcoming battle because of the anticipated pain. But they are also men who need the chance to prove themselves in a competition which few can tolerate.

The race attracts American oarsmen too, who regard acceptance to study a course at the University of Oxford as a great honour, offering too the chance to take that privileged step to row in the

Dark Blue boat against the Light Blues of Cambridge. For it is a step which will set them apart for the rest of their lives.

Some of these American students make the pilgrimage to Oxford with quite illustrious collegiate and international careers behind them – names going back thirty years, like Rubin, Spencer, Howell, Fink, Trippe, Bockstoce, Sawyier, Shealy, Brown and Reininger. They all came, and they all pulled a Dark Blue oar from Putney to Mortlake. Most of them brought their own brand of humour and honour; their cheerful brashness comfortably absorbed by the Oxford coaches, who were happy to introduce an invigorating culture shock to their British squads in return for the strength and guts of the confident big Americans.

Such Americans do not give up. They do not collapse. And they never shirk the ultimate sacrifice the Race demands. In fact Americans have a very good record of success in the Boat Race, and many English oarsmen who have competed with them look back fondly on their days at Oxford and treasure the strong transatlantic friendships they made for the rest of their lives.

In 1986 Oxford suffered their first defeat in eleven years. The ten Dark Blue victories in a row between 1976 and 1985 had been an all-time record and came after sixty desolate years in which Oxford had won but twelve times.

It was Daniel Topolski, a former Boat Race winner, who had suddenly and dramatically changed the world for Oxford.

During his historic reign, the Dark Blues broke the Boat Race course record three times and smashed every other record along the way. They boated the heaviest crew ever, the biggest man ever, the first woman (cox) ever and the most successful oarsman ever (Boris Rankov with his famous six victories). And they provided oarsmen and coaches for British and overseas Olympic and world championship teams winning gold, silver and bronze medals. The 1981 Oxford crew beat the British National Eight at Henley to win the prized Grand Challenge Cup.

Heroism and brilliance walked hand-in-hand during these most glorious years. The conflicts with the Light Blues were brutal, none more awesome than the six-foot victory in 1980 – Oxford battling to hold their lead with their bow man a barely conscious passenger for the final mile.

But the defeat of 1986 was devastating. The crew would not remain as others have, close-knit and forever friends. For Oxford's apparent invincibility was at an end and excuses and scapegoats were needed to ease the pain. Oxford's Boat Race men were to pay a heavy price for that one defeat after so many years of triumph. Now a new, insidious mood replaced the traditional brotherhood.

In the bleak winter of 1986–87, in the aftermath of the defeat, a group of international-class Americans came to Oxford and made it clear that they did not particularly like what they saw. They considered the harshness of the winter training schedule unnecessary. They considered the Oxford chief coach Daniel Topolski to be a demonic martinet of the river, with too much influence and outdated techniques. And they considered the holder of the ancient office of President of the Oxford University Boat Club, the quiet Scotsman, Donald Macdonald, to be below standard as an oarsman and essentially a man to be pushed aside.

They were supremely confident of themselves, of their talent and their value to Oxford. But their actions that winter were unprecedented. The 850-year-old seat of English learning was split asunder by a political battle that raged across the international air waves and through the media, as the suave and accomplished raiding party from the U.S.A. fought for control of the University Boat Club.

At the centre of it all stood the unsuspecting figures of coach Topolski and the Oxford President Macdonald. At first unprepared, they found themselves ensnared in a web of deceit, threat and counterthreat which seemed certain to obliterate the entire constitution of the Boat Club.

But as the conflict grew harder, the unassuming Macdonald grew tougher, and with scores of newspaper, television and radio personnel laying siege to Oriel Square, he began a momentous and sometimes heroic fightback.

At one stage he stood virtually alone, the only rock between total anarchy and years of tradition. He was assailed from every corner, and for a while he remained the sole guardian of the sacred trust among oarsmen which had held the Boat Club together for one-and-a-half centuries. But it was a trust that while strong and resolute in history and theory, was totally vulnerable in the face of what has become, in modern sport, something akin to warfare.

The battle made headlines both on the sports pages and front pages of England's national newspapers for weeks on end. Each night the story made the news all over the world. It made the front page of the *New York Times*. Macdonald himself was once phoned by an old friend in Tokyo to tell him he was headlines on the six o'clock evening news in Japan.

The Times ran the story one day over five columns on its front page under the headline 'Oxford Threaten To Use Reserves – As Crew Mutiny'. The *Daily Mail* devoted its entire news feature page to the uproar with a line over the top which read 'Behind The Gentlemanly Façade Of A British Legend' – and then in the biggest type used on that page : 'Mutiny Of The Oxford Yanks'.

The Oxford Mutiny, as it came to be known, caused rifts among friends that will never be healed. Senior figures at the university were appalled at the seditiousness of the battle, the intrigue, the dogged entrenchment of the principal parties, for months afterwards the university reverberated from the strife.

My own part was strictly that of an onlooker. But the Boat Race has always had a kind of mystical attraction for me, since long ago in the early Sixties when I covered the event for the *Daily Express*. It was a part of my career which was distinguished by my total lack of grasp of the finer points of the sport. I also, on one near-legendary occasion, thundered through the columns of 'The World's Greatest Newspaper' that Oxford 'were so bad they may as well not turn up for the race.' The five-length victory of the Dark Blues that year reduced me to a figure of fun which lives to this day in some unforgiving rowing circles.

Nonetheless I managed to retain a few staunch friendships from those days, but only among those oarsmen who have been blessed with a sense of humour. I still receive wildly amusing letters from time to time from Oxford's American strokeman who blew my 1963 forecast out of the water. His crew mate Miles Morland, the 1965 President, was a regular dinner companion during the many years we both lived in New York.

Another old friendship that still survives is with a young Isis oarsman of 1966, who swears to God he once told me that Oxford were rowing with special oars with holes in the blades to cut down water resistance. And that I printed it! I simply could not have believed him . . . but on a slow news day . . . .

The name of that jester was Daniel Topolski. He went on to row twice in the Boat Race for Oxford, winning once, and became a writer and travel photo-journalist, a world champion oarsman and Olympic coach. He also became the most successful Oxford coach of all time. Which was something of a surprise to me, for Daniel had never seemed the sort of man destined to become a crew-cutted drill sergeant of the river. Daniel, with his fashionably long hair, his charm, his *bon viveur* life-style and beautiful girlfriends, his penchant for rough travelling in far-flung exotic places, always struck me as being more at home in expensive King's Road restaurants than a gymnasium. But I was wrong. He is forty-three-years-old now and still looks more at home in a Chelsea restaurant; but his legend will live in the Oxford University Boathouse forever.

I left journalism and formed my own publishing company in the United States. I also wrote books about my first love – racehorses – and then, in 1985, co-authored a book called *Born to Win*, the autobiography of the great Australian helmsman John Bertrand, skipper of *Australia II* which won the America's Cup.

In the four years following the triumph of *Australia II* I was asked to write several biographies by various publishers and literary agents, but none of them had the personal sense of heroism that unfailingly catches my attention. Nothing was so moving that it would inspire me to devote months and months to the writing of another book. Until that is I began to follow the saga of the Oxford Mutiny. Months later, I was talking to Daniel Topolski about an entirely different subject when I just happened to remark: 'I suppose by now you've nearly finished a book about the Mutiny.'

'Well no. I've thought about it,' he said, 'but my heart isn't really in it and I haven't honestly pushed that much. The whole thing was so bruising I still haven't properly got over it. Even now I wake up in a cold sweat about it.'

'That bad?'

'Bad beyond your wildest dreams,' he said.

We talked about it for a while and I could see the scars went very deep.

'How does Macdonald feel now?' I asked. 'Just as badly, I think.' said the coach. 'I don't think any of us will ever really get over it.'

It took me six weeks to persuade him that the full story should be told, that we could write it together. With Donald Macdonald, he gathered together the mountain of documentation that tabled the events of 1986–87 at the university. I was astonished by the unfolding story as I pored over the cuttings, letters, and the minutes of Boat Club meetings. It was like gazing at the innermost workings of a monastery, attending confidential discussions to which no outsider had ever been admitted before.

At one point, as the crisis was reaching its peak, the President had called Dan to tell him that he was close to breaking point. Topolski told him: 'If you quit, I'll go too and they can have it. But if you stay and fight them, I'll fight the bastards with you.'

Those were the words that saved the traditions of the OUBC. They were the words of Dan Topolski, the only man who could ever tell this true, and most devastating sports story of our times.

Patrick Robinson.

CHAPTER ONE

A FANATIC IN THE ATTIC

He made up for his initial lack of skill and finesse by fanatical commitment and a fiendish aggression. The prostrate figure of Donald Macdonald, half-dead with the fury of his effort in a race, caused one coach to warn: 'I do not especially want a death on my hands.'

He had been waiting for five days now. Once again Mr Macdonald stood alone outside number 37 Albert Road, shivering in the bleak north-east wind which swept up the River Tees. For an insurance inspector, with a pregnant wife and sixteen-month-old baby, he was showing scant regard for the strict rules of punctuality which govern the daily workings of the dour and fastidious business of underwriting policies, as his watch ticked resolutely on beyond the hour of nine a.m.

Again he scanned the deserted street, felt the chill of the wind through his heavy tan Burberry, and paced along the front of his large, terraced Victorian house. He was a big man of enormous strength, a lean 6ft 2ins, with big hands and a shock of dark curly hair. He had a gentle studious face with deep brown eyes which he now cast heavenwards to the December skies in a gesture of exasperation and despair.

He walked a few more yards to his car. 'Perhaps they don't even bother to contact you at all if they don't think you are good enough,' he thought. 'Perhaps at twenty-seven I'm just too old. Damn. I probably never stood a chance anyway. I was only testing myself. So why has it suddenly become my whole life?'

He started the car and drove slowly forward, just as the first waves of sleet began to sweep across the windscreen. Suddenly, he sensed a movement in the doorway of number 29. A grey-uniformed figure was hurrying to the next house. Mr Macdonald wound down the window, and called out, 'Morning. Anything for number 37?'

The postman fumbled in his bag and pulled out a big bulky buff envelope. 'Just this, sir,' he said in a broad North Yorkshire brogue, and hurried away into the now-driving gale. The insurance man clutched the package, stared at the return address in the top left-hand corner. Here was his destiny, and he placed it meticulously on the passenger seat. Then he drove on to the offices of the General Accident Insurance Company at Bishopton in Stockton-on-Tees. It was a drive he would never forget. Sometimes he would look at the road, sometimes he would gaze at the package, which mockingly guarded its fateful secret. Years later he would recall ruefully, 'It was a drive to work of the most exquisite torture.'

He pushed his normal Tuesday morning workload to the back of his mind. The package on the front seat now assumed fantastical proportions – a possible state pardon to a man on death row. There was no life beyond the package. He drove through those drab, hopeless provincial streets of north-east England as if the elixir of life lay just a few inches from his left hand. He parked the car carefully, forcing himself to stay calm, and fought to control his own dread of failure should there be rejection beyond the seal. Thank God he had told no one, except Ruth, not even his father, not even his brother. And now, he told himself, I'm going to open the package, right here in the General Accident car park.

He stared at the return address, Mansfield College, University of Oxford, and he ripped open the envelope. Inside were all of the essays he had written, and written, and written, often through the night, pages and pages, months of work, extolling the virtues of T.S. Eliot, examining the tragedies of Shakespeare, of Hamlet, the lonely Prince of Denmark, of the grotesquely-betrayed King Lear; and perhaps the most demanding of all, the soul-searching studies of the strengths of man in extreme danger and isolation, so beautifully penned by the Polish author Joseph Conrad.

'They've sent the whole lot back,' he whispered in near silent anguish. 'Everything I wrote.' And the dull sense of foreboding descended like a cloak upon him. 'I know one thing,' he muttered, 'I shall find it hard to admit to anyone what I tried to do. Where's the letter? Surely they must have written to me. But perhaps they don't bother if you're so bad. They just return your papers.' And then he found it, typed upon stiff ivory-coloured stationery, from the head of the department of English literature, Mansfield College.

'You will already have heard,' it began erroneously, 'the good news that the college is offering you a place to read English from next October. . . .' A vision of bountiful libraries, of academic pastures, of discussion and study. It all cascaded through his brain. 'A place to read English. . . .'

Even as he read the words which would change his life, he imagined a far-distant river and the mighty whack of eight oars slicing into the water, the rush of the bubbling slipstream beneath the speeding shell. He tensed to the burst of ferocious energy surging through his arms and chest – and in his mind he clutched once more the great wooden handle in his hands, and the cries of the coxswain rang through his brain: '*In-three! In-two! In-one! Go!!*'

And now at last, he thought, those blades are coloured Dark Blue, Oxford Blue, the colour of learning, the colour of culture. The colour of the Titans of the River, 'Dan Topolski's fabled Oxford University Boat-Race crew'.

All alone in the General Accident car park, Macdonald half-expected to feel the pain, the dreadful pain of killer racing that he had once known, and to which he had been addicted.

He dumped the entire contents of the package on the floor of the car, and, still with imperious disregard for the traditions of punctuality in the insurance business, he hurtled out of the car park, heading back home to number 37 Albert Road, Eaglescliffe, to share his triumph. By now it was after nine-thirty, and as he drove out through the sullen Victorian streets in this town of the once-burgeoning industrial north-east, he knew he would miss the place. The people were so warm and friendly – for despite their reputation for pragmatism, they were instantly hospitable and full of charm and northern frankness.

Gazing down the river towards Middlesbrough, he could see only the great iron skeletons of disused cranes still aiming skywards from the old derelict shipyards which once spelled such hope and profit, and now signified only decay and the far-lost prosperity of another age. The grime of the place, showing gloomily between the facile concrete and glass attempts of the 1960s to brighten up the old town was always a source of mild sadness to him. But not on this day. Instead he envisioned once more a bright but fading picture of a great colonial house in a sunlit garden, tumbling with the glorious red, yellow, and orange flowers of the canna plant.

Singapore, in the final days of the Empire, the late 1950s and early 60s, the island city of his birthplace and childhood, the paradise of his earliest memories. What a home it had been, one of the loveliest homes in a land of grand homes – wide cool verandahs, spectacular tropical fruits, tennis courts, Chinese servants, and enormous windows with carved shutters for the cooling breezes. Standing solitary on an imposing ridge it had been the last line of defence against the Japanese. The Madras sappers and miners had managed to hold out for a week before the surrender. After Field Marshall Slim's men drove the Japanese out, it became the home of the manager of the New Zealand Insurance Company – the biggest overseas insurance operation of its type in South-East Asia – the lord of which was his own father, Captain Ian Macdonald, late of the Rajputana Rifles, 2nd Indian Airborne Division. A Henley finalist, man of steel.

Captain Macdonald and his beautiful wife, Mary, were among the last of the colonial empire, living to the full that hard-working but rewarding life.

Everyone called his father Tuan Bezar (the equivalent of Hong Kong's Taipan) – and he could remember the loud threats of 'Will tell Tuan for sure!' as he raced with his first cousin Gordon for the cover of the lacy fronds of the casuarina grove, shouting with laughter. It was carefree laughter which he had not known since. At the time it never occurred to the oldest son of Captain Macdonald that any other form of life existed.

Leaving Singapore in 1964 at the age of eight had been a truly traumatic experience for him and he still remembered weeping tears of desolation as he said goodbye to Gordon and his Chinese friends and flew to England on an old Comet Four, never to return.

It was the kind of upheaval that had been commonplace in his family for more than a hundred years. The Macdonalds were Scottish through and through, tracing their ancestry back directly to the survivors of the massacre at Glencoe. By the middle of the nineteenth century, while maintaining strong roots in Edinburgh and in Stirling, they were mostly to be found adventuring in the Far East, making and sometimes losing fortunes in spices and textiles, tea and property.

Donald's maternal Scottish grandfather had traded in Java and his Australian-born mother had lived there. There were also countless cousins and other relatives running vast sheep stations in New South Wales. In Sydney they still talk of the incorruptible Rhodes Scholar and Queen's Counsel, the Honourable Sir Vernon Treatt, Donald's great-uncle, Leader of the Opposition in the NSW State Government and later appointed Chief Commissioner of Sydney to reorganize the city's chaotic civil service. The Macdonalds were then and still are a tough, resolute and resourceful clan, with friends all over the world – particularly in the east.

'Homecoming' for Donald was a severe shock. His father now worked in the City of London – and the eight-year-old former 'playboy' of the tropics found himself in a world which bore no relation to anything he had known before. The sight of people wearing overcoats and caps amazed him. The cold took his breath away.

Like many a well-born colonial Scotsman before him, young Donald was enrolled in a stern boarding school back in the old country. In his case it was Morrison's Academy, which was established in 1860 in the small granite country town of Crieff in Perthshire, the very gateway to the Highlands. There he learned to cope with the cold, to run in the foothills, to play Rugby football on bleak wet winter days, and to find independence from the family and the servants he had always known.

He emerged from the academy ten years later, at ease with the local farmers and Scottish businessmen and with the world. He had too a finely developed love of poetry and literature which would stay with him for the rest of his life. He was a popular fellow, mainly due to his polite, unassuming and trusting manner, and his keen, droll wit.

Donald was, above all, a Scotsman, born of the blood, with a predeliction for wearing the elegant tartan kilt of the Macdonalds, and for playing the bagpipes, that most mournful of instruments which seems to sound a cry from the very heart of that grim and ancient land. Following the Macdonald's strong tradition of business and enterprise, their eldest son joined Lloyd's of London, headquarters of the world's insurance markets.

Now, as he crossed the River Tees on his way home, his thoughts were still far from the rusting cranes on either bank. Further down the banks were more rural, more like a river should be, with the stream running quite quickly towards the centre. 'That's the place to be,' he muttered, 'just slightly left, cut the next bend tighter, and then hit the stream again. Probably worth about one-and-a-half-boat lengths.' His mind wandered back four years to the time of his last serious race. Here, three miles from Eaglescliffe, on this morning of dreams, he was back in 1978, in the London Rowing Club Eight, pulling the number six oar with a fierce devotion, fighting for victory on the London Tideway at Putney.

If he thought hard enough, he could remember the first day as a twenty-year-old that he ever reported to the club, at the suggestion of his father, and the cheerful welcome he instantly received from the men who rowed there. He had never been in a racing shell in his life, but they adopted him as a friend and a potential crewmate without hesitation. If they needed any convincing his demonstration of strength on the ergometer rowing machine was decisive, and within forty-eight hours he was actually in a boat, with a chance to row in a competitive Eight.

The first five seconds of his first-ever trial were sufficient. He was captivated, a total prisoner of the river and of the cameraderie of the oarsmen, from that moment on. The thrill of a fast boat cutting through the water was like an aphrodisiac. Only stronger. No thrill, no sensation had ever affected him as the vicious sweet opium of crew racing. It affected his every waking hour. He fought for a place in the boat, he trained to become super-fit, he ran circuits, pumped iron. And all day, every day, the thought of the boat was with him.

Within weeks he had progressed from a rough, raw number 2 man in the bow of the boat, into a rough but less raw number 6 man in the engine room. He made up for his initial lack of skill and finesse by a fanatical commitment, and a fiendish aggression which even surprised himself. He pulled so hard he found himself on the verge of total collapse at the end of every outing.

Within a few months he had actually moved into the London Rowing Club; he rented a room in the attic above the bar. He lived for the water, rowed in the mornings before work, rowed in the evenings after work. After a few weeks he arranged for his younger brother Hugh to join him as a resident at the club. By now they were both in the insurance business and they went to work in the

City each morning on Hugh's motor bike. And while Hugh would never become quite the fanatic that Donald now was, he was still very keen and rowed with his brother whenever he could.

By 1978 they were the mainstays of the crew – Donald pulling away with a deranged dedication as the London Eight stormed from victory to victory in regattas up and down the river. He was allowed to train with the National Lightweight Squad which was based at the club, and he drove his body harder and harder in an attempt to stay up with the best in England. One coach, alarmed at the fury with which Donald attacked the circuit training, called him over and sternly warned him that he, as coach, did not especially want a death on his hands.

The prostrate figure of Donald Macdonald, half-dead with effort after a race, was a regular sight in the dressing room of LRC. There was something of the noble savage about Captain Macdonald's son, and he sought victory in these early days of his love affair with the sport with a near-lunatic hatred of defeat, despite his initial lack of finesse.

I was a member of that National Lightweight crew and I remember Donald. He was always eager to learn, and at times quizzed us remorselessly for advice. During one summer, late in the season after the world championships, we combined with Donald and some of his crewmates to race a series of regattas in the West Country. We won everywhere we went. But soon afterwards, Donald disappeared from the London rowing scene and I was quite surprised to learn he had gone to live in Scotland.

There had been one race on the Thames in 1978 in which Donald and Hugh rowed together in a païr. So confident were they of victory they invited their parents to watch the race. On the day, they won every one of the heats easily – but in the final, disaster struck. A passing ferry almost swamped them, when they were in a clear lead, and, not being great watermen, they filled up with half-a-ton of ballast and were beaten by the narrowest of margins.

The usual family commiserations were in full swing when Donald went berserk. He ranted and raved, shouted and trembled, waved his arms, swore and blasphemed. He was white with anger. 'I think I used language on that day that my mother had never heard before,' he recalls. 'I was like a madman. But it was just the defeat. I could not take it.'

Involvement in the sport at this high-class club level heightened his interest in the annual Oxford–Cambridge battle on the Thames which started right in front of his bedroom window at the rowing club. On the big day of the year on the Tideway, the silent thoughtful figure of Donald Macdonald could be seen staring from the attic across the water to the start, the same thought churning over and over in his mind . . . 'Could I do that? Could I, one day, row for Oxford University?'

And yet, in a sense, life ultimately overtook him. He met Ruth on the steps of London Rowing Club. They married in 1979, and after a honeymoon in an idyllic cottage, owned by his parents in Stirling, they elected to bow out of the London rat-race, and to move north of the border to live in the land of his forefathers. Donald secured a job with General Accident in the town of Stirling, and Ruth accepted a demanding post as Training Officer for the Regional Health Board in the same place. Within three years a progressively ambitious Donald seized a promotion in Stockton, and they moved again.

And now, here he was in Stockton-on-Tees – another provincial man in a provincial job, struggling on the lower rungs of a modest corporate ladder. At the age of twenty-seven, like so many others, he now felt the stirring of unfulfilled hopes, of dreams that had slipped away. There must, he thought, be thousands of young men about to enter their thirties who felt much the same. But how many of them dared still to cherish his powerful ambitions in the field of literature and in becoming a top-class oarsman? These were the ambitions of school-leavers, youths of eighteen. How could he have kept them so private for all of those years? And how could they have burned so strongly in his subconscious, and for so long?

In addition he also sought the security of a British home, from which his wife and children would never be uprooted – the old solid yearnings of the children of the Empire in which vast distances and massive family upheavals were, for two centuries, regarded as irrelevant among the hardy breed of people who held it all together. For as long as he could remember he had sought to provide that sense of permanence that he had missed since the departure from Singapore twenty years before.

It was Stockton that had first inspired him to break out of the mundane career that stretched before him. From the moment when he had first parked the little company car in the little car park and walked with a thousand other office workers into his place of employment up on the second floor, he had thought: 'My God, I am really one of them now. Everything I have always dreaded, trapped in a job which leaves me entirely unfulfilled. I have brought my family to this point and here I may stay if I am not very, very careful. Could I ever have a mansion in Singapore, with vast lawns? And where is the river that once made me feel so alive, and gave me such hope?

'They are all slipping away. And I must not let them escape. Because I can still make it. Ruth has challenged me to try, and since she does not care about the financial hardship, I *will* do it.'

For several months Donald fought for a place as an undergraduate. All day long he worked at the General Accident Insurance Company, all afternoon he worked for his insurance examinations, the ones which would take him another small step up the ladder should he fail in his ultimate quest for higher learning and athletic glory at Oxford.

At night he worked on the writings of Eliot, Shakespeare and Conrad. He sought the advice of his friend, the local parish vicar Zolile M'Bali, who was born in the South African township of Soweto and who had fought a far tougher battle for a decent chance than the one Donald now faced. The Rev. M'Bali and his wife were both Oxford graduates and Mrs M'Bali agreed to coach him in the subtleties of passing the Oxford entrance exams. In addition he needed to pass a French examination and he enlisted the help of another local lady, Mrs Janet Atkinson, who had read Modern Languages at Oxford, to guide him through this critical section of the Oxford entry.

He never stopped working. Not for one day, from the moment he decided to try in January of 1982 until the moment he walked out of the examination room at the local school nine months later. He had in truth carried a work-load which would have daunted a less determined man, sometimes he would stumble up to bed at two and three a.m. Once he never made it and Ruth found him paralyzed with exhaustion, slumped over his desk at six in the morning. Occasionally he thought he could not take it any more, and that he must give himself another year. But he had no time. Even if he made Oxford, even if he made the Oxford rowing crew, he would already be the oldest man ever to row in the Boat Race. He could not wait. He had to pass that exam so he just went on working with a desperation which Ruth had not seen in him before.

At last he had his result, and there were a million things for him to do. The house to be sold, his resignation to send to the GA, bank managers to meet, loans to be arranged, a new house to be bought in Oxford.

They were on their way again – to Oxford this time where Donald expected, surely with good reason, to find a hard-working but gentle peace. Leaving Stockton would not be the same emotional wrench as leaving Singapore had been. But Stockton would hold many memories, mostly of people, many of whom would remain lifelong friends; after all both of the Macdonald children, Ian and Alexandra, were born there.

He stopped the car outside the house and stepped out onto the same icy Albert Road which had, just one hour before, seemed like the Valley of Death. Now it was bathed in the warm glow of victory – and Donald shot through the front door of number 37, yelling like a banshee, and scattering his precious essays behind him.

He grabbed Ruth and danced a neat little Scottish reel around the kitchen, knocked over two chairs, sent a frying pan flying, and scattered a box of corn-flakes all over the floor. But no one was 'telling Tuan' this time. There was only Ruth to share his joy, and she flung her arms around him and told him that in her view this was the major opportunity of his life, and that minor details like being broke should not stand in the way of his Oxford degree in English literature.

Together they read the letter from John Creaser, head of English literature at Mansfield College. Its contents were a source of great pride – Donald had done so well in the literary critique section, in which he was required to examine a poem called 'Fencing the Uplands' by Charles Tomlinson, that Professor Creaser was moved to write: 'This was one of the two outstanding essays we read on that poem . . . exceptionally acute and accurate in its detailed analysis.'

The excitement was overwhelming but then Donald looked aghast at his watch. What could he possibly be doing at home at this hour of the morning? He charged back out through the front door and drove all the way back to Stockton, his little Ford moving like a Ferrari. He hit his desk running shortly after 11 a.m. One way or another, the rules of punctuality in the world of Scottish insurance were more or less in smithereens for him at this stage. But for financial reasons he would have to keep his job until the very last minute before he left for Oxford.

The New Year of 1984 seemed to arrive quickly, and before it was more than a few days old Donald steeled himself for a phone call he felt he must now make. The recipient was often on the phone and the line was constantly busy. But finally, he got through and I picked it up with my usual curt: 'Hello'.

'Er, I wonder if I might speak to Mr Topolski?'

'This is Daniel speaking.'

'Oh, er, Daniel. I was hoping you might remember me. Donald Macdonald. No 6 London Rowing Club 1978.'

The conversation that followed was terse and to the point. He wanted to know whether he could do any work before coming up to Oxford so he would be better prepared and I told him the amount of weight training and circuit training he would be required to undertake if he was to have any chance at all of making the Blue Boat.

Donald gulped and I remember him muttering something about being able to manage around twenty squat-jumps at this stage of fitness (this by the way would probably cause an unfit person to collapse).

'Fine,' I replied. 'Work that up to around eighty.'

'I'm sorry, Dan, I didn't quite get that. How many did you say?'

''Bout eighty.'

'*Eighty*,' he yelled. 'I thought you said eighteen. Jesus Christ!'

Anyway North Yorkshire's King of the Overkill went to work. He underwent a regime of training at a local gymnasium which would have put a marine commando in a rest home. Inside two weeks he had stretched and pulled just about every muscle in his back, and the more it hurt the harder he trained. Finally the pain levelled him and it took a specialist to put him right. Ruth was still massaging that back when he arrived at college eight months later. They sold the Ford and the house in Stockton, and bought a much smaller semi-detached in the more expensive vicinity of Oxford. There was £5,000 worth of change on which he proposed to support his family for four years as a supplement to his government grants.

The move south was chaotic. Donald, Ruth and the babies drove down the motorway in a battered old Beetle, and the furniture from the big Stockton house instantly filled every square inch of space in their new residence in Lime Road, Botley. It also filled the cellar, the attic, the front garden and half of the back garden. Friends and relatives rallied, and drove to Botley to remove some of the pieces. Then, leaving the Beetle behind, Donald set off on the train, alone, back to Stockton where he would stay with friends and continue to work and draw his salary for another six weeks. Every weekend he made the 360-mile round trip to be with his family. He finally came home to Oxford in the first week in October.

In fact he was there a week before term started and before reporting to his tutor, he reported to a place which had been for so long a dream, the big imposing home of Oxford rowing, the University Boat Club's historic headquarters on the River Isis.

He was not to know it, but he was walking into the lions' den, where a couple of dozen of the best college oarsmen in the world were fighting for the eight places in the crew I would select to face Cambridge the following spring. They were all younger than him, fitter than him, sharper than him; and on the surface about ten times more aggressive and determined than him. At least that's what you might think, without knowing much about Donald.

He walked in by himself and I said: 'Oh, hi Donald. Nice to see you.' I felt some members of the squad instantly bristle and look up to see who the stranger was. 'Christ! Daniel's called him "Donald" – they must be old friends, another opponent, another rival for my place.'

Right now as the trials were about to commence, this was one of the most competitive little arenas in the world.

Donald himself was a little overawed by the situation. He is by nature one of the most self-effacing people I have ever met. But here, faced with these apparently invincible athletes, he scarcely knew whether to hang on or run. There was the powerful Australian from Sydney, Graham Jones, veteran of three winning Oxford crews, former President of the Boat Club, and one of the strongest men ever to pull a Dark Blue blade. There was Bill Lang, from Wallingford, another 200lb Olympic-class man. Both of them had rowed in the powerful stern four of the record-breaking Oxford boat of 1984.

It was the first time Donald had ever been in the presence of such men in direct competition for a place in a boat. He had seen them occasionally. He had met them from time to time. But never as rivals. And that curious psychological make-up of his must have gone into overdrive, because as a sportsman, and even as a person, Donald is a nearly unique paradox. He will attempt to attain the unattainable, such as trying to become an undergraduate at the age of twenty-seven and then become the oldest man ever to row in the

Boat Race. Once having launched his attack, he then becomes assailed by self-doubt and feels that he must do more than any living human being has ever done in order to succeed. The prime example of that was his entry into Oxford. First he nearly killed himself by working all night every night, and then he produced an almost unnecessarily good result.

Fear of failure is what motivates him, as it does many high achievers. But I will never quite understand why quite ordinary, limited people often seemed so daunting to him. Is it just a natural humility or perhaps a lack of self-confidence? It makes him quite charming, and understandably popular with everyone, a state of grace he clearly enjoys. Politeness and consideration to others are second nature to him, and sometimes those who do not know him well interpret this as weakness, although it is far from that.

Anyway we settled down to training for the 1985 Boat Race and Donald was rather rusty. Compared to his potential colleagues his bladework was a little slow, and he carried his oar too far off the water, which caused him to be a fraction late with his stroke. This may not have showed up much in a regular crew but here at Oxford it was more obvious.

I raced him in a Four in a regatta in Reading, and while his performance showed me he was still a bit slow, I knew there was a lot more to come out of Donald Macdonald. He was a tough, gutsy competitor who loved to race, and while I knew his lack of race sharpness left him light on stamina, I knew that would improve. I also noticed he would row till he dropped, and that he would never give in.

I was actually quite surprised when he came to see me after that race, and asked very quietly and very privately: 'Dan, please tell me honestly, do I have a serious chance of ever making the Blue Boat?' I looked right at him and told him straight. 'Yes, Donald, you do have a chance. Give it time.' More than two years later, as we stood shoulder to shoulder in the middle of the most shocking crisis in the history of Oxford rowing, he turned to me and asked if I remembered that moment. And I told him I did. Vividly.

In the end Donald enjoyed a good first year at Oxford. He made the second crew Isis, and they beat the Cambridge second boat Goldie, easily in record time. Donald was then voted Secretary of the Boat Club, and during that summer his Four rowed a series of tremendous races in the Visitors' Cup at the Henley Royal Regatta.

He returned for the new university year in the October of 1985, an oarsman of considerably improved stature, commanding considerable respect from his peers.

As secretary he took it upon himself to greet and welcome any new undergrads who wanted to try out for the Blue Boat and on his first day he went down to the river to see who had arrived. The first person he came across was a huge American preparing to push out in a sculling boat. Chris Clark, spare man on the 1985 US world championship Eight, a 6ft 6ins Californian, had arrived. Donald hesitated just for a moment at the sight of the laconic blond-haired giant from the West Coast, noted the deep tan and the relaxed confident manner. He walked over and said quietly: 'Good afternoon. My name is Macdonald, are you Chris or George?'

The American smiled. 'George Livingstone is not here yet,' he said. 'Hi, I'm Chris.'

Donald Macdonald, already impressed at the sight of one of the giants of American rowing, leaned over to shake warmly the hand of the man who would become his most implacable enemy.

CHAPTER TWO

CALIFORNIA BLUES

This magnificence of sturdy power – chilled away by the frosty wind – of men who may not gather redundant fruitage from the earth, nor bask in dreamy benignity of sunshine, but must break the rock for bread, and cleave the forest for fire, and show some of the hard habits of the arm and heart.

John Ruskin, *The Stones of Venice*

It is 5,633 miles from Stockton-on-Tees to Newport Beach, California – a quarter of the way around the world. The difference in cultures between the two towns is enormous.

For many of the residents of England's depressed industrial areas in the north, the dawn of the 1980s was a period of no hope, no work and bitterly cold winters in which the elderly poor sometimes died of hypothermia. It was from this melancholy setting that Donald Macdonald moved south to take his place at Oxford.

Newport Beach, which sits on the permanently sun-kissed Pacific shore of California, America's most bounteous of easy-living states, shared not a single common factor with the rusting graveyards of Stockton's shipbuilding industry, save perhaps for one. They each contained one powerful oarsman who harboured a secret desire to row for Oxford University in the Boat Race of 1986.

Newport Beach is the home town of Chris Clark. Its position, thirty miles due south of downtown Los Angeles, makes it one of the most sought-after places on the coast, for those attracted to the somewhat languid, relaxed style of southern California. It sits on a bay in Orange County, so named because of the huge fruit crops produced there each year. Limes and lemons grow freely on tree-lined streets. And the great warm Pacific rollers thunder onto the ocean-side beaches, making it a haven for the local beach-gods, the bronzed surfers and the adoring teenage groupies who follow them before heading north up the freeway to take a crack at the film industry. Most of the waitresses in Beverley Hills have lifelong suntans.

Southern California has produced more than its fair share of top athletes – runners, swimmers, football players, baseball stars, and some oarsmen – although the big east coast schools of Pennsylvania, Yale, Harvard and Princeton still dominate rowing crews in America. The west coast has always been a little isolated from the mainstream, but the University of California at Berkeley has a successful history in international competition. More recently the Washington Huskies have been a major force in American rowing, while Orange Coast College has acted as an early training ground for the big universities. Their success though derives from the presence of one or two top-class coaches, like Dave Grant, rather than any special tradition. Most recently the Polish coach Xenon Babraj at UCLA has brought the Bruins up to the level of the big Ivy League teams. The popular San Diego Classic now attracts crews from all over the world for a weekend of 2000-metre six-lane sprint racing in early April.

Rowing in the States is based almost entirely on the universities while in Britain the clubs and national squads dominate with the exception of the big three universities of Oxford, Cambridge and London. While European rowers operate within a wide club net-work, American oarsmen aspiring to international status, but who have finished their studies, have to attach themselves to their old colleges or to the few clubs like Penn AC on the east coast. However, national camps for selection to the US teams are held after the sprint championships in the summer and are highly competitive and very intense.

Chris Clark was certainly an oarsman of international potential, whose Newport Beach parents lived in a pleasant wooden house near the water and were able to help him financially with his rowing career. At 6 feet 6 inches and 205lbs he was ideally built for rowing.

He took up the sport during his two years at Orange Coast in Costa Mesa, California, just a short distance up the bay from his parents' home. In 1980 he transferred to Stanford University to the north of LA, but what he really sought was a fast crew, and in 1981 he was on the move for the third time in four years, enrolling at the University of California at Berkeley. His rowing career there led him to a medal at the Pan-American Games and to the pre-Olympic squad preparing for the Los Angeles Games.

I met Chris Clark at the international regatta of Lucerne in Switzerland where he was on tour with the 'Dirty Dozen' team from America. This unusual team consisted mainly of high-class non-rowing athletes financed by philanthropist Alan Trant, who were attempting, as an experiment, to reach international class in an Eight under the watchful eye of US coach Al Rosenberg. There were two Pairs of more experienced men attached to this eccentric enterprise. Chris Clark was rowing a coxed Pair with fellow CAL oarsman, George Livingstone, and their friend, Fran Reininger, was rowing a coxless Pair.

Although they all failed to make the finals they showed good form. During the last day of the Regatta they sought me out, having heard that the Oxford coach was in Lucerne with the British Olympic Pair. They were very interested in coming to Oxford to pursue graduate studies and hopefully to row. I explained to them that there were no sporting scholarships in Britain but as long as they had the qualifications and the funds they should apply directly to the admissions department. They returned to America to try their luck in their national trials but they failed to make the Olympic team.

In 1985 Clark, who had acquired the nickname 'Heater', apparently because of his sudden bouts of temper, again missed out on a place in the US team but went as one of two 'spare men' to the world championships. For this role he was required to row on both sides of the boat. It was at this regatta, held in Hazewinkel, Belgium, that Chris enjoyed his finest moment in rowing. On the night before the finals one of the American Pair withdrew because of illness, and much to many people's surprise, instead of withdrawing the crew – because a Pair is a boat which needs a lot of practice – they summoned the 'Heater' to stand in and row the *Petite Finale* with a US Navy officer from Annapolis named Daniel Lyons. This race would decide the overall placings at the championships for the seventh to twelfth positions.

They rowed brilliantly, won it, and were now officially seventh in the world – a feat which occasionally in the future would cause poorly-briefed journalists to confuse Clark's performance in Belgium with that of an Olympic or world gold medallist. However it was an impressive effort which suggested potential and since I now knew he was coming to Oxford I looked forward to working with him. Unfortunately three further attempts to make the US team also ended in disappointment.

He came to Oxford University on a self-financed post-graduate course to do a Special Diploma in Social Studies, following in the footsteps of Fran Reininger who had stroked the Blue Boat to victory against Cambridge earlier in the year. He had the makings of a high calibre rower, very strong and smooth through the water and with a lot of what Californians call ego strength. I liked him though, thought he was good company, and he used to come and stay in my apartment in London.

On the other hand he was very hard to please. On that first day when Donald went down to the river to meet and welcome him, his opening observation was that, although he had been at the university for all of forty-eight hours, no one had been to see him yet, and he really found that a 'little strange'.

Donald suggested they meet that evening for a drink with the President of the Oxford University Boat Club, Bruce Philp, at a pub called The Turf at the back of New College. Bruce, it ought to be said, needed a bit of getting used to at the best of times. Here was one of Oxford's major characters. He weighed well over 220lbs at the time, several pounds too much for his 6ft 2½ins frame. This was due largely to his *bon-viveur* lifestyle, and his propensity to throw down six pints of best bitter ale at a sitting.

His head was crowned with a huge thatch of blond semi-punk hair, and he was one of the best-read men I ever met at Oxford. He loved *avant-garde* literature and music, and I never heard a poem mentioned from which he could not quote. He was also a world expert on traitors from Judas Iscariot to Anthony Blunt. His sense of humour was based upon the advanced teachings of Monty Python – except slightly more obscure. Bruce had the talent to reduce Donald to tears of uncontrollable laughter, however bad a situation was, but he was not everyone's cup of tea. He was a rather unkempt, gently eccentric figure, colourfully dressed and, as far as I was concerned, about the best company in Oxford.

He was also pretty deft with an oar. He had rowed and lost twice in the Boat Race for Cambridge as an undergraduate, and became the only man in history to row for both sides when he transferred to Oxford as a graduate in medical school. He had twice been a finalist at Henley Royal Regatta, in the Grand Challenge Cup and in the Stewards Challenge Cup. He was as strong as a stud bull and one of the more powerful oarsmen to have pulled an oar for the Dark Blues, a fact which was never obscured by his insistence upon wearing delicate pink and pastel-shaded candy-striped gym shoes on his unusually small feet.

He was reading a most demanding subject, clinical medicine, at Worcester College, and after losing over a stone in weight in training at my insistence, he helped Oxford to a dramatic victory in 1985, rowing in the number 3 seat. It was his first Boat Race win, and he was subsequently elected President of the OUBC by the University's college boat club captains. A few people had some misgivings about his appointment because of his unusual approach to practical matters like organization, but he was a most delightful man, strongly committed, and determined to do a good job.

However his work often kept him on all-night ward rounds at the hospital for he was deeply conscientious about his profession. In addition he had the great distinction, but also the added burden, of being President of the Blues Committee which organized all sport at Oxford. It all proved overwhelming, and the next three months until the crew was selected were perceived as one of the most undisciplined in living memory. Desperately overworked, Bruce was invariably late, chaotic and charming.

Donald recalls that first meeting with Clark with icy clarity. After initial introductions in the cosy bar of The Turf, Bruce, who was wearing a neat little set of communist badges from Moscow or Cuba, confided in mock seriousness to Clark, an invented family motto: 'The last thing I need is another friend.' The Californian frowned and made up his mind, there and then, that the President of Oxford was a true goof-off, just 'incredibly unfocussed'. Chris was baffled by Bruce. He had not come across anyone remotely like him in his life.

Fortunately Chris did have a good friend at Oxford who was also from Berkeley. George Livingstone was a very good oarsman, and he too was eager to row against Cambridge. At twenty-five George was an unmistakable gent. He was only slightly smaller than Clark, and took pains to affect an elegant, well-dressed appearance. He was the sartorial opposite of Bruce Philp. But he had a finely tuned sense of humour and while he in fact came from Sacramento, near San Francisco, you might more readily have placed him as some breed of well-born New Englander, possibly even a 'Havahd' man. George was a very accomplished and gutsy oarsman and he grew up in a rowing family. He was smoother and more subtle than Philp, but he was not as strong. He was on an Economics and Industrial Relations course and like Clark harboured ambitions to go into banking when he left university. George was a stone-cold certainty to earn a place in the Blue Boat at Oxford.

Over all of us hung the spectre of Graham Jones, a twenty-five-year-old from Sydney, Australia, unquestionably one of the best oarsmen at Oxford or Cambridge between 1983 and 1986. Graham was a shy, attractive, and very popular Rhodes Scholar at New College. He was also a superb athlete and had won national championships both in Australia and Great Britain. He rowed twice in the world championships, finishing sixth and seventh. He was a cultured and honourable Aussie, and he could beat anyone at anything to do with crew training. He loved rowing. It was in his blood. However after three winning Boat Races for Oxford, his Ph.D degree (D.Phil) in clinical biochemistry demanded his undivided attention. With agonizing reluctance he announced he would be unable to train with us for the annual battle with Cambridge.

It was a severe blow, but he resisted all efforts to persuade him back. The most he could offer was that if we really believed we faced defeat in March, he would consider coming in at the eleventh hour and attempt to save us on the day. Since Graham always kept himself super-fit, I accepted the situation, but with regret.

The role of the two Americans, Chris and George, and how they adapted to Oxford, now became extremely important, because without Graham they were the biggest men and the most experienced racers we had. However the only men with actual Boat Race experience were Bruce Philp and young Matt Thomas, and there were unusually few Isis oarsmen from the year before available to provide that continuity that had always been such a strength at Oxford. This year most of the oarsmen were new to the system.

Chris Clark was extremely angry at Graham Jones, and considered he was just playing hard-to-get. George Livingstone probably concurred in this view, but displayed none of Chris's outbursts of temper, nor any of his abrasiveness. In addition Clark developed an increasingly bad feeling about the President and the seemingly unstructured nature of the squad. He went AWOL on more than one occasion and did not reappear for days.

The first two months of training for that 1986 race were, to say the least, poorly organized, and this was highlighted by the difference in college rowing at Oxford and at American universities, where professional coaches run a single squad. At Oxford there are thirty-six separate college boat clubs all run, like the Boat Race squad, by volunteers, and their separate needs have to be taken into account. Inter-college Fours and Eights races also demanded loyalty from the university squad candidates.

I sensed that the two Americans often found themselves frustrated, mainly because they had believed that earning the lifelong honour of a Rowing Blue for Oxford was going to be easier – with a centrally-organized crew and professional coaches, coolly integrating them into the boat. They expected to turn up at the river for a couple of hours a day, and that would be that. They had all done university-level training years ago and felt they didn't need that again.

Well, at Oxford it simply does not always happen like that. A lot depends on commitment and discipline. A 'finished' Oxford boat is, on occasion, world class and is generally one of the fastest two or three British Eights. In terms of fitness and skill for a long-distance race they are the best. We are the last true amateurs, for there is not one thin dime of reward for the self-sacrifice and dedication. Only the honour. We achieve our results on the basis of mutual co-operation, self-help and personal discipline. No one is spoon-fed, for no one gets paid. So everyone has to pull his weight. Everyone helps with the boats, everyone understands how long it takes to get the crew on the water, and how long it takes to get packed up afterwards. For my part, I have devoted months and months of my time each year from 1973 onwards helping them to win.

Before 1973, when I took over as chief coach with a new team and a new programme, Oxford had won exactly twelve Boat Races since just before the First World War. Between 1974 and 1985 we won eleven out of twelve. For this I neither received, nor expected anything. I drove most days from my home in London to Oxford, Radley, Henley or Pangbourne, wherever we happened to be rowing. It was always over a hundred miles round-trip.

Each year I would have to be asked anew, by the incoming

President of the OUBC, to coach the crew. At that moment I was handed the responsibility for the training programme, selection, choosing a team of assistant coaches, and organizing the logistics of the London end of the preparation. In turn the President, who is always a student and a member of the squad, is supposed to co-ordinate the daily logistics and to communicate training details to the squad and other coaches. The President retains final authority, but he overrules his coaches at the risk of losing them.

I arranged board and lodgings, rest weekends, cooks, diets, and anything else I could to help the crew. I did it for my old University, I sometimes think, because I never got over losing to Cambridge when I rowed in the bow in 1968. No one hates losing more than I. In 1967, when we beat Cambridge by 3½ lengths, I rowed at number 7, at 157lbs the lightest man to row in the Boat Race in over twenty years. In those Oxford crews I rowed with three outstanding Americans, all from Yale, John Bockstoce, Josh Jensen, and Bill Fink, who remain good friends to this day.

My first crew as a coach in 1973 was stroked by a brooding manic powerhouse from Harvard, Dave Sawyier, an Olympic finalist. He was interesting to deal with, because he was at once challenging, rude, exciting, intensely competitive, disruptive and uncompromising. He nursed a deep-rooted hatred of the enemy, and he sincerely believed that a day off from training was tantamount to throwing in the towel. 'We're being *chicken*,' he would roar from the middle of the river. 'We can't go in yet. We're not getting enough done. We need *more work*.'

On a pure pound-for-pound basis Dave Sawyier was at that time probably the strongest man who had ever rowed for Oxford. And in our training races against other crews in the run-up to the battle with Cambridge, he was not at his most attractive if we lost, which was rare. He would stand there shaking with fury, yelling at everyone. Once he accused me of having rowed only 'in dog-shit crews', and of never having coached anything. 'Topolski!' he thundered: 'You know absolutely f---ing nothing.'

But he would have laid down his life for Oxford, and there was nothing he would not have done in the interest of victory over the hated Light Blues.

When in 1973, with Dave stroking, we lost by a shocking thirteen lengths, half-filled with river water, I thought he would probably take a pistol behind the boathouse and do the honourable thing.

Instead he swore vengeance, and stroked Oxford to a famous five-and-a-half length victory the following year, our first since 1967. I do not think I ever saw a happier man than Dave Sawyier on that wonderful afternoon.

During our ten-year winning streak between 1976 and 1985 I worked with three excellent American oarsmen. There was the great Harvard stroke and 1974 World Champion Al Shealy who rowed at number 6 for us in 1977 and 1978. Like Sawyier he too was the most colossal presence, and would stand stark naked in the dressing room shouting with immense authority the speeches of the US General George Patton: 'No bastard ever won a war by dying for his country – he won it by making *the other poor dumb bastard* die for his country!' He wanted to be a Hollywood actor, and certainly had the lack of inhibition for it. Once, in front of the Bishop of London, he told the most rancidly disgusting joke I have ever heard. But there is no doubt that his stirring after-dinner 'blood 'n' guts' speeches really did help psyche up a crew before a big race. By the time Al finished with them they were prepared to go out and win, or die in the attempt.

There was Ken Brown of Cornell University, also from that great US world champion crew of 1974. He too rowed at number 6 for Oxford, in 1976. Then there was Fran Reininger, from the University of Pennsylvania, who learned to be a part of the Oxford system, having been a US national class oarsman before coming to England. As stroke, he enjoyed one of his finest hours when we destroyed Cambridge in 1985 to make it ten in a row. The Evans twins, Mark and Mike, from Canada, rowed for us in 1983 and 1984, and went on from the Boat Race to win the gold medal in their national Eight in the 1984 Olympics. They were cut in the same mould as Sawyier and Shealy – larger than life, confident, witty men.

They were big men in the finest sense of the word. They had all scaled the heights of international competition before Oxford, but they all knew humility, and they recognized the traditions. They all underwent the final intensive six-month training programme, a crucifying preparation often in sub-zero temperatures, spending up to five hours a day on the water and in the gym.

They realized that the Boat Race is like no other rowing contest in the world in terms of racing conditions, international media attention, and as a pure long-distance endurance test. And they wanted to face it as fully trained as it was possible to be. They listened to the experience of the coaches, and they knuckled down to work in the gym, with weights, and on the track for months on end. Like everyone else, they expected to be pitted man against man, friend against friend. Training for the Boat Race has no other standard except its own.

Like all class athletes under pressure they sometimes complained. We all do. Some could be a bit abrasive, even arrogant, and sometimes difficult. A few of them thought they knew it all, but in the end they all felt that they had learned much from the experience and went home with a healthy respect for the event. Without exception they were men of character, and self-confidence, who knew their purpose, knew that in rowing we all pull together. They saw the need for mutual co-operation, and they lived by that unspoken sacred trust among oarsmen that we fight side by side, that no one gives up, ever, and that we are bound together for as long as it takes.

There were times of course when they found our English reserve a little unnerving, especially when they first arrived at Oxford, but as the months wore on many of them became more English than the English.

Chris Clark, though, once he recovered from the initial surprise of a man like Bruce Philp, may well have formed the opinion that the British lack of immediate openness was a form of snobbery. He gave the impression that he felt he was being snubbed, and that, plus his feeling that our freewheeling President gave us no sense of purpose, caused him to sink into a near-permanent state of irritation.

Both Clark and Livingstone were quick to voice their criticism of the prevailing sense of disorder, and certainly at times I was hardly able to disagree with what they said. Nevertheless, next to Bruce, I was probably highest on Clark's hit-list of disapprovals. Basically I think he considered that I did not come to Oxford frequently enough and that I had too much influence. He also thought I should have shaken the President up more, made him take a more efficient approach to squad matters.

It was undoubtedly an uphill battle. The squad lacked the internal dynamic that had motivated Oxford boys in previous years. There was an apathy and destructiveness afoot that was alien, and however much I tried to instill a sense of purpose, each day seemed a retrograde step on our long journey to the London Tideway. None of this was the fault of our basic system for fighting this private river-war between the two great universities; our troubles sadly were endemic to that particular year. We had, after all, just won ten races in a row in a contest which represents the entire reason for the existence of the OUBC; and we had smashed the course record three times, which had previously stood for twenty-six years. Perhaps this success induced a lack of urgency and a belief that all would be all right on the day. As it happened I, too, found things rather difficult at times.

But Bruce was about to become a doctor – and when he had accepted the Presidency six months earlier, he had had no idea of just how much he would be expected to do. He may well have thought I would run most of it for him – but I too had a life and a career as a photo-journalist in London. And from a regular sixty days a year coaching from 1973–78 I was by now spending up to four months of the winter either in an Oxford launch or on a highway.

When I was not there, even my most routine instructions often failed to get passed on. Thus when the squad arrived to train and the President was late no one would know what to do. It was, to say the least, a slow and discouraging autumn; we lacked power, pace and spirit.

In November I always entered a crew for the Fours Head of the River Race on the Tideway, and I usually managed to field a winning coxed Four combination. This year, by way of a much-needed morale booster I decided to put out our very best four, with Chris Clark, George Livingstone, Bruce Philp and Graham Jones who agreed to row on this special occasion. Cambridge also put out their best Four for this race and defeat by them was, for me, unthinkable. The race would be rowed over the reverse Boat Race course and we needed to win. The four men pulling the Dark Blue oars were carrying the entire morale of the Oxford squad.

Well, the race was a disaster. Cambridge, starting behind us, actually rowed right through us, actually overtook us! – and went right away to finish an unacceptable eighteen seconds in front. I had a chill feeling in my bones that we had not fought to the last breath. And when I saw Graham Jones I sensed my worst fears justified. He was seething, having rowed himself nearly to a standstill; he *knew* that something was wrong in that boat. Had someone lost heart when Cambridge challenged?

The Americans experienced a mixture of anxiety and resentment, imagining themselves almost as outcasts in college, being blamed for the defeat. They confided these fears to Donald, as their friend, on the running track. Shortly thereafter we had a very serious and tense meeting in the gym, in which we discussed mental attitudes. At the time, I remember feeling a bit sorry for Chris Clark. He was such a handsome giant that no one gave much thought to his insecurities; he was undoubtedly lonely, and homesick. He found it impossible to let go and join in with the English, just for this couple of years. Chris Clark arrived on the Isis as a pure-bred Californian, and I am afraid that he left Oxford as precisely that. Very little of us ever rubbed off on him.

As November drew to a close I knew we were rapidly approaching a crisis: I had to cope with a despondency which was affecting the whole squad. I noticed they were often wearing grubby kit, and there was a lifelessness about the rowing. If this went on for much longer we could end our winning run with a terrible beating by Cambridge. And through it all, these guys were so demanding, expecting me to be there all of the time like a full-time paid manager. 'Where you been, Dan?'

I read them the riot act, but things grew worse in the boathouse. There was a backlog of repairs building up, little things constantly needed fixing. The end of the term was approaching, the first week in December, which is perhaps psychologically the most difficult time of all for a Boat Race squad – as others prepare for parties, presents, invitations and relaxing evenings of festivities. But not us. As the nights drew in and the weather grew colder, we all journeyed down to London for our first full-course trial, a closely fought contest, flat-out, neck and neck along the whole murderous four-and-a-quarter miles from Putney to Mortlake. I usually divide the best eight men among the stern fours of the two boats, to make them even, and then let them fight it out.

We were not yet at racing fitness, despite the tough and uncompromising training schedule since the very first day of term back in October. The gusting wind made it a very demanding race for everyone and, like all trials, in the end it merely simplified what was already simple and complicated further that which was already complicated.

They finished exhausted but close, and when I reviewed the possible line-up, I still only had Bruce and Matt Thomas who, having rowed in 1985, had that vital Boat Race 'blooding' experience behind them. Then there were George, Chris and Donald as definites. The last three places from three to bow were wide open. It would be a fight between last year's reserve crew men Gavin Screaton, and Mark Dunstan; and the freshmen Tony Ward, Hugh Pelham, Julian Richards and the huge college-taught rower from Wadham, Gavin Stewart.

As everyone else broke for the vacation, we returned to Oxford. By now it was getting dark before 4 p.m. and the lights were on all afternoon in the bright modern shops and arcades which have blended into the old university city. Santa Claus was showing up all over the place and from the big hotels came the smells of roast turkey and the sounds of corks popping as dozens of office parties were unleashed onto this cheerful and festive Oxford scene.

But the colleges were now like morgues. Every day the Boat Race squad emerged from them, heading for the river, big grim men in heavy jackets and long scarves, hurrying through the cold streets down to the Isis where it was even colder. They were men with a lot on their minds. There was Chris Clark, sombre and full of problems behind his sun-glasses; Bruce, often tired and pale after a night on the wards; George, in a niftily-cut overcoat covering his working gear of tracksuit, tights, gloves and sweaters; Donald, ever busy, tearing round the corner on his racing bike, his saddle bags crammed with essays on the tortured syntax of the metaphysical poets and Jacobean gory tragedies.

Every day they took to the water, all of them now consciously fighting for those precious places, rowing hard against a sharp and ceaseless north-wester that chilled the river beyond belief. And every afternoon they returned to the lonely precincts of the university, to the near-deserted libraries and common rooms, trying to catch up on the work that this cruel struggle was now costing them.

We broke for ten days at Christmas and then hit London for the pre-term selection camp. These two weeks, fighting it out on the wide, windswept London Tideway in January, were notorious among all Oxford rowers. The schedule was brutal. Four sessions a day in arctic conditions. This really sorted out the giants from the big men. But in 1986 this squad still appeared aimless and unfocussed. 'What are we waiting for?', they said; or 'Why hasn't that rigger been tightened?'; or 'Shouldn't someone put tape over that crack?'

The fact was an Evans or a Sawyier or a Jones would have grabbed a roll of tape and done it themselves, without a second thought. Moved boats, packed gear, whatever it took, because everyone 'mucked in', all members of the little Oxford rowing family which Chris, in particular, seemed to find so difficult to join.

I was now coming under increasing pressure about the unbeaten run which had unquestionably made me its prisoner. In my own mind I could never leave as long as we were winning, and it would have been considered cowardly if I had left after a defeat. Therefore I decided that if we did lose I would have to return for as long as it took us to win again, and then I could feel free to retire. One way and another it seemed that I could still be in harness here well into my nineties.

We struggled through the first two weeks of the January term in freezing conditions at Henley, with the wind howling under the old town bridge, a raw and merciless blast. The seat racing competition in fours for those last three places in the crew was intense. And at this stage I was still having to give little tactical talks to the Americans, impressing upon them that there was nothing like the Boat Race in all the world as a test of endurance and of character.

I used to say: 'Forget about 2,000-metre racing – forget the Olympic distance, the fast stuff on flat summer water in six lanes. I know that's what you have been used to. But believe me, this is different.

'Just imagine you are Sebastian Coe or Steve Cram hurtling into the straight for the 1500 metre Olympic final. You kick for the line, giving it your most punishing effort. And somehow you get there, and you have made it, or nearly made it, and your explosive burst for victory is over, and your lungs are sobbing for breath and every muscle aches.

That's what the oarsmen feel like in the Boat Race after 2,000 metres in the long fight for supremacy to the famous landmark of Harrods warehouse. Except that the cox is yelling for you to do it *all over again, right now* in the desperate struggle for the inside of the four-minute bend through Hammersmith Bridge. You have got to produce that kick another time and another, and your opponents are in front, and you are on the outside, and it's clearly life or death, and you probably wish you were dead anyway, anywhere but in this hell-hole on the water. NOW COME ON OXFORD!! IN-THREE! IN-TWO! IN-ONE!! GO!!!'

The tactics, and the state of the race often demand these sudden gut-tearing bursts of speed, and even after the *second* 2,000 metres, you are still only two-thirds of the way home, perhaps with Cambridge still in front and your coxswain bellowing for more, pleading for one last power-twenty, a final momentous effort to peg them back. *'Come on Oxford! One more! In-three . . .!'* And all you know is that when the stroke's blade digs this time, a fraction faster, you will match it, no matter what. 'Please God, help me keep up. Don't let me stop.'

Anyone who has not rowed in a really close Boat Race cannot comprehend the level of the pain. The agony of the race hits every man in the boat as lactic acid builds in the body, to replace the aerobic oxygen-based energy which is being depleted with every second of the battle. The body produces energy from food in measurements of kilocalories, just one of which lifts the temperature of a litre of water by one degree. Thus someone cleaning his shoes produces three kilocalories, someone on a long walk five, a cross-country skier thirty. But an Olympic oarsman produces thirty-six. And in the latter half of the Boat Race this may rise to fifty, the most dangerous level of stress in any sport, outside of the marathon.

I told them a thousand times: 'There is nothing in the world like the Boat Race.' Regularly I updated our training methods, to stay in line with other top international squads. As an Olympic coach I was usually at the world championships and I always spent time exchanging views with other coaches, from behind the Iron Curtain, old friends from the USA, Canada and Australia. There was nothing old-fashioned about us at Oxford, although Chris Clark often gave his fellow crew members the impression that he thought I was not entirely up-to-date.

However I was not altogether without experience myself. I had won a gold and a silver medal in the world championships as an oarsman, and I had rowed in two Boat Races; I had also won four Henley and five national titles. Chris's spell with the US national squad undoubtedly gave him a lot of knowledge and I never minded him expounding this. Just occasionally though, I took exception to his assumption that his was greater than mine. I had also rowed in the world championships as a member of Great Britain's Heavyweight Team. I weighed just 152lbs at the time, but then, it's not the size of the man in the fight that counts, it's the size of the fight in the man. What me? Over-sensitive? Never.

The day of the race grew ever closer, and morale improved when they settled into a regular routine as a selected crew. It snowed in February on the upper reaches of the Thames and conditions on the water were grim. The ice froze in the crews' eyebrows as they battled their way through the work-outs, hands almost frozen to the oars. I could see their breath coming in short white bursts on the thin, cold air, and the shouts of the cox Andy Green took on an eerie, echoing quality as he urged the sixty-foot racing Eight along this deserted stretch of river, winding through the silent white landscape.

I watched them carefully, as always, searching for a sign of mental weakness. But there was none. Each man was coping well with the hardship, each one of them locked into his task. But it is one thing to practise, and quite another to race. And the trouble is, you never know who, on the day, will find it within his soul to give more than he has ever given before. It takes a kind of madness to compete like that, because of the willpower, and the ego, and the loyalty. And while some men have it, others have yet to find it; and a coach can only use his best judgement as to who those men will be.

On 6 April 1985, for instance, the Oxford boat went out onto the water to face Cambridge nearly paralyzed with fear. Five of the crew looked like men going to their execution, white-faced at the ordeal which lay before them, in front of a world-wide television audience. But they found it within themselves to fight and fight, summoning up reserves of hostility and ferocity they were not aware they possessed. They won not just because they were better – indeed I believe they were probably not as good as Cambridge – but because they would not let go when the chips were really down. And because Cambridge cracked first.

This year there were a couple of men in the boat I knew could scrap like that, but there were others I knew less about and had not seen under that sort of extreme pressure. Often the least likely ones surpassed expectation, while others, who promised much, fell short.

Then, three weeks before the race, Graham Jones became available. He could tip the balance for us, but it was a big gamble to take psychologically as well as physically. The morale of the crew hung in the balance, and Chris in particular voiced objections. It was important that I recognize that his view of himself as crew leader should not be undermined and that he should not be moved

45

from the important number 6 seat. But even so when he heard of Graham's re-entry he blew a gasket, and swore that Jones would come in only over his, Clark's, dead body. But as we stood, we lacked a winning look. The resident number 3 man, Tony Ward, eighteen, made selection relatively simple by taking a sudden, and unexpected moral stand. He said that it was highly unfair that Graham should be able to just walk back in, not having undergone the full training, and he, Tony, wished to have no further part in the Dark Blue Boat. I argued that we would be running test trials, that he had a good chance of holding his place in the crew. But his attack of 'conscience' was decisive for both of us. I recalled a comment of his earlier in the year: 'If I make the crew then it can't be very fast.' It all made me question his fighting qualities and I accepted his decision.

So Graham went into Donald's seat at number 4 and Donald moved back to 2. For the bow seat we had the tall, ambidextrous Gavin Screaton, a twenty-two-year-old aspiring doctor, with an eye for the girls, and a taste, like his pal Bruce, for a pint or two after training. Mark Dunstan, a 6ft 5ins engineering student from Kent rowed at 3, and the stern four remained unchanged: Philp 5, Clark 6, Livingstone 7, with Matt Thomas at stroke.

Graham Jones had always dominated all the aspects of our training whenever he joined us through the winter. He really was a superb athlete; however his re-appearance had its problems. One or two members of the crew felt I had effectively decided we could not win this Boat Race as we were. And from the moment Graham Jones arrived back, some of them mentally shifted the responsibility for winning the race from their own shoulders onto those of the Australian powerhouse. Clark's threatened 'suicide' did not take place, but there was a sense that somehow he had evacuated his territory, no longer seeing himself as Big Man in the Boat.

With Graham aboard, Donald says the boat did not go faster immediately. 'It shook more because of his enormous strength, but it was not as smooth.' A few days later we lost by nine seconds to the tough London University crew in the Reading Head of the River.

On this rather disappointing note we left Oxford and moved into our London headquarters, a big luxurious house in Putney. There were just fourteen days to go before we faced Cambridge. I was mildly optimistic, and stressed the importance of each man now becoming an integral part of the life of his crewmates. We would enter this house as ten men, but we would leave it as a crew. It was a time to weld together psychologically, a place in which differences must be cast aside, and in which we must think and act as one fighting unit. It was a purifying process. And it had never failed us.

Although I stipulated no fixed rules about booze, girlfriends or late nights, there always existed a concentrated determination that nothing should get in the way of our Boat Race effort. Everyone wanted to savour every moment of this fortnight, and no one wanted to break the spell. So there was a self-imposed discipline. I believed always that an athlete should do what he finds makes him most comfortable. Sudden denial is not a great idea because it disturbs normal rhythms. A customary evening pint or a couple of hours making love in those last intense days were preferable to total abstinence if a build-up of tension and anxiety was the result. I always found the relaxation beneficial. But in fact it was rare that any of them ever wanted to go out, preferring to stick with the group and talk tactics, watch films and joke together.

This year we experienced an extra dimension: Chris and George had brought with them some tapes from California, and would sit listening to the dulcet voices of their coaches from back home, from whom they believed they would gain extra motivation. Instructions from Carlos Castaneda also circulated through the house – in particular, sections from *The Warrior*, in which he exalts those facing adversity to tune into another kind of reality. My view was that if it helped them, fine. Our President was more succinct. 'Load of bullshit,' he observed.

No one could say that Bruce was not doing everything he possibly could to foster true crew camaraderie. He even went as far as to acquire some finely explicit hard-core pornographic movies to while away the hours after dinner. They appointed the stroke, Matt Thomas, presumably because of his position in the boat, to take charge of the remote control, and at this he was bloody hopeless. On three occasions our very pretty cook came into the room suddenly, and Matt, fighting furiously with the controls, was quite unable to remove the copulating figures from the screen in time, for which he was, of course, severely admonished by the crew.

But we still lacked that confident aggressive atmosphere, charged with straining athletic urgency, that had characterized every single one of my thirteen Oxford crews. There was a round-shouldered apologetic mood here, which persisted, and out on the water the crew lacked verve and sparkle. I hoped against hope that we could still develop real racing aggression during the final days but I grew more and more anxious with each passing hour. I had not known such negative sensations before, such a frantic gnawing feeling of doom. Try as I might, I could not help my final briefing from lacking inspiration, for words could not inspire a team which was not in tune, not pulling as one. Somehow it simply was not clicking.

Meanwhile Cambridge were developing one of their better crews in recent years. John Pritchard, the mercurial British Olympic silver medallist from the Moscow Games, was stroking them. They had the Canadian international Gibson, two British international squad rowers and the giant US oarsman, Jim Pew, at four. It was a tough act to beat, but we had pulled off at least three victories in even less likely circumstances in the past.

On Saturday afternoon, 29 March, the boys set off to race Cambridge University, rowing away from the Putney 'hard' twenty-five minutes before the start. We had won the toss and chosen the Surrey station and there was nothing more I could do for them now. I stepped onto the Oxford launch, a helpless spectator of my own fate. The Oxford record of ten-in-a-row was well and truly on the line.

The starter got them away first time, right in front of Donald's old bedroom at London Rowing Club. But this time there was no thoughtful face at the window staring out across the water. Eight years later that same face was set tight with determination above the number 2 seat, Donald's knuckles white with tension as he wrenched the oar through the first three strokes. Oxford dug deep, their strike rate above forty for the first twenty strokes.

Cambridge matched them, gained a foot, and then the Light Blues rate settled back to thirty-seven. Oxford stayed two pips higher through the first minute, but Cambridge now had a man on them. This was critical. Cambridge were beginning to move aggressively over into our water.

The umpire bellowed at Cambridge to get back. Donald, pulling away with the compulsive toughness he had learned at LRC so long ago, now glanced to his left and found himself eyeball-to-eyeball with Jim Pew and he knew in that split second we were two men down. He looked out to the right at the Dark Blue blade for which he had given so much – and he braced himself for the surge of power he knew must come as the Oxford stroke hit the accelerator, to grab back that distance. But nothing happened, and now Pew was moving forward, and deep inside him Donald could hear a voice screaming: '*Come on, Damn you. They mustn't get away.*'

Again the umpire roared at Cambridge to move over, and Donald knew that Oxford must strike right now with a power-20, but it never came. Instead they settled into a steady pace that would lose them the race for certain. At the end of two minutes Cambridge had taken a length, and Donald said later, 'I remember wanting to shout. I wanted to yell out: "For Christ's sake! Fight for it!" Because there was just no fight in that boat. There was a kind of deadness that only occurs when someone has given up.'

Cambridge drew further and further away and won it by seven lengths. The record was gone in the most humiliating way. But that seemed suddenly less important than the fact that this crew had lost on this day, and that somehow they had sold themselves short.

Later that evening Donald came up to me and said: 'Dan, I am really sorry it had to end like this. But we just didn't fight. It nearly broke my heart. Because I seem to have been preparing for that race for half of my life.'

The magic ten-year spell was over. It should have been devastating but curiously the taste of defeat was less harsh than I had expected. I was more irritated than disappointed. But something had been wrong all year, and it had manifested itself in the race. Maybe it was me, and I had lost my edge, my instinct. But I could not go out on a seven-length beating, like this. And I felt that, if invited, I would have to come back next year, to win, if only to free me from this bitter-sweet treadmill I had created for myself. I needed a break, I thought, in the American sense of the word.

On 6 May 1986 I got it. The Old Blues and captains of the thirty-six Oxford colleges elected as the next President of the Oxford University Boat Club, the reserved and scholarly tiger of Mansfield College, Donald H.M. Macdonald. The old Rajputana Rifles would have been proud. He phoned me that night to ask me, formally, to be his Head Coach, and I remember saying something flippant: 'Well, we can't take another beating like that, you know. My nerves won't stand it.'

The phone went very quiet and finally Donald spoke. 'This is a great honour for me, Dan. I am already in the record books as one of the nine men who lost the longest Oxford winning-streak in history. I will not go down as a losing President. We are not going to lose, you know that. I want to win and the university deserves it.'

His words reminded me of my own reaction eighteen years earlier when I too rowed in a losing crew. The over-riding feeling was that somehow, somewhere, I would have to make amends.

And on that note Donald and I set off on a fateful adventure that would propel both of us on to the front pages of just about every newspaper in the Free World, and turn the University of Oxford into a battleground.

CHAPTER THREE

THE NEW PRESIDENT

Donald would drive his sculling boat through mile after mile, in a silent brutal programme of conditioning – he would work all alone, at first light, punishing himself without mercy. His was the private dignity of the lone athlete, with a grim purpose, fighting a solitary war with himself, towards a goal only he can see.

The roots of mutiny tend to run deep, and we can trace this one back to the immediate hours following that horrendous defeat on the Tideway, six weeks before Donald was elected President.

The scene was, by any standards, imposing: the Savoy Hotel, which stands in Edwardian splendour on the steep hillside between London's Strand and the northern embankment of the Thames beyond Westminster. Over the years this international hotel has become something of a citadel for celebrating sportsmen. The great banqueting halls echo to the cries of the scarlet-coated toastmaster calling to order the annual gatherings of Britain's leading athletes. Fighters like Henry Cooper and Barry McGuigan, golfers like Tony Jacklin and Sandy Lyle, racing drivers Stirling Moss, Jim Clark, and Jackie Stewart, Olympic champions Daley Thompson and Sebastian Coe, and from the past Roger Bannister, Tommy Farr and Colonel Harry Llewelwyn, have all risen to speak in these palatial surroundings. 'My Lords, Ladies and Gentlemen, pray silence for The Champion. . . .'

On the evening of 29 March 1986 at the annual Oxford Boat Race dinner, the mood of the assembled Old Blues was subdued because of the seven-length drubbing. This one defeat seemed to have obliterated all of the success that had gone before; defeat throws a cloud of doubt over everything. Here it undermined confidence in a system which had for so long brought nothing but triumph. Shortly before ten o'clock, in response to shouts of 'Let's hear from the Americans,' Christopher Clark rose to his feet. On that darkest of nights some took the view that we had to cast everything overboard and start again from scratch. Chris Clark was one of those and his solution was graphically simple.

'Next year we're gonna kick ass. Cambridge's ass. Even if I have to go home and bring the whole US squad with me.'

There he stood, the 6ft 6ins Californian, resplendent in his colourful bow-tie and his newly-acquired waistcoat, cream with Dark Blue trim. He did not dwell overmuch on the events of the day, save to mention that as he was rowing along behind Cambridge he did think of the Oxford record. 'I thought of Dan's book,' he said referring to my account of the past decade of Oxford success. 'And I thought, well, we sure have spoiled the next chapter of that!'

But in general terms he concentrated on the future, a future in which he saw himself as a prominent and, at least for the next year, a permanent part. 'It's cost me $10,000 to be here this year,' he said. 'And if it costs me another $10,000 next year, I'll be back.'

As speeches go, that one certainly went. It went down like the *Titanic*. As he spoke you could almost feel the shudder of irritation pass fleetingly through the room – upper lips stiffened, eyes were averted, sunny expressions vanished in small flashes of annoyance. Who was this American, they thought, who seemed to think that their beloved Oxford Blue Boat could not win without hired mercenaries from the USA? 'Dammit, during the whole of our ten-win streak there have only been three Americans – who is this bloody fellow?'

There is, of course nothing quite so infuriating to an English amateur sportsman as implied inadequacy from a foreigner, and Chris had surely hit the wrong button with this lot. For in this grand room was a group which had, to a man, undergone its own baptism of fire on the river between Putney and Mortlake; some of them more than once. Others among them had gone on to represent Great Britain in the Olympic Games, and to win medals.

And here was Chris, up on his hind legs, suggesting that he alone, with his friends from across the pond, was all that stood between Oxford and further humiliation at the hands of the despised Light Blues, known affectionately in this room as 'The Filth'. Glancing around the room, it would be an understatement to suggest that, just at this moment, there was little being achieved in the field of Anglo-American relations.

Off to my left was the venerable figure of Ronnie Rowe, Chairman for the night, a hard ex-Army man who had been a member of the elite SAS since the early days, and who had pulled the number 4 oar in the battling Oxford crew which broke Cambridge's outstanding record thirteen-win sequence in 1937. In his speech earlier he had already said that our crew today lacked what he called 'dig and hoik'.

Then there were the heroes of 1980, Tom Barry, Nick Conington, and John Bland, all members of that glorious seven-man Oxford crew which held off the late charge of the Cambridge Eight by only six feet, after the Dark Blue bowman had blacked out a mile-and-a-half from home. They were completely rowed out and it took them twenty minutes to manoeuvre the boat ashore next to the finishing line.

There was Ronnie Howard, the burly President of 1959, who had single-handedly put down a mutiny led by the American oarsman Reed Rubin and then, as the biggest man in the boat, helped pull the weakened Oxford crew to a famous five-length victory.

There was the Olympic finalist and multiple Henley winner Christopher Davidge. In 1949 he stroked the Dark Blues in a defeat of a bare quarter of a length in one of the most murderous struggles ever seen on the Tideway. In 1951 he was back and still pulling, still calling for more as Oxford sank in heavy water in Putney Reach, and in 1952 he stroked them to a thunderous, neck-and-neck victory over Cambridge by just one canvas (about four feet). With Mr Davidge, you are talking strictly Iron Man.

And here was the occupant of today's critical 6 seat in a historically-defeated crew, which had shown about as much fight as a pound of pork sausages, chatting away publicly about how he was going to put everything right. His way. With his friends. The casual dismissal, implicit in his words, of young English oarsmen stung deep. Chris Clark's harmless assumptions of American superiority, did not bother us younger Old Blues overmuch, but it was not greatly appreciated by the older brigade.

At the conclusion of the speeches, Donald, looking like Bonnie

Prince Charlie in the elegant green tartan kilt of his clan, and his beautifully-tailored Highland dinner jacket, murmured to no one in particular: 'What a good way to win friends and influence people.'

There was however a groundswell of opinion among the Old Blues about our basic rowing performance that afternoon. Even Donald, normally the most tolerant of men, was moved to observe that, 'by far the biggest puddle left in the water by the oars on the stroke side was the one left by Graham Jones.' And he made no secret of his frustration at the lack of initiative demonstrated by the stern four.

It was a view which was impossible to quarrel with, and in addition a significant proportion of the blame rested, in truth, at my door. It was after all I who had somehow failed to get them *up* for the race. What worried me most was that apparent reluctance to race in hard side-by-side competition. And the slightly haunting tenor of the words of Macdonald: 'It was the kind of deadness that only occurs when someone has given up.'

At that Oxford Dinner the words of our 6 man suggested a very different viewpoint. It would be many months before I would learn the real meaning which lay behind his words. Chris Clark really did believe that he was the man to reinstate Oxford rowing, and that the men he needed to help him in this mission were all in the United States. Deep down, Chris believed that the existing training methods at Oxford were archaic.

Meanwhile I was enormously busy, for, within a couple of days, the entire Oxford crew was scheduled to fly out to the United States of America to race in two regattas, both over the regular 2,000 metres summer sprint distance. This would be hard for us, straight after a four-and-a-quarter mile marathon.

The first one was to be on the Savannah River in Augusta, Georgia, a couple of days before the US Masters began; and the other was on the west coast against the College crews of the University of California (Berkeley) and the Bruins of UCLA. They would compete upon the very waters where Chris and George had fought their way to prominence – the shallow tidal strip of Ballona Creek, in Marina Del Rey, right up the road from Newport Beach.

The Augusta Boat Club had approached us to play a part in a major public relations programme for a development on Savannah waters. On the other coast, we were going to help the Bruins, who were locked in a struggle with the UCLA governing body over whether or not crew-racing should survive as a part of the athletic programme.

Both sets of organizers had worked out that the best way to make a big splash was to hold a top international regatta, and to invite the most famous crew in the world, the Blue Boat of Oxford University. They split the cost, arranged many receptions and the kindest of hospitality – and we, still stunned by our defeat, boarded a plane bound for the great Southern city of Atlanta. At least most of the Oxford squad did. I, for my part, with a dash of true individualism, managed to miss the plane.

This was a pity as it was on the flight over the Atlantic that Donald noticed the first stirrings of a definite 'lobby'. Clark and Livingstone were having little meetings about the crew. Our spare man Ward, like George, an Oriel College man, seemed privileged to be on the fringe of this. There was general criticism at 35,000 feet above the Atlantic about who had been good enough in that boat and who had not. But it was clear that the Americans had very definite ideas about how the new crew should shape up. Clark was already mentioning the influx of top US oarsmen he would be bringing back to Oxford.

Donald never mentioned any of this to me at the time, but he now recalls that he formed an opinion that Chris Clark was a young man who saw himself as the influential voice at the OUBC in the coming months. Indeed in a heady moment in the Club van, in a discussion about the future, he had said: 'Donald, whoever they elect will only be a puppet President.'

Finally I arrived at the hotel at five o'clock the next morning, and, like the rest of them, became a guest of the Augusta Chamber of Commerce. And for three days we were looked after like kings, wined and fêted, as the élite boat crew we unhappily, at that moment, were not. Chris cheerfully joined in everything, but he was a man on the move, because a day before the race he shipped out altogether, leaving Augusta early in the morning. He had warned me that he was unlikely to stay on for the race although some of the others had hoped he would reconsider once he was over the initial disappointment of the Boat Race defeat. But after four days he decided that he needed 'to spend some time preparing for the US national squad' and he felt he had to touch base with them.

Despite the hospitality of the Augusta Chamber of Commerce and the free transatlantic ticket, the rowing part would have to take place without him. He agreed, however, to join us in California for what would turn out to be a battle-royal on Ballona Creek, against his old alma mater, Berkeley.

We raced without him in Georgia, got beaten narrowly by just a few feet, but rowed to the best of our ability for the Chamber of Commerce. The winners were Temple University, one of the better crews from Philadelphia, and a huge crowd cheered them home against the Oxford Blue Boat. Everyone got their money's worth and with the greatest thanks and goodwill from the Georgians, we headed west for Los Angeles.

We touched down shortly before ten o'clock on Saturday night, 6 April, one week to the minute since the Old Blues dinner at the Savoy. They dispersed us to some of the most magnificent homes in Palos Verdes and we settled down to five days training from the UCLA boathouse at Marina Del Rey, the one we were supposed to be saving from extinction.

It was clear to us from all reports that we would have our work cut out to beat the Berkeley crew. The Bruins of UCLA? We thought we could handle them and the boys were beginning to move quite well together. But it would have helped to have Chris back in the boat. His absence was becoming a bit of a talking point since the organizers had focussed much of their pre-race publicity on the big pair of Berkeley veterans, Clark and Livingstone, rowing for Oxford. It was getting embarrassing.

The Varsity had made a major deal of the event – the actor Gregory Peck, their old strokeman from their Junior Varsity of 1937-1938 – was chairman of the proceedings for the day. Dudley Moore was to be Master of Ceremonies, and we were due to meet the Mayor of the City, Tom Bradley, next day for a special presentation.

Well, Chris failed to show and telephoned to say he was heading back east to join the US squad at Penn AC in Philadelphia. He was not coming to race on Ballona Creek. 'Dan, I feel I must concentrate totally on just this one Pairs competition with Dan Lyons. It's the US trials for the world championships. I just don't want to burn out; I need to save myself and get mentally prepared.'

When the message came I thought for one remarkable moment that George Livingstone was going to explode. We were in an ice-cream parlour in Westwood, and he almost dropped his butterscotch-pecan cone straight down his rowing shirt. No one had ever seen George as angry as that before. Donald, who would shortly find himself beginning his preparation for next years' Boat Race, did not take Chris's excuse seriously. We felt obliged to do something for the sponsors. So I called Fran Reininger, the ex-University of Pennsylvania oarsman who had stroked Oxford so valiantly to that underdog victory in 1985. The spirit of the Dark Blues still burned strongly in Fran and he drove up to join us.

On 12 April – two weeks after the defeat by Cambridge – we lined up to face UCLA and Berkeley before a stiff tail wind on Ballona Creek. With a new stroke, a substitute 6 man, and a much shorter racing distance, this was likely to present a severe test for us. But we hung tough at the start, and grabbed a quick lead. However at 600 metres Cal went by us to win, and we failed by inches to hold the Bruins on the line for second place.

We'd like to think that if there had been another three miles we would probably have put the lot of them in hospital. But, anyway, a big crowd had turned up and everyone was happy – rowing looked secure on the Creek for another year at least, and ex-Oxford undergraduate Dudley Moore remarked that it was so long since he had felt such complete humiliation, he found it quite refreshing.

The absence of Chris on the plane home turned out to be rather more permanent than we at first thought. Our number 6 man did not turn up at all for the summer term at Oxford. The authorities at University College were furious for he had promised he would assist their Eight in the championship bumping races on the Isis. An oarsman of Chris's class could make a huge difference in a boat-load of rookies racing against crews of similar standard; and all year the boys at University College had been looking forward to getting in a few blows against their ancient rivals from Oriel, New College and Christ Church. The American's vanishing act especially inflamed one senior academic who had been particularly supportive of Clark's application in the first place. As a keen supporter of the college boat club, this professor was then compelled to watch the Univ. first Eight, having delayed crew selection waiting for Clark, ultimately fail in their challenge on the river.

There was the inevitable contrast with the events of the past summer, 1985, when Fran Reininger had put his place in the American national trials at risk, by staying at Oxford to help his University College crew in Eights Week. What's more he placed his international future in even further jeopardy by moving – so close to US summer trials – from strokeside to bowside in response to a plea from the college coach.

Donald Macdonald was elected President of the Oxford University Boat Club on the first Thursday in May, and we then faced the task of rebuilding our demoralized squad in time to face Cambridge the following spring. Young Hugh Pelham was made Secretary of the Club, at the age of only twenty. His family lives at Henley-on-Thames, and his father Michael was a former stalwart of the St Edmund Hall crew which was Head of the River at Oxford University from 1959 to 1961. He won twice at the Royal Regatta and is the founder and chairman of the British International Rowing Fund which raises money for the British national squad to compete round the world.

Hugh was very much of the Establishment world of his father. As seventeen-year-old schoolboys they both rowed for St Edward's School, Oxford, and both won the fiercely competitive Princess Elizabeth Cup at Henley. A ferocious hard worker, Hugh is very loyal to the traditions of the OUBC and throughout all the troubles which would confront us, his loyalty to Donald never wavered. At a height of only 6ft 1in he was obliged to fight like a terrier for that precious seat in the bow of the Blue Boat. But Hugh is a racer. It is in his blood. They say that when he helped to haul St Edward's to victory before a packed grandstand at Henley his father almost collapsed with pride.

Another appointment was made at that meeting, and that was of a Vice President of the Boat Club, a position which is not always filled, but is occasionally required by a President who anticipates he will be especially busy. Donald, who was by now thirty-one, with a wife and three children, a near-derelict bank account, and a highly demanding tutor, not unexpectedly assessed himself as 'busy'.

Gavin Stewart, the 6ft 8½ins Wadham College student of American history, was selected for the job, with a formal brief, written into the Club's constitution: 'to assist the President'.

Unfortunately it did not include a brief to advance his Boat Club boss a few grand, because Donald was under severe financial pressure. It was clear that as President he would not be able to complete the degree in English Literature in the prescribed three-year period. The demands on his time would be just too great. He requested permission from the Proctors of the University to give him another year to finish his degree.

The Proctors gave their permission. But the building society which had provided Donald with the mortgage to complete the purchase of his modest house, had a collective heart-attack in the loans department. One more year with no income! The sheer irresponsibility of it! 'We are very sorry, Mr Macdonald, but you will most certainly have to make some arrangements.'

Being Donald, a straightforward formal application for a further grant was nothing like good enough for him. So the old King of the Overkill bought himself a train ticket for £50 and set off north for Middlesbrough, to the office which had helped him three years before. He worked on the theory that a personal appearance might melt their stony civil servants' hearts but it did not. They waved the rule book which said three years in black letters, said they were very sorry and everything, and sent him home, poorer by £50.

His situation was now serious. He could probably scrape by until the end of his third year. But thereafter he would enter a financial wasteland. Times was hard, and threatenin' to get a whole lot harder.

Donald, remarkably, faced all this with a kind of wry amusement and flatly refused to readjust his life. He was after both a top degree and the honour of winning the 133rd Boat Race as President. He was broke, but his resilience impressed the bank manager at Lloyds in Oxford, and he came to the rescue with a loan. The mortgage company was silenced for a couple of years, and Donald began to rally the troops who would be in the running for next year's Blue Boat.

Bruce Philp would, of course, be gone. Jones, too, would also be leaving at the end of the summer term, as would Matt Thomas. Mark Dunstan and Gavin Screaton would be unavailable for most of the year. Clark was AWOL and George Livingstone still could not say whether he would be available as it depended on his job applications. Right now Donald stood alone as the only remaining Blue in the line-up. His good news was that practically the whole of the winning reserve boat, Isis, would be back.

From where I stood it looked like a classic battle from scratch to win the Boat Race next March. But you never knew what talent might turn up in the autumn – British youth internationals, top schoolboy oarsmen, or more experienced graduates. Then there was Chris who had threatened to persuade a bunch of top American Olympians to join him at Oxford for the Michaelmas term. I had heard little about him recently except that he and Lyons had finished last in their first heat of the US national trials, after which they had declined to race again. He wrote later to say he had hurt a rib and was taking a break for the summer.

I was beginning to wonder a bit about his true capacity and I tried to marshall some clear facts in my brain. Since coming to Oxford, Chris had rowed in three major races. In the Fours Head of the River, he and three other proven class oarsmen had been annihilated by Cambridge. In the Boat Race he had been in the key 6-seat in an Eight pulverized by Cambridge. In his own national trials, rowing with a man who would go on to win a world gold medal, he had finished last in the opening heats. Also why would he not race with us in America?

But, then again, I had a clear picture of him and Dan Lyons battling their way home in the *Petite Finale* in Belgium, holding off five world class Pairs to win by seven seconds. He had been racing as a last minute substitute there, with no real pressures or expectations piled upon him. Maybe he was the sort of man who performed better when he could just go out and have a bash, with nothing to lose. The contradictions were baffling. He just had to be able to row. Hell I had seen him with my own eyes scrapping and pulling his way to victory in that *Petite Finale*. And look at his US college reputation. Just look at the size of him. His build, his obvious strength. He had it all going for him. It was only that I had not seen anything from him lately. . . . I don't know . . . I wish I knew what he was really made of. . . .' The guy was a real enigma. But I knew that, somehow, I had to get him to fulfil his potential.

All these thoughts cascaded through my mind every time I thought of Christopher Clark. And apparently I was not alone.

With the elections completed, and our 'executive' now in readiness to pick up the remnants of defeat, Donald called a meeting of his main coaches at Vincent's Club, the historic Oxford gathering place for Blues and current members of university teams – rugby players, cricketers, amateur boxers, and the rest. The club is located, eccentrically, above the former Oxford stationery store of Vincent's just to the south of the High Street, and we hired a room, in case anyone said something too provocative which we might prefer not to fly around the university.

Donald and I were joined by three other coaches, Steve Royle, Jeff Jacobs, and Mike Spracklen, an ex-champion oarsman, and coach to many of Britain's top Olympic and world championship crews, including the Los Angeles gold medal Four.

As chief coach I started the proceedings with the five simple words asked by chief coaches the world over at the first formal post-mortem after a major defeat. 'What happened? What went wrong?'

Spracklen spoke first. 'You know what went wrong,' he said. 'Clark wasn't pulling. Look at the strokeside puddles. You can see it all on the video.'

The table was silent. Donald, who had already had a private meeting with Spracklen earlier in the week, just stared. His own words on the night of the race rushed back – 'The kind of deadness that only occurs when someone has given up.'

I was utterly flabbergasted by Mike's flat statement. But I recovered quickly, and said: 'But surely that was true of most of the crew, not just Clark.'

Spracklen only just agreed. 'Probably,' he replied. 'Yes.' Pause. 'But Clark was not pulling.' It was pointless to argue since no one could ever prove it, one way or another.

He went on to identify what he thought was Clark's unconscious withdrawal from his perceived role as the key man in the boat; he pointed out the mental and psychological effect that the reappearance of Graham Jones had probably inflicted on him. This was the first time I had heard anyone spell it out like that, certainly by anyone of Spracklen's stature. 'I doubt if Clark caused the defeat,' said Mike, 'but he caused it to be seven lengths.'

Now I really did have a major task on my hands, because Spracklen's views were truly damning. Yet it was hard to accept that Clark was not an essential part of the Oxford fight-back because of his past record in the States. However we had to press on with the discussion, and make our plans for the coming year. I decided the best thing to do would be to have a concerted attack of potential Blue Boat squad oarsmen on the Henley Royal Regatta. We needed to see who we had available for next year's Boat Race.

As a strategy it hardly left the drawing board. The Boat Race defeat had provoked all manner of unexpected repercussions. An air of anarchy prevailed, and the boys, who might have been expected to close ranks around the leadership, suddenly scattered in all directions. They all wanted to row for their colleges instead, and we had to abandon plans for an Oxford squad Eight. To me, this was a blow, because a good Oxford Eight at Henley had, over the years, proved to be a critical training ground for the Boat Race crew the following year. We had been unable to raise one the year before as well – and I attributed our subsequent defeat, in part, to that.

Now we were in the same boat again. The best I could manage was a couple of Fours – one in the Visitors' Cup, which was a catastrophe.

This crew, which contained the huge gangling Gavin Stewart, met ignominious defeat at the hands of a Cambridge college. The other Four, which contained George and Donald, plus Ward and Hugh Pelham, made a more determined attempt in the Brittania Cup, but were defeated by Kingston Rowing Club, who were subsequently selected to represent Britain in the world championships.

This was the Oxford that I would work with. It would be interesting to see if anyone emerged from the United States, but meanwhile all of the English oarsmen would find themselves in the annual ruthless struggle for a seat in the Boat. And Donald would be no exception. Fit and experienced as he was, he knew there was no divine right to a place, even for a President. He would have to earn it, with the rest of them.

It is highly unusual for a President not to make his own boat, but there have been occasions in the past, most notably in 1963, when Toby Tennant, the dedicated old Etonian son of Lord Glenconner, anguished over his lack of form, dropped himself from his own crew in what one coach described to me as one of the most heartbreaking meetings he ever attended at the OUBC. Miles Morland, the powerful red-headed freshman from Radley was called in, and Toby watched quietly from the Oxford launch as the American stroke, Duncan Spencer, rallied his men before Hammersmith Bridge, and the Dark Blues came from behind to beat Cambridge by five lengths.

Presidents tend to lose form in their year of office as the pressures of the job are enormous. Before I came to Oxford, the President could normally count on an element of protection from the chief coach. My reputation as a non-traditionalist was made when I dropped, for a while at least, the President, Andy Hall, three months after I started with my first-ever Oxford squad.

Since then Presidents have had to fight for their place. And Donald, determined to lead from the front, now embarked on a furious attempt to become the fittest man in England. He imposed upon himself a murderous regime of sculling. Each day he would be out on the river in his slim racing shell, far upstream from the boathouses shortly after first light. And he would drive himself through mile after mile, in a silent, brutal programme of conditioning. Once I had a very early meeting with a crew up near the lock, and I looked downstream along the Godstow Reach. There was a light early mist along the river and I could see a lone figure pounding his way towards me. The slightly upright style was familiar, big, hard strokes, smacking into the peaceful waters.

There could be only one man at this hour of the morning out there, working with that kind of dedication. I stood, just behind a drooping willow tree for a few moments and watched Donald driving his boat along, all alone, grunting with the effort, punishing himself without mercy, in his quest to become the toughest, strongest President in the history of the Boat Club. That's Donald. But if you met him socially, you would never believe this dedicated scholar capable of such spartan, selfless, quiet aggression.

I did not try to talk to him, for he was rowing as if in a trance. I did not want to break his concentration, nor did I wish to disturb the private dignity of a lone athlete fighting a solitary war with himself, towards a goal that only he can see. I moved back into the long shadow cast by the rising sun, and I thought then that here was a man with a high obsession. If Carlos Castaneda had ever wanted to see his Warrior, he should have been at Godstow that early August morning.

And so Donald went at it, in his own separate time-frame, dealing with the business of the club, and his family, and their worrying finances, and with himself, his fitness and his state of mind for the great battle which lay before him.

In our determination to recover the old Oxford morale, we took the new boys into strict training on the Upper Thames over a month before the new term began. We concentrated on gruelling distance endurance work in pairs. It was intensive stuff and to his own quiet satisfaction Donald finished on top of the Dark Blue heap at the big national Pairs event over the Boat Race course in London. The Oxford boys all performed well and there was, immediately, an optimistic buzz in the camp.

A few days before term began Chris Clark's tough new recruits arrived from the USA. Not that they were all at Oxford purely because of a plea by Chris; two of them had already been hoping to come anyway. But they were a welcome sight, these big, phlegmatic oarsmen from the other side of the Atlantic.

George Livingstone had been successful in obtaining a job in a bank and decided not to return to business school at Oxford. But in his place we had the following men.

Daniel Kevin Lyons was Clark's old partner from the 1985 world championships, and a member of the US Four which had just won the world championship. This was by any standards an excellent start. Dan came from Wayne in Pennsylvania and had grown up with rowing, on the Schuylkill river in Philadelphia; coxed boats at ten, rowed them at twelve. His father sang in the opera while Dan himself was a very useful tenor and planned to sing in an Oxford choir. He had attended the United States Naval Academy at Annapolis, and was now a Navy lieutenant. He stood 6ft 4ins tall and weighed a modest 185lbs – a little on the lightish side but unimportant when you have just won a world gold medal.

As an oarsman Dan was not stylish, but he moved a lot of water, and was very effective. He was clearly a tremendous racer, with a fanatical competitive streak. I think he always believed himself slightly inferior to the very big men in the sport, because after his gold medal victory, which took place at Nottingham, he walked around for days with the medal stuffed in his track suit pocket. His girl friend once asked him why he found it impossible to be separated from the symbol of his triumph; he looked at her very carefully before saying: 'That medal answers a whole lot of doubts I had about myself.'

Dan also saw himself as something of an orator. He liked to talk, and he liked to sermonize. It was also not unusual to find him at odds with national team coaches and selectors, bucking the system despite his naval background. He was a huge fan of Sir Winston Churchill and of General MacArthur. Like Al Shealy before him, Dan brought to Oxford a certain devotion to the creed of General Patton. He very nearly took that devotion to Cambridge, because having seen the film 'Chariots of Fire', he became convinced that Cambridge was the most romantic place on earth and the true home of amateur sport. In Dan's mind Harold Abrahams and the young Marquis of Exeter epitomized what he admired most in life. That was where he longed to study and he secured a place there for the winter of '86–'87.

But it seems Chris Clark convinced him that Oxford was just as good, and that, since the Dark Blues were in his opinion essentially a 'dogmeat crew', he would find himself on the side of the underdog. This was too much for Lyons, and the tall gangling Philadelphia oarsman, at the age of twenty-eight, began a post-grad course for the Special Diploma for Social Studies at Oriel, just down the street from his pal Clark.

Next we had Christopher Penny. He was twenty-four and came to study for an M.Phil in History at St John's College. This 6ft 5ins oarsman from the little town of Middletown, Rhode Island, had rowed for Princeton University in New Jersey. He was a major force in an Eight and had rowed in the middle of the United States crew which won a silver medal at the Los Angeles Olympic Games in 1984, and a bronze medal in the world championships the following year. In 1986 he was spare man. He liked to portray himself as a 'good ol' boy from down home Rhode Island.'

He was, though, a natural oarsman with his long arms and legs and relaxed easy rhythm. And he most enjoyed working in the 5 or 6 seat of a crew where he was outstanding. I first met him at the world championships in 1985 and he had spoken to me then about his ambitions to study at Oxford. Penny would have come to Oxford with or without Clark, for he was a serious student.

Then there was Chris Huntington, twenty-six, a member of Clark's old Berkeley crew. His parents' New York apartment is close to the more exclusive part of Fifth Avenue and his childhood friends were the children of the British Ambassador Peter Jay. He enrolled late at Mansfield College, and while he may not have been quite as flush as some of his compatriots, he was certainly better-heeled than most of his fellow Mansfield students. At 6ft 5ins, and 210lbs, Huntington, too, was an international class oarsman. He had won a bronze medal in the Coxed Fours at the 1986 world championships, and he was in the US world championships Eight which finished third in 1985. I had first met him some years earlier, and he had mentioned then an interest in coming to study in England. Of them all Hunt was probably the easiest to get along with.

Finally there was the garrulous coxswain from New York, Jonathon Fish from Long Island. He had coxed with the United States national team in 1985 having graduated from the University of Pennsylvania. He had worked as an accountant for a while in New York City, plotting and planning a way to get to the 1988 Olympics. Graduate school at Oxford, with this galaxy of US oarsmen lurking around, was of great interest to him, particularly since the '86 'world's' were being held in Britain, where he was coxing Huntington's bronze medal Four.

He had first applied to Templeton College, which specializes in management studies, back in 1985 on the basis of his work at the Wharton Business School at Penn. But Fish did not make it. Even the final flourish with which he finished his application did not swing the balance – 'In addition, studying with people from all over the world would only add to the learning experience for me. My experience at Oxford would become even more complete when given a chance to steer the Blues for their eleventh victory over Cambridge in the Boat Race.'

He finally secured a place at Mansfield, joining Clark on the Special Diploma in Social Studies course. He was a good cox, and at 5ft 8ins he often had to slim down like a jockey to make the 110lbs weight. He had spent £8,000 to be here, both clear signs of determination.

There is no university coach in the world who would not have been pleased to be on the receiving end of this little group at the start of the academic year. Clearly they were strong and experienced athletes, used to national team training, and some years beyond the college sports scene. How flexible they would be with an event like the Boat Race, with all of its unique quirks and demands, remained to be seen. Clark had, no doubt, provided them with some helpful background information.

Donald spent some time helping them to find accommodation in Oxford. He showed them the usual student flats. 'You can't be serious,' came the response. 'Well this is how students live in England,' replied Donald, somewhat taken aback. 'Well that's not how these students live,' they said. It took them quite a while to adjust to life at Oxford.

We spent a few days training in Fours at Radley before Clark himself arrived back for the beginning of term. Macdonald rowed with a couple of them and they looked terrific, long, powerful and mean.

I arranged a dinner meeting of welcome at Brown's Restaurant in St Giles, on the first evening of term, for all of these new oarsmen, to coincide with Clark's arrival back in Oxford. But the night before the dinner I received a phone call from Donald. There were rumblings, he said, at Oriel and Mansfield about the training programme I had given him and which he had distributed to the squad. He had decided to meet the Americans in the bar at St John's College to discover what was worrying them and to head off any serious disagreements before I came up from London to meet them the following night.

Clark, in the end had not turned up, but the rest of them did and it was clear that there was much they were not prepared to do in the way of training. They looked again at my schedule, on which I had ventured to suggest we might do some work every other Sunday until we began to reach serious fitness. Chris Penny took Donald's copy and wrote against the Sunday schedule, the letters NFW.

'What does that mean?' asked Donald.

'No f---ing way', he replied.

It was apparent to him that these Americans did not see the defeat of the Light Blues as a matter of life and death as it did to us. They were interested in many other aspects of university life, and to them a rowing Blue was a foregone conclusion. It was after all only Varsity rowing, not the real thing. He warned me to expect an argument.

We gathered at Brown's, all five Americans, Donald, myself and a big, powerful doctor who had rowed for London University, a plastic surgeon named Tom Cadoux-Hudson. At twenty-eight his credentials were every bit as good as those of the transatlantic newcomers. He had won a bronze medal in the Pairs at the world championships, and was one of Britain's most accomplished oarsmen. He was 6ft 5ins, same as Hunt and Penny, and he was known as one of the hard men among the British internationals.

We had a good cheap dinner in this big bright restaurant patronized by so many students at Oxford. Then I began to outline my programme. I told them how pleased I was at the prospect of working with them and that every one of the men assembled around this table had a major role to play in the defeat of Cambridge. I told them that I regarded this as the nucleus of a very great crew, one which had a chance of going down in history as one of the best Dark Blue boats ever to represent the university. 'I just want to be sure that we are all thinking along the same lines,' I said. 'And you are all experienced enough to know never to underestimate the opposition or the race.

'We cannot afford just to tick over – you have to lead this squad by example, be competitive within the group, and keep the others on their toes. It's a funny old race and it needs a special approach. It's a rough and tumble unpredictable sort of race and it demands a robust training programme. It comes early in the year – you have to peak five months earlier than you're used to – and the thing you have to remember is that there is no second chance in the Boat Race. No heats, no semis, no repechages for first-round losers. Chris has probably told you we were badly under-equipped last year, so we've really put that right. We've bought good equipment for you – an Empacher eight, Stampfli and Empacher Pairs, Burgashell sculling boats video system and six ergometers. So we're in great shape.'

I told them that I had devised the programme with their long term world championship ambitions in mind and had spoken to their US squad coaches.

Dan Lyons, the reigning world champion, said that he thought that that was all pretty interesting but basically he did not much want to do any running. Clark and Penny also voiced objections to the programme on the basis that neither of them wanted to do any work in the mornings. And Clark now began to get excited. Finally, Huntington spoke up, quite embarrassed, and said quietly to his fellow Berkeley crewman: 'Chris, you are out of order.'

Clark swung round on him, blazing with anger: 'That's really typical of you, Huntington,' he shouted. 'Really typical. So Goddammed East Coast. I knew we could never count on you for back-up. Goddammit we're trying to make points here, together. To get this straightened out once and for all.'

I stepped back into the argument, and pointed out the myriad of problems we would encounter in this four-and-a-quarter mile contest, probably in rough water, and high wind, and the special emphasis on hard endurance training it would require.

'Take my word for it,' I said. 'This race is like nothing else you have ever experienced in your whole lives. It is quite simply *different*. And Chris Clark, of all people, should know that.'

The gathering went silent. Then a voice began to speak. 'Dan,' it said. And I glanced up to see it was Clark. 'We all know that you think the Boat Race is different to any other race, and that it needs a special type of training programme. Well we all know that's bullshit. So if you have to say it, then say it just once. Because we don't want to hear it again.'

Nice to have you back Chris, I thought.

But Clark was by no means finished. On behalf of his friends he informed me that they considered running superfluous and circuit training to be of little use. They would not do two sessions a day, especially on Saturdays. Sundays? NFW. Sculling too was out.

'You got that okay, Dan?'

I sat there in stunned amazement, and Clark added, in the nature of clarification, 'These guys are the best. We don't need to train. We are so good we could just turn up on the day and beat Cambridge.'

The attempted take-over of the Oxford University Boat Club was well and truly under way.

CHAPTER FOUR

DISGRACED

It was rubbish, spineless, and the President knew now that he faced the prospect of going down in history as a member of the greatest Blue Boat ever to be defeated in the Boat Race. The man who filled the boat with five US internationals and still lost.

A bright moon shone above Oxford as I started my car and drove back along St Giles into the city, heading east towards London. I could still see them all on the wide stone pavement outside Brown's Restaurant, and as I passed, I waved a cheerful 'goodnight' despite the feeling of unease that was creeping over me. I could see Clark, sitting astride his motor bike, visor up, still speaking forcefully to them. And I could see Tom Cadoux-Hudson talking to Chris Penny, probably still discussing, with mock seriousness, the cost of an operation to reshape Chris's massive chin, Tom being a plastic-surgeon, and Chris chuckling about the cost of becoming a bit less lantern-jawed.

However there was, I later learned, nothing frivolous about the conversation which was going on outside Brown's for practically the entire time I was hurtling the fifty miles home along the motorway. Chris Clark was angry. Very angry. 'It was clear that he felt an opportunity had been missed,' recalled Donald. 'He had wanted to present to us a united front of the five Americans, to insist on what training they would do, and that with which they would have no part.

'They wanted to get control of that training schedule, because they all wanted very much to enjoy all the other things that were going on at Oxford. A couple of them wanted to join the flying club, Dan Lyons wanted them all to join the choir, Chris Penny wanted to wander round inspecting historical places, Clark wanted to tear around the countryside on his new motor bike. They did not want their lives dominated by the Boat Race which they thought they could win anyway, because they believed they were the best.

'And after you'd made one of your special Topolski speeches, lifting the whole thing onto the level of Mount Olympus, rather than a freezing boathouse in the middle of winter, well, Huntington started to waver – then Cadoux-Hudson told them that your schedule was very like the one he used to do at London University. And the united front began to disintegrate. Clark blew his top, and attacked Huntington. But in his mind Clark seemed to feel he had been the victim of some kind of a Topolski magic trick.'

It was a very perceptive, and I am sure, accurate account by Donald. He also remembered that Clark was stressing to the rest of them how they had just lost a golden opportunity, that nothing definite had been decided and that they had not achieved their aims. The schedule was probably going to be adjusted, slightly, but it was still under the control of the 'demonic Topolski', and that was nothing but 'a big pain in the ass'.

I should point out that many weeks went by before Donald went over those conversations with me, and I suspect that the feeling of unease I felt during the journey home was partly caused by an instinct I had that the President was leaning towards the Americans rather than backing his chief coach. What had happened? What had changed the mood of those Americans who had been rowing with us so cheerfully for the past few days?

Although I was not aware of an intention to take control of the training schedule, it was obviously going to be extremely difficult to get them to work-out in the manner I believed was necessary. I also knew that it did not matter how many world champions we had available; if they were only half-fit for the race they could well get caught by Cambridge in March. None of the new Americans had the slightest idea how fit, tough, and fast these Boat Race crews became after six months of relentless training all through the winter, and they certainly had no idea of what that race could do to you. Back home they would not start serious work for their summer racing season until well into the New Year.

And now I sensed Donald being influenced by their high confidence and arrogance about 'college rowing' – and as I drove through the dark, quiet streets of London in the small hours of that Tuesday morning, I was beginning to think this was threatening to be a year at least as frustrating as the last. On the one hand I had the potential for one of the greatest Oxford crews of all time. On the other I had a group of guys who sincerely believed they were collectively bigger than the event.

I wondered whether subconsciously I was loading the schedule a bit as a result of last year's defeat. In any event Clark seemed to be becoming an enemy. As a matter of fact I think that his compatriots found his rather hostile attitude to the training something of an embarrassment. They had, after all, come to Oxford to row in the Blue Boat and none of them wanted Clark to overstep the boundaries of reason and politeness.

There was one other problem that had to be dealt with early on, as there always is with a new squad, and that was to sort out who we had rowing in the squad and which was their normal side. That is, who rows on the starboard side (the left if you are sitting in the boat with your right hand on the end of the oar), and who rows on port. Any coach dealing with this has to make definite decisions with long-term consequences.

It was particularly so in the year we now faced, because we had a very powerful squad in the autumn of 1986, and it was seriously unbalanced.

On the strokeside the strength was exceptional: Cadoux-Hudson, world bronze in Pairs; Penny, Olympic silver medal in Eights; Huntington, world bronze in coxed Fours; Macdonald, Blue and Henley semi-finalist; Clark, Blue and US spare man; Stewart, 6ft 8½ins and 230lbs. All six of them were men who preferred their hard left hands on the end of the oar. Only four of them could make it.

On the bow side (starboard) Dan Lyons, the world gold medallist, stood alone. The rest, Pelham, Ward, and Leach had rowed in the Oxford reserve Eight a year earlier. Hull was a freshman with unknown potential. Worse still: some of those portside men outweighed their opposite numbers by as much as 30lbs a man!

The dilemma scarcely needed explaining. The solution was clear. To even up our chronic imbalance I asked Cadoux-Hudson and Clark, two near-certainties for the crew, both with Tideway experience, and some bowside rowing behind them, to swap sides. In a few weeks they would never tell the difference – because in reality the change is not that difficult – especially for a man like Clark who had been spare man in the US squad, a position which by definition required him to be able to step in, on either side. In any event I had used him on that side in 1986 during training. I not only knew he could do it, I knew he could do it almost easier than anyone else.

It was with an uncomfortable sense of disquiet that we settled down for the six-month haul to the Tideway. I radically restructured the schedule, knocked out some of the running, eased down on the circuits I expected them to do in the gymnasium at the Oxford stadium in Iffley Road and eradicated morning training. In place of this I did include some hard sprinting up a steep hill, a workout suggested by Chris Penny, who had gone through a similar programme of running back in the USA.

They used to run stadiums (up and down the bleachers again and again) at Harvard. Sawyier and Shealy still remembered with awe their work under Harry Parker. In my own second year at Oxford we used to run a series of 200-metre sprints up the steep hill behind the Leander Club at Henley   carrying a crewmate each on our backs.

Donald had the new schedule typed up and the following Monday morning when he drove into Oriel Square the boys were all ready for the rowing at Radley and then the hill sprints at Headington. The horror stories about Oxford training did not appear to have affected Lyons, Penny, Huntington or Fish very much, and they were all sitting on the wall with Chris Clark. Donald handed out the schedules and they all began to read, digesting the output I required from each and every one of them.

Suddenly Clark climbed slowly to his feet, shook his head in a gesture of exasperation, uttered an expletive which I shall now delete, and then walked away. What's more he did not come back for three days. Hated hill runs. Donald says this behaviour really did embarrass the Americans. Indeed Huntington apologized profusely for Chris's attitude. 'Don't take it badly, Donald. He'll come around. He's probably just a bit overwrought.'

At this stage in mid-October I already felt we had compromised the training schedule pretty severely. One of the younger new-comers to the squad asked me if land training at Oxford was always so easy. Donald was playing the diplomat as well as he could, attempting to separate me from any confrontations with the Americans over the time being spent in training. It was quite a difficult situation for him, in a way because of his age. Donald was now thirty-one, not twenty-two, as most Oxford Presidents usually were. And whereas those younger men in the past had been quite happy to leave training programmes entirely to the coaches, indeed grateful to do so, Donald felt he had to respond to the complaints and make adjustments to the schedule on the spot to satisfy them, and then hope to clear them with me later.

Throughout the autumn he was on pretty good terms with his squad and enjoyed the company of the Americans in the group – particularly Clark with whom he had been good friends during their time together in the '86 crew. He thought his problem was one of joint leadership, of having to clear those changes with me in London. But it wasn't. The problem was the most powerful resistance group ever encountered by an Oxford President. He was for ever being boxed into a corner.

Donald had a very pragmatic way of looking at our problems, and one thought was uppermost in his mind. He was not going to be beaten by Cambridge. His view was simple. If we rowed over the winning line behind the Light Blues, then he assumed he would return to 14 Lime Road, Botley, in a coffin. In the light of all this he did not intend to lose those who could help to power us home. He thus became something of a master at accepting the egos of the 'stars', handling the compromises, and preventing me from reading them the riot act. Those US oarsmen represented victory, a big smashing victory, and Donald was not about to let the chance of that slip through his grasp. The memory of the defeat was too painful for him. He was driven both personally, and as President, by the all-consuming fanaticism for revenge.

At the time though he seemed firmly based in the American camp, and I began to feel a sense of isolation. I was worried about our commitment to training, the sort of training Oxford had been doing for fifteen years. But the Americans only saw me as someone presenting a training schedule containing work they considered unnecessary to beat Cambridge.

'C'mon, Donald,' they'd say. 'This race is just not a problem to win. These guys are international oarsmen – you're talking college rowing here.'

We began our training on the Thames at Radley College, moving the shells down to their boathouse, about seven miles from Oxford. We started off in pairs, and Donald's personal fitness put him in a league with the best. He rowed with Chris Clark. Generally I liked the Americans to switch around, among each other and among the English boys to familiarize everyone with various styles. I remember Donald mentioning how surprised a lot of the younger members of the squad were at the lack of speed the men from the US displayed. They may have been expecting the kind of performance normally associated with oarsmen from the planet Krypton – but they did not get it.

As young Hugh Pelham remarked after rowing against the Americans at Radley: 'I've rowed in a pair on the river when Redgrave and Andy Holmes have been practising. I can tell you they would leave any two of our Americans hundreds of yards behind.'

But, of course, the Americans were only just getting into the swing of things and in truth they were still geared up for their normal US schedule directed at a summer racing programme. They saw no need for urgency. Why should they worry about beating anybody so early on in training?

Strangely it was Donald who brought me the first feeling of doubt over our competitiveness. Clark and Donald, who got along pretty well, had been rowing along quite fast one afternoon, when they came under attack from Hugh Pelham and his partner. Hugh's creed is simple: if it moves, race it. They came roaring up behind Donald and Chris; Donald was at stroke, and the American was behind pulling the bowside oar quite cheerfully, never even suggesting a problem in getting used to that side of the boat.

Donald glanced up, saw Pelham out to his right, pulling away as if his life depended on it, coming through in the manner of a Henley finalist with victory in sight. Donald glowered across the river and instantly increased the rate, fighting to stay level. 'Come on, Chris!' he snapped. 'Let's teach the little bugger a lesson.'

'Easy, Don, just stay cool,' said Clark. 'Just keep rowing along, nice and steady. Let him go.' It was, according to Donald, the statement of a big man discussing the antics of a teenager. 'It was like Mike Tyson grinning at an ambitious club fighter. Except Tyson would have hit him!'

It irritated Donald badly, but it inspired the old hero of the St Edward's school crew which won at Henley. Every time he saw Macdonald and Clark, he charged, rowing like a lunatic past them, and every time he did it, Clark asked the President to 'stay cool' and simply would not get into a race with the warlike Pelham.

'Clark's attitude was that such little battles were beneath him,' said Donald. 'But it nearly drove me crazy. Once he said "Don, sometimes I don't know where you guys are coming from". And I rounded on him, like an angry schoolboy, and I said: "Maybe you don't. But the only thing I want to do right now is to row Pelham off the river – and you won't f---ing well help me."'

There are always little frictions such as these around a training camp – and most of them are best ignored. As men become fitter and more psyched up towards their task, so feelings tend to run higher. That's all part of it, and all part of my usual rationale to members of my crews. I believed that inter-squad competition was a vital ingredient.

However, during the first three weeks at Radley I began to detect a rather insidious questioning of my methods and technical observations. It was not, I suppose, much, but it was repetitive and constant.

'Er, Dan, what *exactly* do you mean by that?'

'Look, Dan, could you just explain that to me – I'm not sure what you mean.'

'Dan, I thought you said something a little different the other day. I'm really not clear on this at all. . . .'

'Aw, c'mon Dan, that's not exactly what you said before. I just want to get it straight in my mind. I'm simply not clear what you are asking me to do.'

'Er, Dan, this is really getting a little confusing. . . .'

Whatever I asked them to do, they made me go over it again. I tried to treat it all naturally in a straightforward way, tried to convince myself that they were as profoundly dumb as they were pretending to be. After a couple of weeks I began to realise that it was just a ploy to undermine my authority, to make the younger ones snigger, and to perpetrate this atmosphere of sarcastic superiority, and the assumption of greater knowledge. I felt I was being made out to be a slightly out-of-touch old dodderer for the benefit of the rest of the group. It came as a bit of a shock because I had always felt at one with my squads in the past.

Was I having a good time coaching this crew of Oxford world-beaters? Not yet. And because my track record counted for nothing with them, I found myself on the defensive, while they seemed so certain of themselves.

Men in my British national team crews got on with the work without complaint, so why were this lot so different? There had been other 'star' oarsmen at Oxford before – silver and gold medallists like Bland, Brown, Mahoney, Shealy, Andrews and the Evans twins – but they had taken on the responsibility to set an example for the youngsters. They were competitive in absolutely everything, whether they thought privately that they were above such stuff or not.

Now I was faced with five 'stars', all persuading each other that my demands on their time were unnecessary. And yet deep in my soul I knew that if we did not go through a full programme of training, we would suffer the most humiliating beating on the Tideway. And in the end, I was not prepared to risk that. Neither was Donald.

Nonetheless things were going from bad to bloody awful. We were using a video-tape to sharpen up imperfections in technique. On one occasion at Radley I was talking about the problem of over-reaching at the catch – the beginning of the stroke – and as I did so Steve Royle was saying on the video, 'stretch out, reach for it.' Steve and I seemed at odds over a two-inch reach difference going forward.

This was too much for Fish, who was endeavouring to become the Lenny Bruce of the Thames. He yelled 'Contradiction! We have a contradiction here.' And seizing the remote controller proceeded to re-run it about five times. 'We do have a contradiction here gentlemen. A coaches' contradiction is what we have.' He milked it for every last ounce of humour, and it was pretty funny – the first time. Then a couple of them murmured: 'What a load of ?!?!?!?!'

That did it. I'd had enough. I turned round on them, blazing with anger, and finally read them the riot act, told them they were acting like a bunch of f---ing kids. They were going to have to shape up if they wanted to row for Oxford. Into this they doubtless read an implied threat that it was well within my sphere of influence to ensure that none of them did. My outburst silenced them, in calmer mode I informed them that they were going to have to stop undermining the coaches. They were like disruptive schoolchildren, having a go at a teacher, digging away and challenging authority at every turn in the road. 'This is puerile,' I said. 'And if we go on like this we're heading for big trouble against Cambridge next March.'

Their joint policy of confrontation, argument, and sarcasm was getting us absolutely nowhere, and I was beginning to wonder just how long I was prepared to go on listening to this rubbish. When I stepped back and tried to observe objectively what was actually going on, I could only see myself bending over backwards to accommodate the testing baby-games of a group of out-and-out brats.

One afternoon at Radley, I was vainly trying to get them into order for work on the river and running into the usual difficulties. Like nobody was ready. Actually, on this occasion it was slightly worse than that. I could not even find them. I couldn't find any of them. The boathouse was empty. I checked the clubhouse, and finally wandered into the dressing room. There they were standing in a silent group listening enthralled to the words of a man I didn't even know.

'Shhhhhh! Dan, shut up, this is important.'

'Huh?' I said. 'What's going on? We're supposed to be on the river. Who the hell is this guy? Carlos Castaneda?'

'Look, Dan, would you cool it for a minute? This is our choirmaster – we're just going over a few choruses.'

And with that the whole darned group of them burst into a horrendous rendering of 'You've lost that loving feeling!! Whoa–whoa–whoa–whoa', with their choirmaster conducting them.

If Cambridge could have seen us now. I just hoped to God that this lot could row under pressure a whole lot better than they could sing. In normal circumstances I would have been pleased by this manifestation of crew spirit, but here it seemed to be just another nuisance. It seemed calculated to divide rather than harmonize.

Donald? Well I assessed he was getting just a shade irritated by the choirboys. His polite and reasonable nature kept him affable, but sometimes I looked at him and he was deep in thought. He did not look like a man who knew he could *not* lose the Boat Race. But the rest of the squad were hooked. Several of the English boys quite openly thought the Americans were the crew gods they projected themselves to be. Young men like Gavin Stewart, Tony Ward, and Richard Hull hung on to their every word.

Any disagreement between myself and a member of that American group now escalated as a matter of course into a major split, with sides automatically taken. The basic authority of coach was being eroded away. Now, either I stayed tough, fought every point, defended every inch of territory, or we were going to slip into the anarchy which had reared its head at Oxford before, but had always been dealt with before any damage was done. As I have mentioned previously there is an unwritten code between oarsmen; we, who will go out and bear the pain together, we, who will never give in. It is nothing less than a sacred trust, and all great crews have it. We fight for each other, and there has to be a mental bond between all of us, a bond to hold that trust in place.

Dan Lyons actually came closest to spelling that out during a team talk. He described how an American coach decided one week to recruit eight 6-men, the big power oarsmen who operate in the middle of the boat, the heart and strength of any major crew. Well, this US Eight, with its all-star material occupying every seat just would not go fast. They rowed their hearts out but it never started to sing through the water. And no one ever found out why. The answer to this is slightly mystical, because the sum of a crew is greater than its parts. Those eight heavyweights had not time to develop the bond, the sacred trust, that can make a racing Eight fly.

And here was Oxford blithely heading towards anarchy with coaches neither trusted nor heeded, and two separate factions of oarsmen developing. In short, we stood a very sporting chance of committing suicide, unless things changed fast. Christopher Clark was going to have to row for us like an Olympic champion in order to compensate for the sinister undertones he had created within this squad.

But amazingly, I still believed he could do it. I also still quite liked him, and he still stayed in my flat; and like all coaches who have enjoyed major success, I always believed I could turn anyone round in time, even Clark, even the old 'Heater', who was causing such heartbreak, and such unrest. 'Come on Chris, let's give it a try. I want to see you row like the great oarsman I know you can be. . . .'

This last phrase of inspiration might have sprung from my lips with more alacrity if I had just a little bit more to go on in this direction. The trouble was I had, stuffed in my jacket pocket, the beginnings of the performance records I compiled meticulously every year. On the orange cover was written in black ink, 'Oxford 1986–87'. But for Clark there were still no weights lifted, no circuits run, no ergometers pulled. Nothing chronicled in there.

On page 6 were the races we had entered, single sculls, pairs and fours, starting with the Pairs Head of the River on the Tideway in the late summer – first Oxford boat home: Donald and Tony Ward.

Then came the Wallingford Sculls – first Oxford man home: Donald. Followed by Hugh Pelham, then me, with the international Cadoux-Hudson fifteen places further back.

A week later: the Reading Sculls – first Oxford man home, by miles, Donald, with Pelham sixteen places behind, and me nine behind him. The rest of the squad spread out among the other 150 scullers.

In the Marlow Sculls, won by Olympic Champion Steve Redgrave, the Americans competed for the first time. Our first man home was the ferociously competitive Pelham, with Donald twenty-three seconds back, our second best. In this big regatta Dan Lyons, a former US National Lightweight Singles Champion was twenty seconds behind Donald, with Clark twelve more ticks back. Huntington and Penny who were still learning to scull were a further minute in arrears. For what it's worth I finished mid-way between Pelham and Macdonald. In the Henley Sculls, Pelham was again our first man home, eight seconds in front of Donald. Then came the improving Lyons, nine seconds further back, with Clark out with the washing, one minute behind our President, and thirty-seven seconds behind me, his ageing and very modestly fit coach.

At this stage last year, the picture had been very different. At Henley Donald, Clark and Pelham had finished within five seconds of each other, in that order (twenty seconds in front of me). By the end of term – the Oxford Sculling Trials held in December – Clark chased Pelham home, leaving Donald fourteen seconds back in fifth place. Last year the American had been twice the sculler he was now.

What was wrong? Did he lack motivation? Didn't he realise that by avoiding training he would not regain his fitness? Dan Lyons was improving week by week, and even Huntington, who could not scull at all, was catching Clark, by minutes.

I also made a weights chart of the maximums each of them had lifted, and at the top of this was Christopher Penny, second was Oriel's Mark Machin, then the burly aggressive Pelham, then the towering Gavin Stewart, then the Australian world under-twenty-three silver medallist Rob Leach, then Donald, who had improved his bench-press by thirty per cent over the year before.

Christopher Clark's strength with the weights was more difficult for me to assess, because he had not completed any tests. So I had to use his last year's weight totals, when he was, in my opinion, stronger. Even then he was behind Macdonald, and in this year's chart he was 31lbs behind the President. Which was not too bad considering the performance of his cohort, the world gold medallist Dan Lyons. He finished last, 241lbs behind Donald, which I hoped was only a little demonstration to emphasize his disapproval of squad testing, rather than a true reflection of his strength.

If it was possible to lead this group by sheer example, only someone with a particularly churlish turn of mind could possibly suggest that Donald, and the OUBC Secretary Pelham, were not doing just that. But their example of determined hard training was not rubbing off. The crew was plagued with minor illnesses. There was always an American voice protesting about a cold, 'flu, 'just not feeling too good today,' or 'I really need a couple of days rest.'

I said little about this. In fact Donald was more angered by it than I was. But every time the subject of these little illnesses was mentioned we heard the same world-weary retorts from the Americans. 'Relax, Donald. We'll win the Boat Race, no sweat. It's in the bag, stop worrying. Cambridge aren't good enough to even practise with us guys.' But Donald knew, just as clearly as I did, that the results in the sculling, pairs and weight-training did not support such overpowering confidence.

And so it went on, compromising the schedule of normal Boat Race training at Oxford. Every time the work was stepped up a fraction Donald found he was listening to the monotone bleating of little Fish, ever protective of his flock of US giants. 'You can't do this to these guys, Donald. You're burning them out. You're frying them. You just *can't* ask them to do that.'

Try as we might to be accommodating we found ourselves facing a situation in which the star oarsmen from the United States were balking at everything and quibbling about what they would and would not do. 'Dan, we really don't wanna do that . . .' or 'Dan, that's really asking too much . . . we just don't wanna spend that much time. . . .'

What they did want to do though was to row together in a Four in the big national annual event, the Head of the River Race over the reverse Boat Race course on the Tideway in mid-November. Now this was always a rather hazardous adventure, because both Boat Race camps often entered at least three and sometimes as many as six crews. It was a key form guide, and it served as an important boost to morale to the university which did best. Needless to say I regarded it as a matter of honour for the carriers of the Dark Blue blades to come out on top. On the whole we usually beat the buggers out of sight.

Three times in the last four years an Oxford crew had triumphed – the exception was, of course, last year when Clark, Jones, Philp and Livingstone were beaten, actually were overtaken by Cambridge and that had really felt bad.

This year I wanted two evenly-matched Fours – splitting the Americans equally, the portside men, Penny and Huntington, each stroking a boat, backed by the starboard men, Lyons and Clark, in the 3 seats. I reckoned Andy Lobbenberg should steer the coxed boat with Penny, on the basis of his greater Tideway experience and his heroic performance in steering Isis to victory on that water against the Cambridge Reserves last March. Into this permutation I planned to insert Cadoux-Hudson, Macdonald, Gleeson, and Hull.

You would have thought I had proposed that Shirley Temple take a place in the crew. This was not acceptable, that was not acceptable. The other undermined the spirit of the crew. 'How can you even think of this Dan?'

In the coxed boat Lyons, Gleeson and Clark would sit at bow, 2 and 3 with Penny at stroke. In the coxless boat behind Huntington I would put Cadoux-Hudson, Donald and Richard Hull at bow.

I designated Penny's crew our top Four, and we gave them the best boat we had, a German-built Empacher I had leased from a Tideway club. So now there were no excuses. Oxford needed, and expected, victory, especially since I'd heard nothing but promises of brilliance from these guys since they had arrived. Now it was time for them to deliver.

They prepared to get down to work in the same mildly serious vein they had adopted all term. 'No big deal. Just relax. We'll be fine on the day.' But soon there was another problem. Lt. Dan Lyons, using some kind of body language technique he had doubtless picked up at Annapolis, walked up to Donald and placed his rather inexpressive eyes about four inches from Donald's, peering at him with the kind of deadpan look last seen on television on the face of another US military officer, Col. Oliver North.

'We wanna make some changes,' he said.

'What changes?' said Donald, barely supressing a sigh of resignation at the endlessly tiresome hand life was dealing him.

'Chris Clark wants to go back to stroke-side.'

'Well, he can't. We've already agreed that, with Dan and Chris. You know he is rowing for us on the bowside. He's been rowing with *me* on the bowside in a pair for almost a month, without complaining.'

'Well, he's not rowing there any more,' replied Lyons. 'We are not going to row with him on the starboard side. Either we cancel the whole thing, or we make the changes.'

Donald pondered the matter and decided not to get over-excited. 'What changes are you proposing?' he asked, 'because I'll have to have a word with Dan.'

'These changes are not for debate,' said Lyons. 'We either make them or we're pulling out of the race. We want Penny at stroke, me behind him, Chris at 2, Gleeson's out, and we'll bring in Tony Ward to row in the bow.'

Donald now had the uncomfortable task of explaining all of this to the ex-Brentwood schoolboy Paul Gleeson, who had only been rowing for a year and was making dramatic progress. 'I'm sorry, Paul,' he told him. 'But you're not going to row either way. If you stay in, the boat does not race, if you withdraw you are on the bank anyway. It's a no-win call. And believe me I am as fed up with all this as you are.'

And so, to keep the Americans happy, we nearly broke the spirit of Paul Gleeson, and promoted Ward to row in the bow. Then they thought he was not good enough either, and he had to go. Then they wanted Rob Leach, the bespectacled Aussie from Adelaide, so he was promoted. Ward was demoted. Training went on as before, not too tough, just enough to keep everyone ticking over on the premise that, 'It'll be just fine on the day.'

The Saturday of the race dawned, a grey, damp and cold November day. The London river was dank and gloomy and up by the Bandstand at Barnes, nearly 400 Fours were preparing for the 'Off'. As guests of London Rowing Club at Putney, we had paddled upstream to the start, both of our crews going easily, and at half-pace they looked encouragingly well together.

Penny's coxed Four started before the Oxford coxless boat and Donald was able to watch them move into their stride and pull away down the three-and-a-half mile course, with Chris Penny driving along the crowded river at a good racing pace. They looked smooth, fast and well within themselves. Huntington's Four charged off shortly afterwards, with Donald at 2 as usual bent on overtaking every boat on the river – police launches, ferries, anything that happened to be going in the same direction. Any crew threatening to pass – attack back, never let them through.

However it quickly became apparent that they had a steering problem. Hull in the bow was in charge of keeping the boat straight, but he kept slipping off the ebb tide, and Tom Cadoux-Hudson called repeatedly: 'C'mon, Richard, ease her back, just a little, head back to the right, that's good, shade more, that's good.'

But Hull was not a fast learner on this day. Finally the autumn air along Chiswick Reach was split by a bellow of: 'For f---'s sake Richard steer the bastard! Are you f---ing blind or something . . . get back in the stream you useless prick.'

What followed was a ridiculous argument, halfway down the course, and the erratic path of the boat continued, unabated. 'Shut up!!' yelled the President. 'I'm not shouting at you!' bawled Cadoux-Hudson. 'Shut up anyway,' bellowed Donald.

Finally they crossed the line, Penny, Clark and Lyons looking very cool, Donald and his group looking a bit harrassed. This race was of course all worked out on the clock, and the full result would not be known for about two hours after the last boat finished. The boys decided to head back to Oxford, but I went along to the Auriol Kensington Boat Club to wait for the result.

When it came I nearly jumped off Hammersmith Bridge. Penny, Lyons, Clark and Leach had finished 28th – our top crew in our best boat. Adjusting the time on the watch, twelve seconds for the cox they carried, they finished dead equal with Donald's Four, and we know what a supreme example of slick racing and steering they had put up.

What was infinitely more depressing was the fact that two Cambridge crews had finished in front of us, the first coxed Four by seventeen seconds. The *third* damned Light Blue crew was only *one* second behind Penny's Four. This was not just serious, this was absolutely diabolical. The room was full of Cambridge oarsmen. I could not take it, I made myself scarce.

I called Donald and told him how disappointed I was. He was very upset and explained in more detail the performance of his own crew – issuing a typical Donald remark, 'Dan, we were not perfect.' He added, sardonically, that in his view a timed dead-heat with his boat was not a matter for major celebration! He promised however to pass on to the Americans the exhilarating news.

By now I was finding it very hard to sleep. I would lie awake churning over in my mind what I had to do to get this squad into shape. Donald, too, was very worried. I knew that. But he was still trying to face both ways, and protect the egos of the Americans. Between us we were faced with a group of international class oarsmen who were determined to go their own way. We were in my view approaching anarchy. And we were going to lose the Boat Race unless something was done. I found now that every time I went to Oxford I was beginning to work out a number two schedule in case they objected to the first. And sometimes during the car ride from London I was even working on a number three schedule, should number two also prove unacceptable.

However I had never known Donald quite so pre-occupied before. He knew now he faced the prospect not only of being a losing President, but of going down in history as a member of the greatest Blue Boat ever to be defeated in the Boat Race. He also faced the likelihood of being remembered as the President who set aside the claims of the young English students at Oxford – and instead filled the Dark Blue boat with five US internationals and *still* lost. Things were looking bleak. And not just for Donald. With this much potential talent at my disposal, defeat was unthinkable. I simply had to make them work. But how? They wouldn't.

I arrived at the Radley Boathouse on the Monday afternoon in a mood which might safely be described as black. I called a meeting of the squad and told them how disastrous the result on Saturday had been. 'Not one of you was interested enough to phone me over the weekend for the results. All the Cambridge boys were there waiting to know how they'd done. They're hungrier than you are. They want it more.' As far as I was concerned a big question mark hung over both their level of fitness and their commitment.

I told them this could not go on for one day longer. 'We are not going to win like this. I have tried to take your views into account, but you are now working less hard on land than any Oxford squad in the past thirteen years.' I said that I had cut back on the time they spent training in the belief that they would reciprocate by working harder. But some of them were showing an alarming reluctance to get tired. They were letting down themselves, the University, Uncle Sam, President Reagan, the United States Navy, Uncle Tom Cobley and all. I expected heavy contriteness. What I got was a level of complacency that was close to pure recklessness.

'Aw, c'mon, Dan, it was just a Mickey Mouse race.' I don't even remember which one of them said it, but one of them did. And I will not ever forget it. Their arrogance remained inviolate. They continued to insist it would all be all right when it mattered. They were offhand, dismissive, and patronizing. I told them that surely they recognized they had been given a valuable and punishing lesson by the Tideway, that the river has a mind of its own and it must command their respect. And they must now know they had to do the proper training in order to be able to cope with it.

'You have just been walloped by Cambridge,' I concluded. 'Disgraced publicly.' But they showed not one sign of humility. 'Relax, Dan. We're here to win the Boat Race, and we will.' They also spared me a few moments to blame the boat and suggest that the Australian, Leach, the man they themselves had insisted on using, had hindered them badly. Rob never recovered his confidence and was to drop out of the squad after Christmas.

I returned to London in a state of despair. I was pale from lack of sleep, and I was making myself ill with worry. The truth was I could not get through to these people. The powers of persuasion I have used for so long to coax exhausted oarsmen to victory after victory would not work with this group. And I was growing sick of trying. What I did not know was that Donald, beneath that calm and polite veneer of his, behind that conciliatory, 'Now come on boys, let's talk it over properly,' was at this moment steaming with anger. The old spirit of the Rajputana Rifles was rising within him, and when that happens he is a formidable force.

Let me explain what this gentle Scotsman can really be like. Join me, if you will, on the Isis just below Donnington Bridge last summer. Donald was stroking a crew when suddenly a good-sized rock flew past his face and splashed into the water. Then another whizzed by, missing him narrowly and hitting the water right next to him. Donald looked up and saw two louts aged about seventeen on the bridge, leering over the parapet. He ordered the crew to pull into the bank, beneath some trees, out of sight of the bridge. He disembarked and set off at a loping run and reached the bridge just as these two shaven-headed thugs walked down and met him face to face.

The iron grip of Donald wrapped itself somewhere between a scruffy t-shirt and throat, and lifting the rock-thrower into the air he hurled him into the river. The second one froze with fear, somewhat too late, for Donald grabbed him and flung him into the river too. He gazed down at them and said quietly, 'Don't throw stones at me, laddie.'

When he returned to the boat, he just climbed back in, pushed off into the stream, and in answer to the question: 'What happened?' he just said: 'I threw them both into the river.' Someone asked: 'Did they drown?' And Donald said, 'I don't know.'

Donald's anger at the defeat of the American Four on the Tideway, in the wake of all the unrest they had caused, was somewhere close to the level of fury he had felt on Donnington Bridge. Not that he was planning to throw Clark, Penny and Lyons into the river – though I would not have been surprised to see Fish hurtling into the Thames at Radley – but, as President, he felt terribly let down. So he waited until I had gone and called another meeting in the clubhouse. And there he delivered the first tongue-lashing anyone had ever heard from him. He told them that the defeat on Saturday had in his view been a direct result of the lack of proper training. He told them they had had their way, taken advantage with spurious illnesses and other excuses, and now Oxford University had received a bloody nose in public, and that he was not going to put up with it for one moment longer. He told them he would not tolerate anyone else cutting training, and that the programme they had agreed was out of the window, that the full Topolski schedule was going into effect as from right now, and anyone who did not like it could get out.

'I know one thing,' he snarled. 'Last year I was not able to crawl up the stairs to bed I was so tired after Dan's training workouts. Pedalling home on my racing bike I used to get overtaken by old ladies. And that's not happening this year. We're all going soft in my opinion. And the whole sorry mess came back to haunt us on the Tideway.'

Donald let them know he would view any more claims of illness with the greatest scepticism, and he said to them: 'I want you to treat every day as if it is the day of the Boat Race. And I wonder how many of you would allow all your little illnesses to prevent you stepping forward to claim your Blue on the day of the Boat Race.'

Only Dan Lyons took half-hearted issue and said to Donald

afterwards: 'I do not like being spoken to like a child either by coaches or Presidents. I do not find it helpful.' But he went no further.

The position of Chris Clark was under severe scrutiny. I had now been associated with him through four major races – last year's Fours Head in which we were humiliated; last year's Boat Race in which we were humiliated; the US trials in which he and Lyons were humiliated; and now this Fours Head in which we had been humiliated. You would imagine that I was developing serious doubts about his capacity to *race* – particularly in the light of Spracklen's comments. But I *still* thought he could come through for us if I could just find the right button to press.

Donald, I think, was no longer so sure about this. He began to inflict an iron regime upon the crew, forcing all of those who wanted to row in the Oxford Blue boat to stick to my original unedited programme. Once when we made an adjustment in the gym, switching the entire squad from the weights to the big rowing machine, the ergometer, Fish came over to complain: 'You just can't do this to these guys,' he said, his voice rising. 'They gonna be fried, man, fried. It's too much.'

The President spun round, white-faced and shouted: 'I don't give a f---. If you don't want to train, don't. Just get out.'

On reflection I suppose Fish was lucky not to have found himself sailing through the window onto the running track. But it silenced him and the rest of them. And for the next ten days they continued to take what they regarded as punishment like men. And sure enough Oxford began to improve. On one evening Donald claims in all seriousness that he was overtaken on his racing bike by two very old ladies, on Botley Hill. And that evening there was a smile on his face as Ruth helped him into bed – battered, exhausted, and aching, but content that our ship was finally back on bearing.

CHAPTER FIVE

WALK-OUT

'My position at Oxford is bloody impossible,' I thundered as I stormed through the door. And that night I lay awake for hours, sometimes dozing off, only to wake sweating, fighting off the spectre of a Light Blue boat driving past Oxford on the outside of the Hammersmith Bend. It will always matter so much to me.

The defeat of the American Four ended my happy little tradition of sending out a crew to win the Coxed Fours battle on the Tideway. And with that twenty-eighth position came the end of another Oxford tradition in Putney – that of staying as guests of the London Rowing Club, a privilege the members had extended to us for the past fifteen years. We stored our boats there, ate there, rested there, showered and changed there and generally treated the place like home. It was a wonderfully comfortable old-style Thames-side rowing club, right opposite the Boat Race start.

No sooner had we left London on that gruesome afternoon than I received a message informing me that the Oxford University Boat Club was no longer quite so welcome – our nominal fee was about to go up by 300 per cent. There was no justification for it. But I dug deep for the underlying cause. It was apparently the general rudeness of some of the crew. I hoped it was a case of some Oxford oarsmen failing to show sufficient deference to members of the club rather than of active offensiveness. So I had to arrange a new

London base for our forthcoming training camps on the Tideway, an annoyance I did not much need on top of everything else.

I told the boys not to worry too much about it because previous Oxford crews had blotted their copybooks in equally auspicious establishments. In fact Oxford had once been thrown out of our autumn headquarters, Radley College-boats, oars, rowlocks and all.

And it was not hard to get to the bottom of that little matter either. It had happened in 1977 with the arrival at Oxford of the mighty Al Shealy from Harvard, one of the best strokes America ever had. Al however had a further important talent, he was one of the world's greatest exponents of the comparatively modern Stateside art of 'mooning'. His timing, perseverance and positioning were supreme in the limited experience of the young English oarsmen at Oxford.

I suppose, in retrospect, Al had three sensational moments during his two years at the university. Two of them were Boat Race victories, one by seven lengths, the other when Cambridge sank in rough water. The third was when he performed a full 'moon' for the entire length of the M4 Motorway from the Chiswick Flyover to the Henley turn-off. He executed this devastating feat of endurance from the sports car of our cox, Mr Colin Moynihan, who is now Minister of Sport in Her Majesty's Government.

As a straightforward achievement Al's Motorway Moon would rank among the major sights of the post-war years in Berkshire, especially since the rest of the crew drove alongside in the OUBC van to ensure fair play throughout the thirty-mile route. However it should also be born in mind that he pulled it off in mid-February and that when his ice-blue buttocks were finally withdrawn from public view, a hero of near-mythical proportions was born.

This in turn caused a competitive spirit to emerge among the English boys and finally they seized their moment. On the way home from training on the Radley Reach, they sighted from the van two ladies on horseback, and they snapped into action. Down came their track suits and four pairs of buttocks were pressed into the long windows of the van. The horses panicked, bolted across the fields; the local village was outraged, and I received a letter from Radley College in very much the same tone of voice as that from London Rowing Club ten years later.

It specified that the Oxford University Boat Club was to remove itself forthwith from the school territory. It was a terrible blow to me, because we need that stretch of water, and it took more than a year for the authorities to reconsider their action against us. I am told that the mooning incident lives still in certain common rooms there, and that some Oxford colleges have never been allowed back to practise on that stretch of water to this day.

I'll say one thing for that Radley ban though. It never killed the Dark Blue spirit. When they arrived on the Tideway for the 1977 Boat Race they mounted a full crew moon for the benefit of the Cambridge boatman Alf Twinn. This is an extremely rare event, a moon of the full ranks of the Oxford crew – I suppose the nearest military equivalent would be Trooping the Colour. But it did not throw the sharp-tongued Twinn off his stride for a moment. 'Looks a bloody sight prettier than their faces,' snapped the old Fen waterman.

Down the years certain names always crop up when you reminisce about remembered laughter or high triumphs, and one of these is Al Shealy, probably because he came to us with the biggest reputation of any visiting oarsman in the history of the Boat Club. He had stroked Harvard through four seasons of almost unbeaten battles (they lost only once in all his time there). He won three US national championships, he smashed four course records, and he stroked the US national Eight for four years from 1973, winning the world championship of 1974.

He loved Oxford and he settled into our ways as if he had been there all of his life. He did a lot of shouting, a lot of bellowing encouragement, and quite a bit of mooning. But when he left Oxford, I think he left a part of his soul there. None of us who worked with him in the Blue Boat will ever forget him – and even now when I cross the quadrangle of University College, I still see Al in my mind, striding through the big gateway, with his huge grin and full moustache. 'Just remember, Dan – no bastard ever won a war by dying for his country. . . .'

He once said something about the Boat Race which says much about him, and a little about us: 'In the early months of training you're thinking "What the hell is all this for?" Because the race is so far off. There's so much tedium and discipline and brutal effort to hammer through. You have to resist the subconscious desire to put an end to all this self-inflicted hardship. But as the days pass and you feel yourself geting stronger, you begin to live for the day. You punish yourself with a will in training, because you know you're facing a twenty-minute race which will suspend your life for that time.

'Somewhere around Hammersmith Bridge (seven minutes into

the race) you find out what it is you've been working for. And you're asking big questions of your body, and when the right answers are coming back, it's a feeling you know you will never forget.

'The work is like an investment. The more you sink in, the more determined you are to get the dividend. And in the Boat Race, there's only one dividend. And that's winning!'

There had been times in the past few weeks when I considered taking Al's words and marching into University College and ramming them down the throat of one of their current students. I resisted the temptation.

Now, in November 1986, my world headquarters was Radley, the peaceful corner of Oxfordshire where the first foundations were laid for all my winning crews. It is a wonderful stretch of the Thames, four miles long between the old pound-locks of Sandford to the north, and Abingdon to the south, both built during the 1600s. The city of Oxford itself lies further to the north, beyond the upper lock where Matthew Arnold wrote of 'the grassy harvest of the river fields . . . down by Sandford.'

The southerly lock guards the waterway to the seventh-century town of Abingdon – and between them the river flows deep, clear and often fast. For its banks narrow along here, and after rain the stream gains speed, flowing past a small island almost forming rapids, which test a coxwain's mettle.

The big Americans, and the Canadian Olympian twins Mike and Mark Evans, and Graham Jones always loved it along here. For the cross-river territories of Radley College and the great eighteenth-century Palladian mansion of Nuneham House guard the river for a long way, making it almost inaccessible to the public.

In comforting privacy the oarsmen of Oxford fight their fights on this lovely reach, beneath lush parklands fashioned by Capability Brown, and clipped lawns which fringe the waterway, making cover sometimes scarce for the grebes and the moorhens, and the occasional old dog otter.

'Sweet Thames, run softly, until I end my song.'

Somehow on the river's broad back I had to coerce this weak-kneed complaining squad into some kind of a Viking warship, and give it spine, and determination. This reach had often, in the past, sifted the faint-hearted in the early stages, for though it is easy racing before its fast southerly current, flowing in flashes of silver on the winding way to Abingdon, it's a back-breaker rowing home against it.

We always lose a couple of guys in our first weeks at Radley, but they are always the ones without real commitment. And now, with our disgruntled transatlantic all-stars apparently trying to make up for past sins, and fearful of the President's wrath, the next few weeks promised a productive and rift-healing panacea.

Saturday, 29 November, saw us almost two weeks into the 'new regime' – two weeks since the big defeat on the Tideway – and the crews were working hard on the course. They'd been up past Arnold's grassy river fields to Sandford on their warm-up, and had raced down on the fast stream, back past the boathouse and on towards the weir at Abingdon Lock. Above the 1,000-metre straight the stream was swirling around the island, and both boats had been thrown towards the bank, the coxes fighting for control.

Now they were driving back, hard against the stream. Penny was looking good stroking one crew, and I could hear Lobbenberg bawling at his Eight, urging them on. The oars crashed into the water as they powered on, struggling for mastery on the little right-hand bend beneath the old Great Western Railway Bridge. They hauled the shells along one behind the other, in gruelling tandem on this silent autumn morning.

And now the island would thrust the crews to one side as they threaded their way past, and I could see Donald working away aggressively, in one of the number 6 seats. Huntington and Lyons were going at it too, and it was heartening to see Chris Clark pulling away on the bowside with big hard, confident strokes. This was more like it. I worked them steadily, in two pieces, all the way back up to the lock, both boats rating at between twenty-eight and thirty strokes a minute just below the anaerobic threshold. No build-up of lactic acid. Every time they stopped to rest, I could hear them breathing heavily in the damp foggy air. Some heads lolled back, others slumped briefly forward. But upon the command, they picked up the oars again, and dug into the ancient waters once more.

Back at the boathouse the boys carried the shells up the bank. They took ashore our video camera on which I hoped there was a full record of each man's performance that morning. We were now getting into the real blood and guts graft that makes boat-crews. There was big pressure on the two coxes and, personally, I thought Lobbenberg was reacting to the unusual challenge of this stretch of deep, fast winding water rather better than Fish, whose strength remained his in-boat motivation of the crew. I shuddered, though, to think of what might happen if I decided that Andy's Tideway experience gave him the edge.

The senior crews had been on the water for an hour and a half and needed a break. I had to go out on the launch again because I needed to spend a half-hour with the third crew, who ought always to feel a part of the Oxford effort to beat Cambridge. In their boat I hoped were men who would pull in the Blue Boat next year, or even the year after.

'Okay guys,' I shouted to the others. 'Don't put the boats away. Leave them on trestles, and get into some dry kit. Grab a cup of tea and a bar of chocolate. I'll be back in half-an-hour to go through the video with you. We'll make the second outing short. Just technique.'

Albert Andrews, our longtime Oxford boatman headed the launch back out onto the river for my appointment with the third crew. As ever they worked hard, anxious to please, their dreams of Blue Boat glory not so far away. Shortly before midday, I arrived back, and as I disembarked the first thing I noticed was that both of the big racing shells had been put away behind the doors of the old Radley boathouse. 'Oh, no,' I groaned. 'Trouble.'

'No, it couldn't be,' I thought to myself. 'You're over-reacting. Maybe they put the boats away because they didn't hear. Don't get excited. . . .' 'Oh Lord. Here we go again.'

I tried to pretend I thought everything was fine, bounded up the stairs into the clubhouse, where they were all sitting around, and I said 'Okay, let's have a quick look at the video together.' This was strictly a technical discussion. I was looking for 'late catches', when a blade goes in just a fraction behind the others making the overall cohesion of the boat look a bit rough; for bodies leaning out, off the true line; for blade heights too far from the water; for co-ordination of the leg and back movements as each oarsman drives off the foot-stretcher, the oars firmly anchored in the water. I was looking for big puddles.

I could tell they were tense, and not really listening to me. I knew something was afoot, but still I pressed on, thoughtfully explaining to each man the areas I felt he should concentrate on.

'Right, let's go out for a short one. Just some technique paddling, to see if we can work out a few of the problems, while the video is still fresh in our minds.'

Chris Penny shuffled to his feet and turned to Dan Lyons, who nodded. Then he began to walk towards me. 'Dan,' he said, 'We don't feel we should go out for a second outing. We've done enough.'

'Oh, c'mon Chris. We've just watched the video. Everything is sharp in our minds. We're not going to work. Don't worry. I only want to practise a few points of technique together.'

'We're not going.'

'Now wait a minute, what's the problem? You know this second outing's on the schedule. It's been there all the time. You know that. I just want these crews on the water for a quick half-hour of technique.'

'We're not going, Dan. We just don't wanna do that.'

There was total silence in the room, as I faced Penny. Every ounce of aggression I possess was flooding into my body. I stared at him, and forced my temper under control. I looked at the rest of them. And they were all standing rigid, like statues. No one spoke. No one moved.

I turned my gaze back to the big country boy from Rhode Island, considered the sweet prospect of landing a cricket bat on the point of his huge chin, but I just said to him quietly, 'I don't want to discuss this in front of everyone. Come out onto the balcony.'

That was a big mistake. I went first, and looked down to see a gathering crowd below. There were the Radley schoolboys beginning to assemble, and the girls from the Oxford lightweight squad, and they all looked up as I stepped out onto the balcony, overlooking the forecourt and beyond that the river. 'Christ,' I thought to myself, 'We're going to look like Romeo and bloody Juliet up here.'

Penny followed me out, and the other Americans came out behind him, Lyons, Huntington, Clark and Fish. And then Donald. He stood slightly to one side, and the other five, unsmiling, formed a semi-circle in front of me. My back was to the river as well as to the wall. This was very, very ugly.

I decided to try reason, for a start, to try to get them for once to see things from my point of view. I explained to them that I was driving 120 miles a day to help them as best I could. I was getting nothing out of it, financially, or any other way. I was just wearing out my car. All I wanted in return was for them to reach peak fitness and then go out and beat Cambridge. 'But right now,' I said, 'I'm hating it. This is giving me no pleasure.'

'It's not giving us any pleasure either,' said an American voice.

I knew that I must reason with them powerfully, try to persuade them. But on the other hand I knew all of this had to stop. This confrontation was psychologically terrible for everyone. You can't win Boat Races with this kind of stuff going on. And it was wearing me down. I said to them: 'Now listen. Your individual techniques must be attended to after we video an outing. You know that. All of you.'

'Yes Dan, we do know that. But not today. We've worked hard.'

'I know you have.' But I could not hold back the edge of sarcasm, as I found myself saying, 'And thank you very much for working hard'. I tried to describe the effect their constant objections were having on morale, mine included. 'Every day,' I said. 'I get into my car and come here to coach you. And for the first time in my life, I am doing it with the greatest reluctance, which is only a short step from resentment. And all the way here, I'm trying to think of a training programme to back up the one we already have, just in case you refuse to do it. Then I'm thinking of a third, then a fourth, just to make sure we can always do something. Something which you as a group will approve of.

'Well, I would like you to know here and now that I really cannot operate like that. It's no good for you, and it sure as hell is no good for me. As a group, on paper, you are a truly formidable line-up, but all of the evidence I have so far says you have a bloody good chance of getting beaten by Cambridge. Can you imagine the embarrassment of that for you and for me? Six internationals and we *lose*. You seem to have no idea of what the press in both your country and mine would do to us. And deservedly so. It would be truly appalling for all of you, in your rowing careers, and equally appalling for me.

'I have had enough. Unless this gets resolved now I'm finished.'

Huntington stepped into the discussion for the first time. 'Dan,' he said, 'There is no question in our minds about your ability. We really respect your coaching. All of us do. And we all know there is no one like you for the last two weeks on the Tideway before the race.'

By now every one of the dozens of eyes below us were fixed on the balcony, and the other guys in my squad were coming through and asking 'What's going on?'

I turned once more to face the Americans. 'Well,' I said, 'I hope I have made my position clear. Let's go out on the river for half-an-hour, and let that be an end to it. Let's just do the programme. Sort yourselves out and get ready to go afloat. And please, please no more arguments.' And I pushed my way through them and went downstairs.

I walked down to the water to talk to the third Eight. After a few minutes I turned around to see all five of the Americans, with their bags, getting into the van. What, however, I did not expect was that the President and the whole British contingent would meekly join the walkout. But they did, and they followed the Americans, sheep-like, into the van. I felt sickened by how deep the rift had become, and shocked by Donald's passive acceptance of the action. I was left standing in total isolation, both physically and emotionally. I felt betrayed, in a sense, by all of them. I went out with the third Eight, rather sadly. At the end of their work, I said goodbye to them and drove myself back to London. In my mind I could not see myself coaching the Oxford boat again. It had all become too painful.

That evening Donald phoned. I think he knew that I felt he had let me down terribly. The conversation was very tense, and very distant between us. Almost formal. Donald took great pains to try to explain to me that his actions at Radley had a firm objective – to remove the insoluble crew impasse from public view. I told him that I thought the writing was on the wall after our pathetic defeat in the Fours Head of the River. I felt I could fight back from that, but not with a crew which would not listen to me. How could I possibly work against that? Get them motivated? Get them to win? 'Donald,' I said 'Can't you see where we're headed? There is no point in me coming back. I don't believe in those guys any more. And they don't believe in me. That's the bottom line. I'm sorry. But I'm finished.'

The Oxford President rang off, our partnership in ruins. I did not know then what he felt. But for myself I felt utterly drained. My relationship with Donald was not the only one under pressure. A couple of years earlier I had settled down with the English actress Suzy Gilmore, and she was watching my decline with growing concern. She remembers me coming home each evening, angry and upset, and increasingly impatient with everybody around me. 'The situation at Oxford is bloody impossible,' I would thunder as I stormed through the door. But she recalls that at this stage things were beginning to pass over her head a bit because she had other matters on her mind. We expected our first child at the end of January – nonetheless she remembers how grey and ill I looked.

On this particular night I lay awake for hours. Sometimes I dozed off, only to wake up sweating, fighting off the spectre of a Light Blue boat driving past Oxford on the outside of the Hammersmith bend.

I am, I know, a lifetime prisoner of the river. And until now I had been a prisoner of the Boat Race, of Oxford, and of all the marvellous characters that have passed through, mostly, I am pleased to say, on their way to victory. Because of my obsession with the race I suppose my career as a journalist and photographer had suffered. I had made up for the lack of big financial rewards by finding much real contentment and fulfilment, the kind that eludes so many people. I was a member of a huge international family of oarsmen, but above all I was permanently involved in the passion of life, in the fight for victory, in the glorious moments of triumph, and in the aching heartbreak of defeat. I felt alive, out there battling, every day.

It often seemed that my whole existence was on the line, especially in late March. And as I lay there pondering what Christopher Clark, Dan Lyons, Christopher Penny, Christopher Huntington, and Jon Fish had done to the OUBC, to me and to Donald, it seemed so unreal. For they were but passing figures, who would soon be gone, leaving the river to the ghosts of Matthew Arnold and Edmund Spenser, and to the grebes and the swans, to Oxford, and to me.

Would I return when they had gone? Would some other President in the future call me one day and ask the question I had heard every year for so long. 'Daniel, would you consider coaching the Dark Blues this year?' Or would they fight now without me? Would I become one of the fringe figures who is occasionally invited out on the Oxford launch to watch a crew of strangers? It would never matter to Lyons, Clark, Penny, Huntington, or Fish, because they were at Oxford only for themselves, and their diplomas. Soon they would all be on the other side of the world, with hardly a fleeting thought for the deep waters running fast past the Radley Boathouse after the rain.

Clark would doubtless be watching the surf in Newport, and Lyons in his white Naval uniform would be issuing his breezy greeting to young Americans: 'Hi, I'm Dan Lyons. You've probably heard of me. I won a gold medal at the world championships.'

Perhaps one day they would come to regret all this. Perhaps in some twenty-first century American boardroom one of them would find his mind wandering from Wall Street, to recall with sadness the deep divide he and his friends had once caused in the Dark Blue boathouse. Maybe he would look back at these years at Oxford, not with pleasure, but as a time of conflict and strife. How could any one of them know how much this university beside the River Isis would come to mean in their lives?

But for now it did not matter to them, and they hurried and bustled their way through the immediacy of their student lives. But it would always matter to me. My life would not be the same again. Which is why I could not sleep.

Back at his home Donald slammed down the phone and said 'Damn!' Then he said to Ruth, very quietly, 'I've lost Dan. We've had it. I don't think we have a prayer of winning without him.'

Ruth was sympathetic to his plight, and worried about her husband generally. He had a huge academic work load, that MA in literature at Oxford being renowned as one of the toughest degree courses of all. Ruth knew he could cope with rowing as well as being a father, head of a family, and President. But now he appeared also to be fighting a war, which was tearing him apart. On the one hand he could not stand to lose the Boat Race, and he believed he needed the Americans to prevent that. But he regarded me as a friend, and now that relationship was, in his mind, in shreds.

'I should have moved; right outside the Radley boathouse,' he told me months later. 'I should have said to them, "Well, *go*." And I should have told them they could not leave in the OUBC van which I required. I should have pounced, made my stand there. Insisted that the oarsmen did as the chief coach said, or got out if they did not like the system. I suppose the Americans could have gone and sat in the van but they would have looked pretty bloody stupid.

'I realize now that that was my chance. And I did not take it. Instead I was consumed with the thought that nothing good was going to happen there at Radley on that day. I felt I should get Clark, Penny, Huntington, Fish and Lyons out of there, gather my thoughts, and hope to God I could get to a phone quick enough to stop you from resigning.'

On the way home Donald had warned his men of the problems they now faced, that he would almost certainly lose his chief coach, and with him, he thought, the Boat Race. Clark was elated: 'Oh my god!' he shouted. 'That's beautiful. Just get rid of the guy. I warned you all about Topolski. And now you think he'll go? That's beautiful.'

Donald says he was most concerned as they drove back to Oxford with balancing the two sides. Trying to keep me on board would be difficult, he knew, but he had to try to get the Americans to stop regarding me as some kind of monster, who apparently had the power to summon them all to the river at midnight if he wished, for a moonlight four-miler.

He believed they were utterly spooked by me, although I had never asked them to do anything I had not done myself or that I had not asked every other Oxford crew to do in the past. What Chris Clark had done, his one most effective contribution, had been to instil a sense of utter paranoia into the squad, a perceived belief that I held life or death sway over their lives. In any event, after the phone call to me, Donald went into action in one final last ditch effort to prevent the OUBC from succumbing to the destructive form of anarchy which now threatened, and which comes when crew oarsmen decide to answer to no one but themselves.

Unbeknown to me he decided to call a meeting and to recruit Graham Jones as a formal adviser. The other man he elected to contact was one of the Oxford legends, the great Boris Rankov, who had studied at Oxford for as long as anyone could remember. He had rowed in six Boat Races, and won them all. He was a terrific guy, looked like a Cossack, and I had coached him throughout his long and glittering career as an oarsman at the university.

In 1978 Boris had rowed at 4 on the strokeside behind Al Shealy in the crew stroked by the brilliant Australian World Lightweight Champion Ag Michelmore; in 1979 the big Russo-Yorkshireman conquered the pain of a badly injured back and was still there hauling away as we crossed the line nearly four lengths in front of Cambridge; in 1980 he switched to the bowside as President and nearly killed himself inspiring his crew home on that fateful afternoon when the bowman collapsed and we still held on by a canvas. Boris could not walk for three days after that, but he was back again to help Oxford's superb eight-length win in 1981. He was there in 1982 when Cambridge led us for the first mile-and-a-half, and in the great crew of 1983 he held the 5 seat right in front of Graham Jones. Three times a winner on strokeside, three times a winner on bowside.

Here was this true Titan of the Isis now being asked to help mediate between a President who was about to lose his chief coach, and a bunch of guys from the USA who were refusing to train properly. God knows what he must have been thinking. As for Graham Jones, who on his own admission had missed no more than twenty days rowing since he was sixteen years old, he too was an Oxford oarsman of considerable standing. He had rowed four times for Oxford and twice for Australia, once in the finals of the world championships.

Donald however knew the extent of the crisis he faced. He understood the American resentment at what they considered to be my hold over them, even though he himself disagreed with them. In Jones he thought he had a tough Aussie who would just say 'Do what Dan wants, otherwise get out.' But he thought Boris might have some understanding for their situation. After all, Boris, a wonderful individualist, celebrated one of our great victories by producing t-shirts for all of the crew, which read across the back: 'I have satisfied Dan Topolski'. Boris knew I was hard to please but that the reward was immortality. Now, as a Professor of pre-Roman archaeology, Boris would, it seemed to Donald, be a calming, reasonable, experienced influence on what might be a volatile meeting.

He then telephoned the History don at Mansfield, Dr Mike Mahony, himself an impressive rower for the college in his day, and booked the great Council Room for a formal meeting of the Boat Club that Sunday evening.

He recounted to me, months later, the lengths he went to in order to convey how seriously he viewed the situation. He contacted all of the Americans and told them it was imperative they attend. He informed each one of them that Oxford had lost their chief coach, and wondered if any of them had any inkling of what reaction that was likely to cause. 'This will be headlines in all the national papers tomorrow,' he said. 'The popular Press sees Topolski as one of the biggest men in rowing in Great Britain.' He added: 'In case any of you are still confused by the significance of this, consider it on the lines of a national disaster, and you'll find yourself in roughly the frame of mind I am looking for.'

At eight o'clock that night they all trooped into the imposing Council Room, with its tall windows, and portraits of academics who have worked at Mansfield since its foundation in the middle of the last century. Donald sat at the head of the table and began the proceedings with the words: 'We have probably lost Dan, and as President I am obliged to regard that with the utmost seriousness.'

Chris Clark, who was vainly trying to keep a low profile behind the stronger characters of Lyons and Penny could not contain himself. He apparently found this news a source of overwhelming delight and shouted loudly: 'Who cares?' Donald demanded silence, and Clark replied with a groan, 'Oh My God, isn't it over yet? Why don't we just get rid of the guy? This is our chance'.

Donald called in Graham and Boris to try and cool the meeting down, and says that Boris in particular spoke with great force.

'Listen you guys,' he said, 'Dan Topolski has inflicted these iron regimes upon an entire generation of oarsmen, for good reason. To make sure we win the Boat Race every year. It's the same for everyone. We all managed to deal with it. And you guys should be able to ride with it too, cope with it, slip a few of the punches if you like, but stop fighting it.

'Of course Dan knows a few corners get cut from time to time,' he said. 'It is just not necessary to turn everything into open warfare. Like all grown-up people you've got to be able to ride with the situation, just keep doing your best, but if something is truly impossible for you, there is still no need for it to end up in a stand-up row with the coach.'

There were a few appreciative American sounds at his revelations. But Donald, who was now thinking and acting rather more decisively, knew he would have to present something very definitive for me to reconsider my position. He insisted they specify their grievances and demanded that they draw up some kind of charter to lay out precisely what time they would all allocate to training, including travelling time. This should signal an end finally to the endless argument over training.

This was duly agreed, and translated into American space programme parlance as 'core-time', which not only took into account where exactly you were coming from, but was very specific about the precise space you were in. It was less specific about meaningful human relationships, and taken literally meant that I would be expected to arrive two or three hours early to do all the rigging for them (the half-hour or so all rowers spend making little adjustments to the rig of the boat – like raising rigger heights, or re-adjusting the angle of blade pitch).

During this meeting, Penny and Huntington, sensing the magnitude of the uproar which would undoubtedly break out if the peace was not quickly restored, apparently behaved with reason and common sense. Clark was fairly non-committal except when my name occurred, at which he tended to lose much of his cool. Fish was extremely militant and Dan Lyons continued his increasingly obvious role as one of the main forces behind the unrest.

The meeting broke up shortly after ten o'clock, and Donald left with the draft of the document in his pocket. He knew it was the last chance the Boat Club had to establish a lasting peace. There could be no more excuses for anarchy flaring up during his Presidency. He wrote in his diary that night: 'The Radley affair had been the perfect opportunity for me to isolate the Americans, and thus divide and rule. Instead I chose conciliation, thereby strengthening their position and undermining Dan's.' It was a course of action he bitterly regretted, and has done so to this day.

At home he completed writing down the details of the 'core-time' programme and telephoned me early the following morning, Monday. I listened to him with an air of resignation. I viewed the American promises with something less than overpowering optimism. But he assured me they had sworn this was positively the last time. He did not feel at the time that he could afford to tell me he had also written in his journal 'When I walked out of the meeting with that piece of paper, agreed by the Americans, I felt like Neville Chamberlain on his way home from Munich.'

I am not a quitter. Leaving this mutinous ship was something I could not do in the face of a plea from the President. Donald promised again this was the end of the trouble. And wearily, without committing myself to anything, I agreed to turn up to see them towards the end of the week. Since it was now Monday, and they had their major full-course trial scheduled for Thursday on the Tideway, I was disinclined to return to Radley that week.

Instead I sat at home and did some very solid, and I hoped, constructive thinking. The root of the problem, I concluded, was that our American visitors sincerely believed they could win the Boat Race, with some ease without going through all of the training I knew to be necessary. They misunderstood the nature of the battle in its entirety. One of the deep psychological barriers I faced here was that they were used to hitting peak form for their own national championships and the world championships at the end of the summer, and for some reason our late March date had not really struck home. I suppose that in October or even November it still seemed ages away. And they just did not seem to be able to switch on to my key requirement for a high level of fitness by Christmas.

They were dismissing my urgent calls for hard individual conditioning in December as the rantings of an eccentric, their lifetime habit of idling their way through the late fall and winter as strong within them as the call of the south to the swallows in October. And yet I kept telling myself, there had never been such turmoil with the other American and international rowers I had worked with in the past. Before there had been a definite feeling of all being involved together. Dave Sawyier's crew had, if anything, to be held back. The Evans twins, who went straight from the Tideway to an Olympic gold medal, had terrific drive and competitiveness in every aspect of our training. The way they went round the gym and the running track in 1983 with Graham Jones, Boris Rankov, Olympian Bill Lang and John Bland, the British world silver medallist, used to set my pulse racing with excitement. Isis men like Chris Long and the huge Australian Dave Rose, who would row for Oxford the following year, were inspired, and revelled in the chance to work alongside these outstanding athletes.

With all of them, the commitment had been there, deep-rooted, throughout everything. But this 1986–87 experience was something entirely new – this tight knot of sullen resistance, and lack of acknowledgement of what the Boat Race means to Oxford University and its austere and stringent demands.

Part of the trouble had probably started last year, with loveable Bruce Philp and the sense of disorder of his Presidency. Something was missing then throughout our training because there was no one prepared to provide that internal dynamic that is so vital within all crew rowing. As soon as Donald's new regime came in I had felt that here was the chance to take this Boat Race by the short hairs and bring it back under control. I immediately had put much more of myself into the job, and I was demanding as much from the guys, for it would be hard to get back on top again.

The instant counter-action of the Americans had inflamed the situation because I could see us wallowing once more. The whole approach to training now had a bad smell about it, which apparently was offensive only to me. And I knew we had to get a grip, and put a stop to the messiness and the lack of commitment. As long as they were permitted to pursue their current attitudes, the atmosphere would slide inevitably back to the way it had been last year, and surely end in confusion, chaos and defeat.

Last year had been atypical. Atypical of the previous fourteen years in which there had been a demon driving Oxford. I was not that demon, but I had helped to create that powerful unseen force which hates the sight of the ghastly duck-egg Blue of Cambridge University.

From the beginning of the century until 1973, Cambridge had been regarded as the 'winning' university, Oxford as the perennial underdogs, defeated on all but twelve occasions since the beginning of the First World War. Losing had been etched deep into the Oxford psyche. The Light Blues cynical toast was: 'Please God let Oxford win – but not this year.' In 1974 we had broken the mould.

In the fourteen years that followed, only *six* out of all the men who pulled for the Dark Blues suffered the despair of not winning the Boat Race – two Americans, a Canadian and three Brits. And although Boat Race lore is liberally sprinkled with the names of great American athletes, in fact only three – one of them a Harvard man – participated in our miraculous ten-year run of success.

Our defeat on 29 March 1986 was a shuddering blow for me. The four new Americans had not suffered that humiliation, that emotional battering. I had. And I wanted revenge. It did not affect Christopher Clark as it affected me, and with his new group of friends, he did not feel the intensity, the hunger and burning urgency to get back on top that assailed me all day and most of each night.

How could they know how hard it had been to win those ten Boat Races in a row? How could they know what it took? How could they ever understand the years of planning and sacrifice and effort? No. They could never understand the pain of last year's defeat. And why should they?

Each and every one of them, Clark, Lyons, Penny, Huntington, and Fish, had come here to this greatest of all universities to ride in glory upon the bandwagon we had created here on the River Isis. And when they realised the bandwagon was temporarily rolling a little less smoothly, not one of them was prepared to get off, roll up his sleeves and push the sonofabitch with me. Not one of them. And now they were playing a part in slowing it down more. Their resistance to training was a symptom of the still-lingering poison of last year's failure, which, like a cancer, can spread so rapidly. Since they did not fully comprehend the anatomy of last year's beating, they certainly were not going to be able to grasp the ramifications of the fight back.

Every sportsman knows that it is a great deal harder to get *back* to the top, than to attain the pinnacle in the first place. For years, more than a century, the old fighters' saying, 'They never come back,' held true. That is until great modern boxers like Floyd Patterson, Mohammed Ali and Sugar Ray Leonard punched that old theory on the nose. But basically it still holds true; thousands have tried to come back, but it takes the fingers of only one hand to count the ones that made it. I'm not saying it's impossible, I'm merely suggesting that it's not easy.

I imagine that the great motivators of the past would never have tolerated their attitude. Can anyone imagine any Notre Dame lineman ever having said to Knute Rockne, 'Sorry, Knute, I've done enough today. I'm just not doing any more.' Or a Green Bay Packer to Vince Lombardi? Or a Dallas Cowboy to Tom Landry? In their own country such behaviour would never be endured.

Here at Oxford, where top-class oarsmen are less common and have to be created, more allowances are made for truculence, but at this stage I was very unsure how much more of this we could take. Because, just below the surface, we had brewing an ugly sedition and a sense of active ill-will towards we who formed, for want of a better word, the establishment at the OUBC.

It was symptomatic of the new brattishness which has been abroad in sport, worldwide, throughout the last dozen years, insinuating itself into places where before there seemed to have been only decent manners, and a sense of respect for the occasion and all that had gone before.

Remember Jimmy Connors in 1977 refusing to attend Wimbledon's hundredth Birthday parade of the great champions of the past, because he wanted to practise a hundred yards away for his forthcoming match? And what of the antics of John McEnroe? Of sportsmen going before law-courts to uphold their rights and be reinstated? And other big stars being arrested for assaulting opponents? And players going on strike for hundreds of thousands of dollars? And even a man like Denis Conner declaring to the world's Press in 1983 that America is still number one – right in front of the great Aussie skipper John Bertrand who had just destroyed him, three races in a row, to claim the America's Cup.

Is the pleasure really going from it altogether? Is the loser's handshake and the gallant gesture of goodwill from the winner becoming a thing of the past?

Petulance, I am afraid thou art wearing a track suit.

Of course professional outfits can cope with these kinds of matter, either by throwing money at the problems, firing people, or issuing fines and suspensions. None of these remedies are available to us, because we are amateurs and supremely vulnerable to a hostile cartel of big stars. We were simply not geared to deal with so many giant egos all at the same time.

In 1987 the setting for most of the dissent in the crew was the bar in Oriel – the fourteenth-century college of the adventurers, Sir Walter Raleigh and Cecil Rhodes. A small inner-city college which spawned the notorious nineteenth-century 'Oxford Movement', with its inflammatory doctrine of 'spiritual and moral awareness'. Now it was the college of Dan Lyons, Peter Gish, Pete Baird, Richard Hull, Tony Ward and Mark Machin. Right around the corner was University College, home of Chris Clark. Jon Fish and Chris Huntington of Mansfield, and Chris Penny of St. John's, also tended to gravitate there. It was a big influential group, highly political and highly motivated in the cause of bucking the system and getting your own way.

Donald rarely, if ever, went there, because mostly he had to race home and attend to all of the countless little details of the Presidency, issuing instructions, making phone calls and holding his family together. During his absence, that gathering of oarsmen travelled across the unseen divide from *ésprit de corps* to become a lobby, or a quorum of complaints and unrest.

This, then, was the Oxford camp to which I was being invited to return. And I felt no sense of flattery. Just a dull, tired feeling where once I had looked forward, eagerly, to the challenge. Now I could see no joy in it whatsoever.

And yet I had to go back. For that unseen demon still lurked in my soul. And there it would stay until Oxford had once more defeated the boat with the Light Blue oars.

CHAPTER SIX

WINTER OF DISCONTENT

Blizzards came and went and there was no shelter. Ice from the spray stuck in their hair, fingers froze, and the water of the Thames froze solid on the oars. As the boys ripped them out at the end of the stroke they were dripping, by the time they had flashed back to the catch position they were frozen over with ice.

I agreed to return to the river to see Oxford on the Thursday after the walk-out at Radley. The date was 4 December, a cold blustery day, and the squad was scheduled to row a full Boat Race course trial between two more or less equal Eights on the London Tideway. This was always a difficult time for the oarsmen, as the university packed up for the Christmas vacation and it required, if anything, even more single-mindedness than usual.

Early that morning the boys began to emerge from the rapidly emptying colleges. They carried their heavy rowing bags, crammed with winter gear, to protect them in some small way from the villainous December blast they would find howling down the Thames sixty miles to the south-east, and they piled into the two OUBC vans in Oriel Square.

By now the squad was beginning to take some sort of shape, and the best men, the near certainties for places, were joined by younger less experienced, but ambitious men, each one of whom felt he had a genuine shot at one of the seats for the battle against Cambridge in March.

We also had a new commercial sponsor, Beefeater Gin, which had come up with £330,000 to help the two Boat Race crews over the next three years. In honour of their greatly appreciated input of cash, we named the trial crews 'Gin' and 'Tonic'.

The first, coxed by Andy Lobbenberg, would be stroked by Chris Penny, with Tony Ward, behind him and Donald in the 6-seat. Chris Clark would row behind Donald at 5 on the bow-side, and the bow four would consist of Paul Gleeson, Tom Cadoux-Hudson, Mark Machin and Hugh Pelham.

'Tonic' would be coxed by Fish, and stroked by Huntington. Dan Lyons would be at 7, in front of big Gavin Stewart, and Richard Hull at 5. The bow four in this crew would be the inexperienced American freshman, Peter Gish, from Dartmouth, the Australian Under-23 silver medallist Rob Leach, Chris Chinn at 2, and Pete Baird at bow.

In the broadest terms, if a final Eight HAD to be picked before the trial, it would be the stern four of each boat, with Ward, Clark or Hull probably losing his place in the next month to Cadoux-Hudson, who was still getting used to the bowside. However the entire thing was now subject very much to performance in this, the first formal race over the full course between our two combinations of the Oxford first and second Eights. Tensions would run high this morning.

At much the same time as they drove out of Oriel Square, bound for London, I too climbed into my car and began the old familiar journey down to Putney. I must have made it hundreds and hundreds of times in my rowing life. But I could not pretend it was just another routine journey out of the West End through the 'yuppie reaches' of the south-west, and out along the King's Road towards the river. Because it was not. The last time I had seen the Oxford squad was when they all trooped into the van at Radley, leaving me standing there like a fool.

For myself I found little pleasure in my impending return to duty. I had not formally resigned, but neither had I given Donald my guarantee that I would coach the Blue Boat. My indecisiveness was not caused by any form of contrariness, merely that I did not yet know what I intended to do. On the one hand I did not think I could stand any more warfare with the American cabal, but on the other hand I felt unable simply to walk away from the problem. It went against the grain. The demon I had helped to create was still there.

The drive down to the Tideway was curious because of this paradoxical mood that weighed heavily upon me. Oxford University had been such a part of my life, and even at those times when I wondered how I could ever extricate myself from its pervasive spell, there was still that old recognition of satisfaction which forced me to go on for yet another Boat Race victory. Now I seemed to have one foot on the outside, indeed I had made up my mind that I could not possibly go on as before, making myself ill with worry over the state of the crew. And yet, I could not just leave them. As individuals none of them could have kept me at Oxford. But as the Eight, the fighting entity that would take to the water to do battle with Cambridge, well that was different.

They might in time become known as Topolski's Last Crew. They might perhaps be known as Topolski's American Crew. But if they should lose badly, they could become known as The Crew Which Finished Dan Topolski. Even if I turned this car around, right now, and drove home, never to set foot on the Oxford launch again, I could not disassociate myself from the argumentative rebels who awaited me at Putney. If they lost this Boat Race, they would take me, and in a sense all that I had done, along with them.

Over the past fifteen years the Oxford team had been energetic ambassadors for rowing, travelling all over the world in response to invitations to help establish regattas. Seven months ago we were helping the City of Savannah in Georgia, and then helping UCLA in California. The Dark Blues were flying the flag. In the years before that we had raced on the Danube in a World Wildlife Fund programme in Austria to save the Vienna Woods from destruction by a proposed dam. We raced in Egypt, on the Nile in the 1970s, several times, to help that country's government programme. We had raced in goodwill regattas in Turkey, Brazil, Japan and Canada and all over Europe, in Spain, Portugal, France, Holland and Germany, Denmark and Yugoslavia, Italy, Hungary, Sweden and Belgium. By any standards we were the most famous rowing club on earth, and I had done everything I could to nurture this comradeship, and to cooperate with this wonderfully diverse international network of countries, who all loved Oxford and everything we stood for, our sportsmanship, our good manners, and our spirit of international friendship. I was really proud of that reputation, as were all of the people most closely involved on a year-to-year basis.

I parked my car on the windswept concrete of the Putney Hard, and entered the slightly less familiar surroundings of Thames Rowing Club, in which I had now arranged for the crew to make their headquarters. I met Donald briefly and went over the crew positions with him, which were the same as I had left them the previous week.

I watched both Eights pull out into the rough, choppy water, on this freezing cold morning, and once more I stepped aboard the Oxford University launch. I saw them through a light outing and we broke for lunch. Afterwards, they got afloat promptly and were on the starting line early, alongside *Enchantress* which was carrying the Press, out in force today to witness the trial.

Chris Huntington, coxed by Jonathon Fish, was drawn on the Surrey station in a slightly superior boat, our big wooden Empacher with which we had beaten Cambridge three years earlier. Penny, stroking the rival crew lined up on the Middlesex station in one of the grey carbo boats which lay a little too low in the water for the big crew aboard. We were short of good quality Eights. The wind was now gusting hard, west-south-west, and there was no way they were going to avoid the big waves breaking up beyond Hammersmith Bridge.

Both crews got away cleanly, fighting for position, Huntington leading with long sure strokes, Lyons as usual moving a lot of water on the end of his blade. Over in the carbo boat Penny was working hard and behind him at 5 and 6 Clark and Macdonald were powering through the first twenty strokes with immense determination.

Inexorably, though, Huntington's crew began to edge ahead, their specially-designed aerofoil riggers slicing through the turbulent water just a little more efficiently. In the first one-and-a-half minutes they got maybe half a length, and then added another quarter in the next minute. But Penny, on the inside of this first short bend, was sprinting furiously to get back on terms, with the hard men in the engine room, Macdonald, Clark and Cadoux-Hudson, backing him up and the cox Lobbenberg roaring encouragement as they fought their way along Fulham Reach.

Then Fish, not knowing the Tideway, started to cut the corner, a little bit early, pushing across to his right. Lobbenberg, watching from behind was having none of it, and held his course, driving his men forward, sticking to his line. I grabbed the megaphone and shouted a warning: 'Jon! Get back to your station! Move left!!' Lobbenberg kept coming, and now they were really close. I shouted another warning to Fish to steer left, but he ignored it and cut right across the bows of Penny's boat which rammed him hard. The air went blue with obscenities.

Pelham, white-faced with anger, swung round and lashed out at Fish with a vicious right hook, aiming a glancing blow high towards the coxswain's head. Mark Machin also took a swing at him, missed and nearly fell out of the boat. Pelham hit out again, driving his fist into thin air, but by now the Surrey crew were well out of reach, wallowing, with a broken rudder.

I'll say one thing for Oxford that year, life was never dull. But now I had to get them repaired, because there was only an hour of the flooding tide left, after which it would turn and render the race impossible. I spent ten minutes hanging over the bow of the launch up to my elbows in the freezing water trying to fix the rudder with Albert the boatman clinging on to my ankles. But it was no good, we had to return to the boathouse. It took another twenty minutes to fix it, and we headed back out again on the fast-diminishing tide.

Again they got away very fast, both crews striking over forty as they ploughed through the first twenty strokes. My main intelligence from the first clash was that Fish had no idea where to go on this river, and Lobbenberg, who had come off the stream in the first race, was not a whole lot better. I picked up the megaphone and tried to talk Fish over the course.

Once more Huntington's men grabbed a fast half-length, but with great courage Penny's boys held them. They raced hard past the Mile Post still separated by that small distance, heading virtually neck and neck for Hammersmith Bridge. By now the wind was howling through that famous centre arch and the two Dark Blue boats buffeted their way through, the coxes shouting and urging them on.

Once through the arch, Fish steered left and his big wooden shell ran into the slightly calmer water off the main tidal stream. Lobbenberg steered straight up the middle, driving hard into the roughest water on the river. They hit it like a brick wall, instantly dropped two-and-a-half lengths, and the fight went right out of them. It was not really their fault, they were in the smaller boat, and had got stuck on the outside of the big Hammersmith Bend. Yet I would have liked to have seen just a bit more grit and determination when they ran into trouble.

As it was they rowed the rest of the course still separated by that three lengths. Actually they looked quite good, better than I had seen them before. Could this be some kind of turning point?

If it was I would not have long to assess it because it was already clear that some of the Americans were going home early, rather than remaining as a group for the whole two-week training camp we always hold on the Isis during the first two weeks of the university vacation. And so I prepared to let them take the next day off before regrouping to take part in the Oxford University sculling competition we usually organized in the week after the end of term. Chris Penny had an idea to make the day a bit more fun, and suggested a scratch regatta in the afternoon, all in Fours, drawn out of a hat. 'Just row some sprints together,' he said, 'It's more fun than straight training.'

It sounded good to me, and on Saturday morning we all reported to the freezing Isis. The river banks were utterly deserted, a hard frost still glistened in the grass, and in that raw silence of thin winter air we went afloat for our last sculling competition.

I got the boys away one at a time, with a stop watch on everyone to decide the winner. Donald and Hugh Pelham went off like tigers, whipping their blades into the icy waters over the mile-and-a-bit course from Haystacks Corner up through Donnington Bridge, and the Gut, past the boathouses to finish at Folley Bridge. Donald was determined to put Hugh in his place, once and for all, but Hugh, who angers so fast and can be so volatile, was equally determined not to give him that pleasure.

They raced over the course like cat and dog, Donald finally beating Hugh, who scraped the bank, by two seconds. Thirteen seconds behind Hugh the lanky Tony Ward, then Cadoux-Hudson six more back, just about level with Hull who nicked another boat. In sixth position was Clark, twenty-three seconds behind Macdonald; then five more places to Penny, who was seventy-six seconds behind the President, with Huntington four seconds behind him. Lyons had already gone home to Philadelphia.

Donald's victory did not surprise me, nor did it concern me. He had after all been our top sculler all year. Everyone knew that. Pelham's tenacious performance was also predictable. The interesting one was Huntington, who was really just learning to scull at Oxford. Remarkably he had capsized in mid-race, but lost only forty-five seconds. He climbed back into his boat, freezing to death, got going again, and was catching Penny at the end. If he had not capsized I estimated he would have been up with Clark at the end of the race. The result then was not exciting, because what I really wanted to see was Clark right up there with Donald and Pelham as he had been the year before. Nothing would have pleased me more than for the big Californian to demonstrate conclusively he had finally decided to get properly fit.

The Fours regatta in the afternoon was a lot of fun, but it ended abruptly. Suddenly boats stroked by Penny, Huntington and Stewart who had been enjoying himself immensely, started heading for the dock. Clark's was not far behind them. The explanation from them was simple: 'Core-time, Dan, as agreed'. Even when they were having fun this lot knew their rights. While we were on the subject I asked them if they still considered it reasonable that I should arrive a couple of hours early and rig the boats for them. No, they were happy to do this, but if they did it it came off the designated two-and-a-half hours. 'That's your time man, not ours.'

They still could not cope with the absence of professional coaches and 'riggers' at Oxford, and what's more were not prepared to make any allowances whatsoever for our amateur way of life. What they apparently wanted was for me to get there an hour or two early and do it all for them. It was true that the Americans had been working harder this past three weeks, but their underlying attitude had changed not one jot.

In the past, the guys had always mucked in and done much of the small day-to-day adjustments to their own rigging, while I, or one of the other coaches, would deal with the bigger jobs, assisted by the crew. I am afraid that my continued sense of weariness with them as a crowd, remained. My over-riding view was that I would stick this out, because I don't like to leave in mid-stream. I did not think I was going to do this ever again. But disillusionment was settling deep within me.

My pleasure in the Boat Race, after all this time, was dying fast. Like it or not, I had to acknowledge that these Americans were now pretty much in control of the OUBC. As long as I went along with them everything was fine, but the moment they disagreed with me, the sky fell in. We had lost that sense of mutual co-operation that I had always valued so highly in all my past Oxford squads.

Towards the end of the following week, after a few days on the Isis, we planned to get down to some concentrated seat racing over on the flat water of Thorpe Park some forty miles away. It is a tough game, seat racing, and it can throw up some useful facts. This would be an important camp. Chris Clark, however, left on a plane for America without a word to us.

The format of these gruelling tests which can so isolate a man, within his squad, is to let two crews row a three-to-six-minute piece. The coach then calls the two boats together in the middle of the river and asks two men to change places. Now we *know* how the two boats finished the first time, and since none of the rowers knows in advance who is due to be swapped over, you can get a pretty fair reading of a decline or increase in performance in either boat. The system of course can lay itself open to some skulduggery, with men occasionally trying to get their mates in, rowing hard for them, and weakly for opponents.

The key to seat racing is thus secrecy, the first race being hard rowed, with none of the oarsmen knowing whom I will swap. From then on it would be dangerous for anyone to slacken off, because they might be next to change. It is rare for people to try to influence results because everybody wants the coaches to select the best men. But it can happen.

We coaches might be a bit slow-witted, but we're not dumb, and it's not that easy to fool us. In fact the only time I can be truly hoodwinked in seat racing is if the strokemen, most unusually, decide to influence the result, because with our system they are never being raced. They are only required to set the pace, keep the rate even, one with the other, and pull consistently and hard. Conceivably they could help a friend if they so wished, because there would be no consequences for them.

Anyway Clark took off right behind Lyons. But the other two American oarsmen stayed and for three days we raced some tough and impressive competitions at Thorpe Park. At various times Gavin Stewart fought a dead-heat with Penny and narrowly beat Macdonald. Huntington beat Stewart, Pelham beat Ward, and Cadoux-Hudson, now comfortable on his new side, finished top of the starboard men, just ahead of Hull. The Aussie Rob Leach failed to make the top five on this side, and sadly withdrew from the squad.

The seat races with the most far-reaching consequences were those between Donald, Stewart and Penny – and my view of them was tempered by the fact that I knew, although he himself probably did not, that Donald was getting a bit worn out and jaded. The pressures of the Presidency weigh heavily on even a man as fighting fit as Donald was. He had covered a mountainous workload of training, a lot more than some of them, having started in August. He rose to every challenge and prided himself on never missing a session.

He wanted to be the toughest, most highly-trained man in the crew, and few who were there could take issue with that. However, I could now see, occasionally, a rather drawn look to his face, displaying the tell-tale signs of an athlete getting run down. Both of the two previous Presidents, Bruce Philp and Lynton Richmond, had suffered a pre-Christmas physical slump for the same reasons of overwork. Actually the pressures of the Presidency have more often than not affected athletic performance over the years.

But I did want to see just how good Gavin had become. In the first race the President's boat had clear water, when Gavin's crew, stroked by Penny, flew the last hundred yards and failed by only a canvas to catch up. I swapped Donald with Stewart for the second race, which ended soon after the start when one of the shells hit a log. We then went back and started again. Stewart's boat took a slight lead which Donald and Penny grabbed back and after a tense battle Stewart's crew moved ahead to win by just over a half-length.

I then seat-raced Stewart and Penny and the result was a dead-heat. Stewart had clearly made great strides, for here he was rowing neck and neck with an Olympic silver medallist. Huntington was a length in front of them and with Donald only two-thirds of a length behind them we were clearly in bloody good shape on the strokeside.

We were racing two crews during training now, and the atmosphere was noticeably better in that fortnight. It had improved with the disappearance of Clark and Lyons, and suddenly we seemed to be developing some real spirit in the squad.

By the last two days of the two-week camp, the rest of the Americans had gone home for Christmas as well. It was with great interest that I selected an Eight, to fly to Spain over the weekend for an invitation regatta in Seville. We were to meet a Cambridge Eight, the hated enemy, for the first time since they had wiped us out in the Fours Head, and the second time since they demolished our winning streak in last year's Boat Race.

I recruited an old Blue from 1979–80, Mike Diserens, to stroke us; Ward was 7, Gavin Stewart 6, Hugh Pelham 5, with two or three more Old Blues to make up numbers. It was a real hotch-potch, but seven of them had something in common; they were all extremely good scullers. Only Gavin Stewart was not really accomplished in single boat racing, but he was so big and strong, as the Americans say, 'He sure as hell couldn't hurt.' Donald remained training in Oxford to spend time with his family.

Cambridge, who were on the same plane, had a very good crew, with several internationals and Old Blues. They were tough and heavy. We would also face a top Spanish crew plus the Italian World Lightweight Champions. It was going to be hard, but I liked these guys and I thought we could do well. On the plane I talked to every one of them in turn, and told them that, although we might appear a rum bunch we were all fast individually and I thought we might just pull it off. Everyone knows I believe the best scullers ultimately make the best crewmen.

In two days in a strange boat, this tight little group of Dark Blues welded together very nicely indeed, and we entered the 3,500-metre race brimful of confidence. We thumped Cambridge and we raced level with the world champion Italians all the way, losing by about five feet in the last fifty metres. The Spaniards, on their own waters, were marginally faster than all three of us, and won by about a length-and-a-half. But it was a smashing race, very close and very competitive. I was well pleased, and the crew were full of optimism having beaten this very strong Cambridge outfit. It was the first beam of sunlight in my life for God knows how long.

In the bus on the way back to the airport all three of the boys from the current Oxford squad were saying that surely we did not need the Americans, that we could race and beat Cambridge as we were. Before they went home for Christmas, Stewart, Pelham and Ward made one joint request – that they each be given the chance to seat race against Christopher Clark, whom they believed they could beat. After their performance that afternoon, I could hardly argue.

I began my answer with the words, 'Well, if he does actually come back . . .' and the rest of my sentence was drowned by howls of derision. All of us knew that so far, it had proved well nigh impossible to get a test result out of him at all – no weights, no seat racing, no erg but mucho walk-out as they said locally. Events however were to overtake our new-found optimism and comradeship. Soon this unity would be smashed beyond repair.

By the time we touched down at Heathrow Airport the first piece of intelligence from Clark was received by our President. It was a letter, about which Donald had noted in his diary, 'received after he had flown home.'

It confirmed that he was well on his way to recovery from illness. However his future with Oxford was uncertain: 'But as far as Oxford rowing is concerned, the point is moot.' He complained about 'another hassle' with me, and proceeded to state: 'There is something gone awry with a crew that allows their coach to rule even though he makes the lives of the team members miserable. No one is indispensible including Topolski. Actually the most loose and productive practices of the year were held during the period of his ersatz "resignation".'

And he added: 'I received some mail today from my coach in the USA. I noticed that our national squad coach has a squad weekend in Philly on the 13th and 14th. I'll probably do that. I would enjoy being involved in some rowing with, one, "professional" coaches, two, good rowers, and three, sensible work-outs.'

He then castigated in writing some of the younger crewmen (Hull, Ward and Stewart) for caring about just 'making the boat', placed himself in a class of 'élite oarsmen', confirmed that winning 'is the key', had another go at 'the likes of Topolski', and signed off with a veiled 'suicide threat' – 'this move on my part ought to make them (the "Boatmakers") happy.'

During the Christmas break I pondered the problem of Christopher Clark. Was he, even as I cut the family turkey at a full Topolski gathering in London, powering through the waters of the Schuykill River, inspiring the US National Eight to ever greater efforts?

Was the American head coach Kris Korzeniowski gazing in wonder at the losing Oxford number 6 man with his new-found zest for the sport? And would I, in the end, welcome back a super-fit Clark, hard as iron from his exertions on the Schuykill? If that were to happen then our problems would be over. We'd be able to put out our strongest crew against Cambridge and I could get on with my life and allow rowing to take a more subdued role in the future than it was at present. If however he came back unfit, I might have to cut another turkey.

Finally I could bear the suspense no longer. I picked up the phone and dialled Kris Korzeniowski in Philadelphia. We had a chat for a while and then I asked him how Clark was getting along with his training. 'Clark?' he replied. 'You mean Chris Clark? Oh, I only saw him for one outing. He was hardly here. He's gone.'

Gone where? That was the question. Was he following the training programme or was he at rest on some beach?

The New Year arrived. And on 2 January the whole squad reported to the Tideway in London except for the Americans. Penny, Hunt and Lyons were all late but were ensconced in our training camp within two or three days of our scheduled start. Clark did not show.

The weather turned suddenly much colder than it had been at any time during that winter, temperatures dropping well below freezing; blizzards came and went, and ice formed along the banks of the river. Conditions were becoming arctic and on the wide expanse of the Thames at this point there was no shelter from the stiff icy wind, which seemed to eat right through even the warmest clothing. Some of the boys wore bobbled ski hats, which quickly became frosted over with ice; others went bare-headed and the ice from the spray stuck in their hair. Some wore gloves, but it is extremely hard to row when you cannot feel the oar against the palm of your hand, and the first half-hour of every outing was agony, as fingers froze before the warm blood flowed back in, causing almost unbearable aching.

The water of the Thames froze solid on the oars. As the boys ripped them out at the end of the stroke they were dripping; by the time they had flashed back to the catch position they were caked over with ice. Sometimes we worked through snow flurries which turned the big grey factories along the river into distant mirages of another world. Sometimes the coxes lurched left or right to avoid ice-floes, but we never missed an outing, never funked it, because, as I continually told them, 'It could be like this on the day, and we don't want any surprises. Let Cambridge miss outings; that would make them easier to beat.'

I reminded them of the words of Daley Thompson, the Olympic decathlon champion: 'I train twice a day – including Christmas – because I know the others will take the day off. That puts me two sessions ahead. And that's the way I like it.'

Most of the crews wore three or even four layers of shirts and sweaters, but this kind of cold was relentless. I listened to protests about the conditions, I heard the Americans assure me that this was the craziest thing they had ever done. Tempers frayed. Some of them just did not want to go on. And one of the squad oarsmen decided to call it quits.

But this was an exercise as much in mental toughness as in anything else. Every day we went out and fought the icy blasts on the river. Sometimes I would look up at the bank, or a bridge, and see people standing there, staring incredulously at these madmen, crashing their way down the Tideway in the middle of winter. And in the faces of the crew I could begin to see real character forming.

The most bullish of them all I would say were Donald and Hugh Pelham, exhibiting a high degree of toughness, and resilience. Cadoux-Hudson was impervious to the pain and just kept rowing. Like me he had done it all before – every winter for years on the Thames for London University. Stewart hung tough throughout, asked for no mercy. All of them came out of that breed of oarsmen which never flinches, and treats the worst conditions as a new hurdle to conquer, a new battle to be fought. There is great pride in dealing with such adversity. Oxford crews grew in courage into hardened giants during these confrontations with the elements. I thought Huntington coped very well, but Penny, Fish and Lyons had turned moaning into such an art form it was hard to distinguish a true protest from their natural way of behaviour.

Into this arctic hell on water, at the end of the first week, stepped Christopher Clark. He checked into the luxury St Ermine's Hotel I had organized for the crews a short walk from the Houses of Parliament and Big Ben. He joined us for dinner at Rollocks, the noisy Chelsea restaurant we had booked at a fixed price for the whole of our two-week stay. 'I guess those starboard guys, Pelham, Hull and Ward aren't too glad to see me back,' confided Chris to his pal Macdonald when they were alone.

On his first day back I put him in a Four, specifying a three- or four-mile low-rating training row with another Four which would work alongside them. It looked all right to me, both crews were working adequately, in these freezing conditions, and they headed up to Hammersmith Bridge in good order. On the way home the other crew began to edge in front of Clark's and it was obvious to me that he was less than happy when they docked half-an-hour later.

There was much growling and ill-temper, I presumed because

one crew had slipped behind. But it was only training and of little importance. Tempers are always short when athletes are working hard and no one likes to finish second no matter what the reason. Coaches like this attitude because it suggests good competitive spirits. But this malaise was somehow different. Back in the boathouse Clark threw a major tantrum and hurled a cup of vegetable soup against the dressing room wall. Then he stormed out, shouting that he was leaving for good. 'Are you going to fire him now?' asked Tony Ward, hoping to see the back of one of his main rivals for the last bowside seat in the Blue Boat.

When I heard of the soup-hurling incident I must admit my first thought was that if we were not careful we could find ourselves thrown out of the Thames Rowing Club as well as LRC.

Someone told me Clark had gone and the wall had been cleaned. Huntington and Penny, always more reasonable, asked for a meeting with me and we adjourned to the balcony room overlooking the first mile of the Boat Race course for what turned out to be a long and winding discussion. I thought by now they must see that Clark had burnt his boats and that he had to be dropped from the squad.

Instead both pleaded his case with immense passion. 'Dan, Dan, I'm telling you, the guy is like a hothouse plant. He has to be nurtured.'

'In time he'll come through, if we can just get him the right conditions. God he has so much potential.'

I asked them both why they were displaying such remarkable loyalty to someone who was showing none to the squad. 'Surely you must see that this has to be the end of it,' I said. 'It has to be finished now. He is having the most detrimental effect on all of us and Donald for one wants him out for good.' I said I believed that he had shown potential back in '85 at the World's but that nothing he had done since had lived up to that performance. He was tearing us apart. We were only weeks away from the Boat Race and with all the will in the world I had to call a halt. But they went on and on, pleading his case, refusing to take 'no' for an answer.

They listened to all of my arguments for nearly two hours, and then said: 'Fine, Dan, but we think he should have another chance.' I should have at that moment said that he was out and that if they felt unable to row without him, then they had better go too. But like a fool, because I always prided myself on being able to get people to see sense, I relented. It was a major mistake which would cost us dearly.

To my eternal shame, I backed down and, in the interests of conciliation, agreed to allow Clark back in, as long as it was they, Huntington and Penny, who made themselves responsible for talking to him, explaining that he was now balancing on a knife-edge and that I expected him to move into the second crew, Isis, and try to work his way back, over a period of a few weeks on the *bowside*. I told them I thought it would be better coming from them, because he clearly saw me, quite unnecessarily in my view, as some kind of *bête noire*.

For someone who was supposed to wish him ill, I seemed to have been excusing the behaviour of Christopher Clark for as long as I could remember. In spite of everything, I had still not lost faith in his potential as an oarsman – and here I was giving him yet another chance. Perhaps, though, upon reflection, I was being not only scrupulously fair to him, but I was also being mindful of the consequences there might be, at this moment, in picking a fight with these Americans, who banded together so tightly, and were not afraid of using their collective clout to achieve their own ends. But was I being fair to the rest of the squad, the men who had been training so long and so hard since September?

So Huntington and Penny left, presumably in pursuit of Clark, promising me they would have a long and serious talk with him about his future behaviour.

The next day I was extremely busy because we were racing London University that morning; this is always a tough and competitive fixture for us. What was more, Penny and Huntington were late and they were both in the crew I had chosen for the race. I was furious with them as we all waited to join London out on the water.

Then Clark came back, reported to me for duty, said he was sorry and told me he would be happy to work with the Isis crew and to do what I deemed best. Because I had no time to discuss anything with him at that moment I told him I needed an ergometer test result from him and, assuming he had been told by Penny and Huntington that he was to row on the bowside, I said that, yes, he should get to work with the reserve crew.

When Huntington and Penny finally arrived they told me they were late back from a visit to Oxford and had not yet had a chance to talk to Clark. I told them I felt they had not honoured our agreement, but there was no time to talk about it now and would they get changed and for *Christ's sake* get into the f---ing boat.

Meanwhile, out of my sight, Clark had paddled off *on the stroke-side*, a fact which I only noticed later on in the day. However we finally set off to race London University and did some quite good pieces of middle-distance work against them and came out well on top. I was quite pleased with that result, and at the end of the day when I did at last see Clark sitting in the reserve boat, in the wrong seat, I decided that I could not at that moment face yet another fight with him. I neglected to go and confront him over the very issue that should have been central to him being allowed back in the squad, the bowside seat I had been asking him to sit in for the best part of four months. That was my second major mistake of the week, if not the decade.

At around this time Mike Spracklen came down for a look at the crews and to have a chat. He knew of all the problems, of course, and advised me to be firm; I should decide on a course of action and follow it. He thought I was being too compliant. Good tips, I thought, very helpful, full of specifics.

The overall atmosphere was still no better than it had ever been. On the river, I mercifully, did not have to listen to that special brand of American sarcasm very much; but in the gym behind Thames Rowing Club, it was always there. 'Come along now boys, you all know how important Dan thinks these exercises are for winning the Boat Race.'

They really closed ranks around Clark, pushing and helping him to get round the circuits, shielding him from scrutiny. Despite everything, he managed to convey an aura of amazing cool and confidence – surrounded by his friends, whom I think he believed rendered him unsackable. He counted on them not to let him down, and he was right to do so, for they never did. Also he stayed on strokeside where we did not need him. At least though I thought he might settle down to getting fit and proving himself so that I could in a week or two swap him back and include him in an 'A' boat selection for a trial. To be frank I could not face another confrontation at that moment.

He did however appear to be more positive on the water within the Isis crew. Whenever I put the 'A' crew next to Isis and sent them off together, at a fixed rate for a set piece of work, I could hear him gearing up his crew: 'C'mon! C'mon! C'mon! Let's go! Go! Go!'

They would go off rating far too high, and of course would get out in front, too far in front, because the 'A' crew with Hunt at stroke, was rowing at the controlled rate they had been set, unusually diligently, on these occasions, following instructions. But it did suggest that Clark was trying to get back to form again which was a welcome sign. The Isis boys enjoyed the jousting with the 'A' crew and credited Clark for their performance. I was relieved too, for while he was happy revving up the second crew he was out of my hair for a bit; and the fact that he was at last training every day, on the water and in the gym, was a major improvement in itself.

But we still had no significant individual results from him as we had for everyone else. Only last year's weightlifting results, a couple of poor sculling results, no seat racing results and a low score on the Concept II ergometer machine, well below the other serious contenders. On the London sweep machine test at the British Amateur Rowing Association headquarters in Hammersmith, Donald had finished first, Huntington second, with Cheatle third, and Stewart fourth. Clark was seventh, Lyons fifteenth and Penny ill. A year earlier Chris Clark had been top ergo man. However maybe now at last we could begin to look ahead to smoother waters.

But as Chris Clark rowed along, charging up that Isis crew he must have realized at last that his future was on the line and he had pushed his luck to the limit. His instinct for survival took over, refined by his colleagues. Furthermore, it would emerge later that what Chris had decided he wanted was to get back into the 'A' crew on the strokeside, the side where Penny, Huntington, Macdonald and Stewart were rowing.

If you ignored all the other tests that had been carried out so far and took the result of one test only, the one in which Stewart had narrowly beaten Macdonald in a seat race, you could make out a case that the President was the most vulnerable man in the boat on strokeside. The first man for the chop if you like. But that would disregard all the performances in other tests where he had finished well above Stewart let alone the others. He was for example the fastest sculler in the squad and the grittiest and most consistently reliable of competitors – a good man to have on your side in a scrap. The difficult and painful process of selection has to take all results into consideration which are then measured against an analysis of compatibility, psychological suitability and ability to deal with the special demands of the Boat Race. Macdonald was one of only two men in my squad who had rowed in the Boat Race before, which was a significant advantage.

With Stewart and Macdonald separated as they were by little more than a second, it was clear that we were dealing with two very strong athletes. For, on that same day just before Christmas, the Olympic silver medallist Chris Penny had been unable to beat Stewart. With Hunt ahead of all three, our strokeside was probably the best strokeside in the country. Our bowside however was just as clearly a good deal weaker. Probably few in the squad cared to remember the time I swapped Gavin and Donald in a Four down on the Tideway and Donald's boat moved out immediately to a three-length advantage. This did not mean that Gavin should be thrown out at the first opportunity. It meant that Donald was in better shape in January than he had been before Christmas.

But in Christopher Clark's mind Stewart's victory at Thorpe Park made his re-entry to the 'A' crew simple and straightforward. All he had to do was to beat Macdonald in a single test, a seat race perhaps, and all would be clear. The logical step would then be for me to tell the President to fire himself from the crew in favour of Christopher Clark, who refused to train, kept quitting the squad and had been beaten by Donald in every test so far.

That was not how we went about choosing Boat Race crews, and the record of the previous decade suggested that our selection assessments had on the whole not been altogether wide of the mark.

One part of this logic however was correct. I definitely needed to seat race Chris Clark. He was the only man who had by all manner of means avoided any testing so far. I might put him up against Cadoux-Hudson, Hull or Stewart or maybe even Penny, Macdonald or Pelham. But that race would be run to test Clark, rather than his opponent. I knew all about his opponents. They had already proved themselves many times over. Clark was the only man I needed up-to-date information about. And what I wanted to know was simple: was Clark fit enough to warrant a place in the crew?

Because the fairest local course at Thorpe Park was iced over, I resolved to race him over part of the Boat Race course in the Wednesday of the second week. I also wanted to take a good look at Dan Lyons, who also had not produced much in the way of test results, but as a recent world gold medal winner his place was pretty secure. Testing everyone was always good for squad morale as it was important to demonstrate that no one could just walk into the Oxford crew. I picked two Fours, with Macdonald and Paul Gleeson each stroking one of them. For the bow seats I selected Pelham opposite Tony Ward and for the 2 seats I put Huntington opposite Clark; in the 3 seats sat Cadoux-Hudson against Lyons. I decided to have four races of around seven minutes, from the Boat Race start at Putney Bridge straight up to Hammersmith.

We set off in cold windy weather and rough water, which I thought would provide a searching test of character. Conditions were pretty bad but they came through well and after the first run I swapped Lyons and Cadoux-Hudson. This was difficult. We manoeuvred the boats together interlocking the oars, and held them close as the two men stepped gingerly aboard the opposing boats. It looked, and was, bloody dangerous. The two Fours paddled back down to the start. Then we raced them with both crews once more fighting their way through the waves in the bitterly cold wind, stroking rates held at a constant thirty-two a minute. The race was close but Cadoux-Hudson got the verdict by some two or three seconds – or about a length. It was impressive.

It meant that Cadoux-Hudson had done an excellent job in preparing himself for the Boat Race. Like Clark he had been asked to swap sides at the beginning of October. He had done it when asked, and had just beaten a reigning world champion in a seat race after just three months on his new side.

The two crews sat in the middle of the tossing, pitching river just below Hammersmith and I asked Clark and Huntington to swap seats. For the first time there were objections voiced about the nasty conditions although at the time I failed to attach any significance to this. I called to them to get on with it and they swung the boats round.

They settled in and began the mile-and-a-half paddle back down to the start. On the way down the wind seemed to grow colder, ice was caking into their hair and there was much griping and moaning as they ploughed through the rough water. Those with some experience of the Tideway understood the need to persevere, but Lyons, Huntington and Clark wanted to go in. It looked as if Chris would once again avoid a test. The subtleties were becoming clearer now but reluctantly I agreed to call it off and we abandoned this rough turbulent stretch of river for the day.

There was now no time for our usual three-day break after the demanding Tideway fortnight. We struck camp and headed off thirty-six miles upriver to the calmer waters of the Henley Reach to finish the seat racing quickly in case the river froze right over and drove us off the water completely.

The town is, of course, the scene of the most famous regatta in the world. Every summer for the past 150 years it has been held on this lovely stretch of the Thames, with its dead straight 2,200 metres so loved by the world's rowing community.

Henley itself is one of those ancient riverside country market towns peculiar to England, with a fine historic stone bridge spanning the Thames. It has quaint riverside pubs, and is the headquarters of the world famous Leander Club, whose members are required either to have rowed for Oxford or Cambridge in the Boat Race, or otherwise distinguished themselves in the domestic and international rowing arena. It is probably the most exclusive rowing club in the world and the members are identifiable by their bright pink club socks, caps and ties, which give rise to the Club's irreverent nickname, the Pink Palace. However the Club has for years attempted to disassociate itself from anything pink, and in its handbook it firmly asserts that the true colours of Leander are in fact 'cerise'.

On the other buttress of the bridge, on the Berkshire side of the river stands the new headquarters of the Henley Royal Regatta. This organization devotes its entire year to staging the boat racing jamboree which brings out boatered and blazered Englishmen in their droves; all sipping Pimms, roaring on their old schools in the Princess Elizabeth Cup, and yelling for any English crews against the invaders from the USA, Italy, Canada or the Soviet Union. Henley being Henley, foreigners were foreigners, and the chauvinistic British made no distinction.

There was no pageantry awaiting us when the Oxford squad arrived there on that freezing Friday morning in January. The river was deserted, the banks were tight with packed snow and ice floes floated just beneath the surface of the water. The launch wouldn't start and hands and toes were quickly frozen. The wind had come round out of the north-east now, and though the water was calm up here beyond the tidal reaches, the air was bitterly cold, and the harsh gusting breeze howled in from across the Chiltern Hills like a blast from Siberia.

My intention was to seat race Clark and Huntington as I had been about to on the Tideway two days before, but Hunt called in sick so I decided to substitute Gavin Stewart who was by now extremely close to the American camp. But he also called in sick.

So I set Donald to race against Chris Clark since I still had to get some guide to the American's state of fitness. Although as far as I was concerned, it was not strictly a test between the two men, athletes being the competitive animals they are, I have no doubt both men were determined to come out on top and the others in the two boats were just as keen to know the outcome.

Unfortunately, a great deal more was read into this race by Clark's friends than there was in my mind. I believe they thought 'If Chris can just win this, just get home in front, we can insist that he be brought in on strokeside. Macdonald is the weakest man on strokeside, right? Lost to Stewart, right? If Chris wins, he's gotta be in, right?'

Wrong actually. I was at this moment concerned with assessing Clark's fitness for the last seat on the bowside. The fact was that whether he knew it or not, he was on trial, all alone, against no one but himself. Indeed the situation was in itself ironic, since a man of Clark's size and potential should have been contesting a seat in the stern of a university boat, not struggling for the last seat in the bows. Even if he showed up well today, he had proved so unreliable in the past, many of us in the coaching team reckoned it a serious risk to even consider including him at all.

But the Americans apparently regarded the test as a life or death chance for Chris and a feeling had been introduced within the squad that it was to be a fight for the last strokeside seat in the boat.

The fact was, Clark's antics had by now made it very difficult for me to take him seriously because I was always half-expecting him to vanish again. How did we know what he would do next? And why should we risk undermining our chances against Cambridge? He had become a side issue, more a source of constant irritation and discontent than a serious contender.

It was in this exasperated frame of mind that I named the two Fours as we all stood on the tow-path – Gleeson, Hull, Clark and Ward in one boat; Penny, Cadoux-Hudson, Macdonald and Pelham in the other. The old bell in Henley's twelfth-century church solemnly chimed twice as the freezing little Dark Blue convoy eased out onto the windswept reaches of the upper Thames.

CHAPTER SEVEN

THE TAKEOVER

'Clark's had his test,' said Lyons. 'On Friday. Against you. We don't want any more tests. As far as we are concerned this is over. We represent the majority in this boat, and you are out. Relieved of command. The crew will not row with you.'

We turned downstream into the teeth of the wind, and the two Fours began to paddle with long, slow, powerful strokes, letting the boats run towards the distant Chiltern Hills. At Regatta time, all along here, would be log booms lining the most famous rowing racecourse in the world. There would be throngs of people on the water in punts, rowing boats and launches, with thousands more packed along the banks, cheering the oarsmen, eating their strawberries.

Today there was nothing. The river is very wide and desolate here, and the stark white summer houses of the riverside residences stand like guardians of a lost July. And the boys ploughed on, downstream through this silent Edwardian ice-age. In the hills high above to the right are two great English mansions, Park Place, the boyhood home of the future King George III; and Remenham Place, a school once attended by the great Antarctic explorer Captain Oates. It was easy to see where he received his early training.

I glanced at our two frozen Christophers, Clark and Penny and debated whether to tell them that Americans were generally expected to doff their caps going along here in honour of His Late Majesty, King of the Western Colonies. But I decided against any jokes, no one being at that moment in much of a mood for levity. This was especially so of Clark who must have felt that his entire rowing career at Oxford was on the line. Presumably his pal Penny thought the same. Donald, being the competitive bulldog he is, must also have believed that his reputation too was on the line.

He had written in his diary the night before: 'I know it's going to be close, and that it won't be easy. But at the same time I feel so much better than I did before Christmas. I know I came close to Penny, who everyone knows is better than Clark. It should be a winnable race for me. But the problem is they all know I'm racing Clark, and I am at the mercy of the other rowers.'

They paddled on down to the island, in the middle of which stands a little classical Greek Temple, its columns set beneath a green cupola. It is an eighteenth-century folly, designed by James Wyatt and its strange white presence in the middle of the Thames has marked the start of Henley races for generations. The drooping branches of the island's willow trees were trapped now in pack-ice along the banks, and the freezing Temple itself looked grey against the pure white snow. We worked along its right bank, and swung windward at the end.

Unfortunately, contrary to my normal practice with seat racing where no one knows who is on trial, everyone knew I was going to seat race Donald and Chris, which made either oarsman vulnerable should somebody choose to influence the result unfairly. In one boat sat Chris with Ward and Hull of the Oriel bar, and in the other Donald would have Clark's friend Penny in the stroke seat. We paddled back up to the traditional finish line to complete our warm-up, then turned to prepare to race down the course.

In the very first race the writing was probably on the wall. Penny's boat lost it by one-and-a-half lengths, although Pelham's stretcher worked loose during the race and probably reduced his effectiveness. Yet with such powerful pullers as were in the boat the margin was greater than I would have expected.

As they pulled up at the regatta finish Donald said quietly to Penny: 'Are you feeling OK?' But in his diary that night he recorded, 'I wanted to say: "Why aren't you f---king pulling?" I'd rowed with him a lot in Fours and I knew by the size of his puddle what he could really do.'

For the second race, to everyone's surprise, I swapped the bowmen, Pelham and Ward, leaving Clark and Donald still in their original boats, and a curious kind of battle royal exploded on that freezing river. Clark hauling away behind Gleeson was shouting short staccato cries of 'Go!' – 'Go!' every time the blades hit the water. When I then called to Clark and Donald to change seats, the President stepped into the other number 2 seat aware that the outcome of this seat race could be decided by Christopher Penny, believing deep down that the big stroke from Princeton would probably row his heart out for Clark.

They paddled back up to the starting line, and on the word 'go' Penny with Clark at 2 rocketed off the line – they were rating four pips higher than Gleeson in the other boat. The ratings were supposed to stride down to even thirty-twos after the first ten, but Penny maintained his high rate for a further twenty, forging into a lead of over a length. I yelled across to him to bring his strike-rate down, which he finally did having established his advantage. I had to keep shouting to stop his rate from creeping up and all the while Gleeson's crew was reeling back that initial lead. Then I heard Donald. Thinking I did not know what was going on out there he decided he must go for it too and he shouted to his stroke: *'Go! Paul, Go!'* Gleeson pushed the accelerator and they began to close more rapidly. Penny was responding and there was nothing I could do to stop them driving the striking rate up and up. Gleeson's finishing sprint was an effective reply to his rivals' initial first minute.

Their blades dug in harder and Donald shouted once more, his voice edged with anger, *'Up! Paul. Come on up!'* as the boats battled for the line. This was no longer just a seat race. This was a most bitter grudge match.

I could see Clark and Penny vainly trying to match Gleeson and the infuriated Scotsman for speed – but the lead was being slashed away, stroke by stroke. The boats flashed across the line with Penny about a half-length up. Twenty seconds more and the second boat would have been through. On paper the verdict went to Clark, by a canvas, albeit a rapidly diminishing one. A canvas was no great distance, certainly not one on which to make a selection decision. But what it did tell me was that Clark was getting into better shape. If there had been any plan to compromise Macdonald it had failed.

At least that was how it looked to me, and that was how it looked to Steve Royle who was in the launch with me. In any event I was not so much interested in the detail of such a close verdict: what interested me more was whether or not Chris Clark was getting fit and whether he was taking his training seriously. The answer to both questions after today was clearly 'Yes'.

In the race there had clearly been a hint of partisanship – and by the middle of January, as a result of Clark's behaviour, the squad was in a high state of paranoia. But now that he was back on song and more confident with a successful test under his belt, maybe we would all be able to relax and get on with our preparations for the race against Cambridge. During the tensions of selection the old Light Blue enemy was often put to the back of our minds, but we would soon be settled into an 'A' crew and able to concentrate on the men from the Fens.

But I was not quite finished yet. I still needed to see how effective Clark was on the bowside since that was where he would be rowing in the end, so I asked him to change seats with bowsider Tony Ward in the same boat. Tony would swap to stroke side. It was not an altogether satisfactory way of doing things because it placed two men who had just swapped sides in the same boat against an unchanged crew. With only a few minutes practise they would be at a disadvantage, although both men were relatively ambidextrous. But we wanted to finish the day's seat racing and I also wanted to prove both to Clark and to my own satisfaction that he was perfectly capable of changing sides and remaining effective.

So I seat raced him again, this time against Cadoux-Hudson who predictably beat him by a length-and-a-half. Since Tom had raced his first trial in an unchanged seat order, Clark's effort was pretty respectable. Tom had after all beaten the gold medallist Lyons a few days back, and this race showed that Clark could certainly operate on the side of the boat I most needed him; and if he wanted to row in the Boat Race he was going to have to get used to it.

I called a meeting with coach Steve Royle, Chris and Donald, immediately after the racing, and we huddled out of the cold in the downstairs lobby of Leander. I told Chris that I believed he was now training properly and asked him to promise that there would be no more bad behaviour. He agreed. I explained that we still needed him on bowside and that I was intending to put him into the 'A' crew at 3. He replied: 'That's fine with me. I'll go for that.' I told him that the race against Donald had provided the proof I needed to show he was returning to competitive strength while the second seat race had demonstrated he could handle the bowside without discomfort. In a month or so he would scarcely feel the difference. He agreed to take his place on that side of the boat.

He asked that he not be seat raced on that side and I told him I would give him as much time as he needed to get comfortable, and he concurred. Steve and Donald agreed with everything and so our initial 'A' crew would now be as follows – Hull at bow; Donald at 2; Clark 3; Stewart 4; Cadoux-Hudson 5; Penny 6; Lyons 7; Huntington stroke; Fish cox. It was clear we needed to settle the squad down first and further seat races would now have to wait.

I then said: 'I really believe we can put the whole mess behind us now, and go on as a team to win the Boat Race. From now on, no fooling about; let's just get on with the job, do the training and we'll win.' Everyone nodded their assent.

The only thing in my mind that now remained was the choice between Hull, Pelham and Ward for the bow seat. Ward and Pelham, the two Isis men had been seat raced before Christmas against Hull, the new man from Cambridge, and both had been beaten. Pelham had been well on top of Ward then, and this afternoon's result between Ward and Pelham had been pretty shaky since Pelham's stretcher had given way. But this was still only the first day of term and for the next three weeks we would be able to see all the various bowside candidates in action. I could make changes to the initial line-up to test for compatibility, before deciding on the final Oxford crew to be announced formally in mid-February. This had been the form now for fourteen years. It would also enable me to get a proper form line on the two coxswains, for I was far from convinced by Fish's abilities on the Tideway.

Donald recalls one small interchange in the van on the way home, and it came from Hull, Dan Lyons' Oriel colleague.

'What will you do, Donald, if you are picked for the crew, and Dan Lyons says he will not row? What exactly will you do?'

Donald was alarmed at the depth of the question, and at the clearly implied threat, for it was the first indication of organized trouble and it came from out of the blue. But he answered it straight: 'If the coaches pick me, then of course I'll row. But if they do not pick me, then I'll accept their decision. But I won't be intimidated by the threat of mass resignations. You've got to be adult in this game. If you're picked, you row, if you're not, you're out. That applies to every one of us.'

'I don't think Dan Lyons is going to like this,' said Hull.

Meanwhile over in the other car, Christopher Clark was saying that he would not row on bowside. He'd beat Macdonald and would claim his place.

Penny tried to dissuade him from rocking the boat yet again, believing that he would be thrown out this time for sure. But Clark was adamant.

Clark clearly thought I had arranged the seat races for his benefit, rather than for my own information, but by that evening it was clear that Clark certainly, and possibly some of the others too, felt that he was entitled now to claim a strokeside place in the crew and that the President should be thrown out. Donald, who was closer to the situation on that Friday evening, says he had a strong feeling on the way back that the seeds of real trouble were being sown. Indeed I too received a warning of unrest to come with a phone call from Christopher Penny complaining about the 'unfairness' of the seat race between Clark and Macdonald. He cited what he thought to be my one-sided approach in that I called his rate down after he had snatched that early length in the first minute. He believed that I had been clocking him at a higher striking rate than he estimated he was doing. 'Jon Fish who was coxing agrees with me,' he said. He would, wouldn't he, I thought. 'I was truly matching Gleeson rate for rate,' he insisted.

'Wouldn't that suggest that Gleeson's boat was going faster than yours in the middle of the race after your initial take-off sprint?' I asked him. 'They did close from over one length down to a canvas. Anyway let's not argue. Chris did well and he's in the prospective 'A' crew.'

From Tony Ward's attitude in the van after the seat racing, Donald felt he should speak to him to ensure there would be no misunderstandings. So over the weekend he phoned Tony Ward, telling him that for the next three weeks Chris Clark was being tried in the 3 seat and that we would like Tony to row with Isis. Ward was silent for a moment and then said: 'Donald, Dan Lyons isn't going to like this.'

On the Sunday evening the Oriel bar group held a meeting in which they firmly took up the case of Tony Ward. Why should he have to sacrifice his place for the second year running? Seat races are seat races, Clark beat Macdonald. Why should Ward be the victim of this power struggle between Clark and Topolski?

Apparently Ward, flushed with success at beating Hugh Pelham in that first seat race, had called his parents to tell them he was in the Blue Boat; a little premature since it was the only time he had beaten Pelham in nearly four months, and especially since Pelham had slipped a stretcher in the race. In any event the crew was not due to be announced for another three weeks. Nevertheless the group had their twin causes – the ill-fated Ward and the bitterly complaining Clark, who was now busy reneging on his undertaking to me just forty-eight hours earlier.

That same evening Donald had dinner with an old friend of his, the brilliant American literary scholar and trainee Jesuit priest, Michael Suarez. Over coffee Donald told him, 'I know disaster is right around the corner. By tomorrow I think there will be battle lines drawn.' Donald did in fact call me that evening and expressed his fears, but said he could prove nothing. It was just a powerful feeling he had. I told him it would probably not be that bad, since I had Clark's word that he would settle down and row in the number 3 seat, and in my opinion he had seemed sincere. Donald said he had heard too much in Oxford to think nothing would happen. And he hung up with what sounded to me like a troubled sigh

Donald and Ruth talked long into that night. They reminisced about how far they had come together, only to be faced now by this crisis that threatened to plunge Donald once more into battle with the dissidents. Two days ago if anyone had suggested that Donald should not be in the Blue Boat they would have been dismissed as a lunatic. Soon there would be so many people saying it, that it would start to be believed as the truth. A minor seat race result of a few feet, arguably unfairly influenced, was suddenly being cracked up as a finally decisive selection trial.

The following morning, 19 January, Donald worked for a while in the library at Mansfield, went home briefly, and at 1 pm swung the OUBC van off the High , past Vincent's Club and into Oriel Square. He pulled up next to where the squad were all standing, and Dan Lyons came over to the van followed by Hull. He put his face very close to the side window and said, 'Don, we gotta talk.'

Donald told him that was not a great idea, since they had to get to Marlow. It was the first formal outing of the 'A' crew, Mike Spracklen was waiting, and no, he would have to wait until later. Hull chimed in, said it would be better to talk now. And Lyons spoke again – 'We should talk in my room.'

Donald stepped reluctantly out of the van, and with Hull on one side and Lyons on the other, he was, he says, 'virtually frogmarched' back towards the High, into a rabbit warren of college rooms and into Lyons's 'first floor garret'. And there he was told that he did not deserve a place in the crew, that Topolski was protecting him, and that the boat would be much better served by Clark and Ward.

Donald exploded, 'Are you seriously telling me that after all of the tests we have done over all of these months, the guy who comes out best should be left out of the top Eight. That's crazy. I am supposed to stay on the bank, rather than Clark or Ward or even Hull. Any one of you want to race me in a fair test?'

'Don, we perceive the tests are bogus.'

'You what?'

'The test on Friday was rigged by Topolski. Clark should have won by miles. But Topolski kept calling Penny down. Basically Don, we will not row with you. The crew do not wish to row with you.'

'That's correct,' said Richard Hull, nodding, unaware of what Donald describes as 'an overpowering feeling that was developing in me to smash my fist into his grinning face.' Hull clearly had no idea how dangerously he was living, because he kept nodding, kept agreeing with Lyons and kept confirming that 'no one' wanted to row with Donald.

Lyons pointed out that it was no disgrace for Donald, since the Cambridge President Quintus Travis had excluded himself from the Boat Race in 1986. He added: 'Anyway, you're out. If you row, we don't. It's that simple.'

'Simple,' added Hull, oblivious to the stare of pure contempt being levelled at him by the President of the OUBC. Donald tried once more. 'If you really think Clark is better than I am, put him in a sculling boat, and you, and him,' he snarled in Hull's direction. Then in more reasonable terms he offered to conduct any tests they wanted in order to work out which of the nine men would fit into the eight places.

But Lyons was adamant. 'Clarke's had his test,' he said. 'On Friday, against you. We don't want any more tests. As far as we're concerned this is over. We represent the majority in this boat, and you are out, relieved of command. The crew will not row with you.'

Donald walked to the door. He remembered how he had felt

after a beating at Morrison's Academy . . . 'never let on to *anyone* that you are hurt. Keep control. Smile if necessary. But never look wounded. Like a fighter who has just taken a count. Be ready to defend yourself.'

How test results could be rigged was not explained by Lyons and Hull. The lists were, after all, issued to everyone and since the squad members and coxswains recorded the details themselves, it was hard for Donald to understand the logic behind their argument. What was clear was that in some irrational way they had convinced themselves that the lists were phoney, and they were now busy spreading the delusion. He remembers being astonished at the capacity of people for self-deceit. Back in Oriel Square, Donald could see Clark standing alone, and, remembering there was still a kind of bond between them – they had been good friends the previous year – he walked up to him and said: 'Is this what you really want to do, Chris? Do you know what you are doing? Do you have any idea what the consequences of this might be?'

Chris mumbled something; then he said 'I don't see we have any choice, Don. The crew perceives me as being better than you. The test on Friday was bogus. And the other tests are irrelevant. This is the crew the crew wanna go with. And you're not in it.'

Lyons, sensing that Clark might be weakening, quickly walked up to them. Donald, out in the air now, felt no further constraints. He swung round on Lyons and snapped: 'F--- off!' And Lyons, showing a sight more native perception than Hull had done, did so, at the double. Finally Donald said: 'OK. Get into the van. I don't intend to walk home.'

He need not have done this of course. He should have just taken the van and gone to the river, explained the situation to the coach Mike Spracklen, cancelled the outing for the afternoon and called a meeting at Marlow the following day for all those who wanted to row for Oxford against Cambridge.

However Donald felt that he needed time to gather himself and to see how I would react. He had a dull feeling that I might adopt a pragmatic stance, regard the revolt as a *fait accompli*; that since I was there solely to win the Boat Race I might tell him to accept the situation and resign. In which case he thought, he would have no alternative but to capitulate.

His diary descriptions of the main characters on the ride to 14 Lime Road were, in retrospect, sharply perceptive and very funny.

Hull he described as 'a man born to serve, but looking for a Finest Hour, so pleased to be on the inside of a Great Occasion'.

He called Lyons 'Cassius, so grim, so jealous of Caesar, so lean and hungry, so proud of his gold medal.'

Clark? 'He just seemed kind of happy, as if we were in a cruise wagon, headed for the beach.'

Halfway home he stopped to make a phone call to me. But I was out and Donald considered my answering machine a bit impersonal for the type of message he was about to impart. So they pressed on towards Botley. Donald felt that he did not want them anywhere near his house, and he parked further along the road.

He got out of the van, and, fighting back his emotions, he smiled and wished them 'Good luck'. And then he walked the fifty yards to his front door, his self-control falling from him as he went. By the time he arrived at the door his eyes were suffused with tears, and Ruth just looked at him and said: 'My God! What have they done to you?'

Donald replied: 'I have never done anything to harm any one of them. It's hard for me to understand that I do not have one friend among them. That most of the twenty-five guys in the squad are against me. It's just hard for me to cope with that. Nothing seems to be making sense any more. That's all. I'll be all right in a minute.' Ruth was shocked at the sheer callousness of her husband's betrayal. But it was the day of Alasdair's first birthday party and Donald resolved to join in entertaining a riotous group of children. He recovered his composure and prepared to join in the party games.

Meanwhile, that van-load of what he describes as 'smirking guilt' set off down the steep escarpment of Botley Hill – except that now it was no longer merely the OUBC van; it was a roller-coaster labelled 'Mutiny'. And having creaked to the top of the hill, it was now on its way down the other side, gathering speed, on a headlong collision course with 150 years of tradition, trimmed in Dark Blue.

While there may have been a sense of euphoria in the van, not everyone was fully convinced. Huntington sat tight-lipped, worried, and sure in his own mind that they were committing the most dreadful blunder. Some weeks later he phoned Donald and told him: 'There was a moment in that van when I could have called a halt to the madness that was about to begin. I could have and I should have. I should never have let you get out of the van. I knew, as you walked away that it was all the most terrible, terrible mistake.'

Huntington was, I believe, the only one who realized that what they were doing was crazy and wrong. But he was swept along with the euphoria of what was a kind of Palace Coup. Somehow they had captured the radio station and were on the march. Old Hunt was on this bandwagon and he did not know for the life of him how to get off.

Clark was, as ever, unable to bring his mind to bear on the subject of 'unpleasant consequences' – that of course was why he had been in and out of so many ridiculous confrontations and problems ever since he arrived at Oxford. There was a childlike quality about him, shameless about throwing a tantrum. Nonetheless Clark was not altogether the harmless child-man of the boathouse. In fact Donald says he will always remember Clark's last words to him at Oriel Square: 'Topolski had it coming to him, man. Too bad you got burned.' And with that he settled back among his friends.

His friends did not now just include the Americans. There was a group of English oarsmen who were firmly entrenched in the rebel camp – Gavin Stewart, Tony Ward, and Richard Hull. There would be no support for the President from them. For in a sense they too were protecting their positions. If Clark were included in the crew, one of them would lose his place. Donald's demise was the result of a 'marriage of convenience' between two self-interested groups. For the Brits to keep Ward and the Americans to retain Clark, Donald became the scapegoat. There was safety in numbers if they all stood together. And so they were all in the forefront of the mutiny, bound for Marlow and the unsuspecting Mike Spracklen. They were an illegal crew about to take possession of the Oxford University Boat Club equipment over which Donald had total authority. And they were about to try to work under a coach who had been appointed by Donald, in preparation for a challenge against Cambridge which could be made only by the President of the OUBC.

I am not certain whether Dan Lyons quite understood the magnitude of what he was undertaking. He undoubtedly did not understand the staunch establishment of Oxford rowing which would have to be convinced of some truly reprehensible behaviour by the President even to consider lending its support to the action he had taken.

They arrived at Marlow and made ready to row. They had been

out on the water for fully twenty minutes before Mike realised that someone was missing. 'Where's Donald today?' he called. There was a sort of 'Oh, don't worry, Mike, we'll explain later,' reply, and at the end of the outing they informed him that there was some kind of problem with Donald, and that they would not be rowing with him. Mike stayed non-commital and waited for the OUBC President to call.

Meanwhile Donald made sure that 'musical chairs' was well under control at the party and began to ponder his future as President, if indeed he had one. He wondered if in fact he still held that office. Initially he considered the possibility of simply resigning, giving the whole thing up, and concentrating instead totally on his studies.

But there is a powerful sense of righteousness in those who are accused of perpetuating evil, where in fact there is none. And it burned strongly in Donald as Alasdair's party drew to its close. He decided he would call me, but first of all he went upstairs to his journal and wrote down some of his thoughts. 'I am now in a positive and philosophical frame of mind,' he wrote. 'The prospect of resignation is attractive. But there is another voice in me saying: "Fight the bastards." This call to Dan should sort things out. But I must remember that although he is an engaging and mercurial character, he is more importantly, the calculating, dedicated, complete match-winner. Which is precisely what a coach should be. He is our Campaign Chief, and now I am going to have to tell him that his Company Commander has been shot and injured.'

'Dan's view may very easily be that we are shortly to engage the opposition, and this is a strong platoon, and there are other able-bodied men available. We must keep going forward. "Somebody have a quick sympathetic word with Macdonald – give him a shot of morphine – but let's press on.

'Except that this Company Commander has been shot in the back by his own troops – and Dan may not approve of that.'

Shortly after seven o'clock Donald dialled my number in London. With military brevity he explained in about four swift sentences what had happened.

It took me a few seconds to realise the enormity of what he was saying. I heard myself bellow: 'They have done *what*?'

'Well,' said Donald. 'They have sort of taken over.'

'*The bastards*,' I yelled. 'The *unprincipled arrogant bastards*!'

'Well,' said Donald in that thoroughly charming, ingenuous way he has; 'It was a bit of a shock.'

'The *bastards*!' I confirmed. 'This is unbelievable. Well they're not going to get away with it.'

'Well,' said Donald. 'I had rather thought you might suggest I resign.'

'Resign?' I spluttered. 'Resign? Are you out of your mind?'

'Not quite yet,' he said.

'Now listen Donald,' I said, rather unnecessarily. 'This is bloody nasty. First though let me make my position completely clear. If you quit, I'll certainly go too, and they can have it. But if you stay and fight, then I'll fight the bastards with you.'

For me their actions, with all their broken promises, was an example of cynical opportunism at its worst. Because deep down I knew they had broken that sacred trust, the very fabric which holds all Oxford Boat Race oarsmen together. Loyalty to the cause, to crewmates, to the elected President and his coaches, the bond that for me was the cornerstone of our long period of success. We were like a family – Dark Blue men of the Tideway who had shared so much pain and triumph together. To breach that trust was unforgiveable. And in my view that was what they had done.

'Make up your mind, Donald,' I told him. 'Will you run, or fight?'

His answer was immediate. 'That's all I needed to hear. We're going to fight. Who the hell do they think they are? Christ, Dan, do you know how many times I've beaten them all in the gym and in the sculling races?'

'How many times *you've* beaten them?' I said. 'What about the times *I've* bloody beaten them this year. You're right. Who the hell *do* they think they are?'

Donald said quietly, 'I have to go out tonight. But I'll speak to Mike Spracklen, and I'll talk to you again in the morning.'

In those brief words I sensed that his whole manner had changed. He suddenly sounded like a different person, and it was clear that all of that stern Scottish character in his soul was being summoned. There are close friends of Donald's who swear that on that day his face changed, and a certain hardness began to lurk behind his easy smile.

As he got off the phone he was beginning to formulate a plan of action. Lyons, Fish, Huntington, Penny and Clark had a serious fight on their hands now, and their English supporters would have much time to reflect upon the wisdom of taking their side.

Donald then called Mike Spracklen, and said that he would like the crews to carry on working for a couple of days in the normal way, that he would prefer Mike to go on coaching as if nothing were amiss. However he explained, things were very much amiss. He told Mike that the crew was gravely mistaken if they thought they had won. 'I propose,' he said, 'to take stringent, and decisive action.'

He also asked the coach for his assurance that he would coach only a crew selected by Donald. Mike promised that he would answer only to the President of the OUBC. He restated his position that he had placed himself at the President's disposal for the two weeks as agreed, and that the training schedule and any politics involved were entirely under the jurisdiction of the President and his chief coach. If the mutineers had hoped that Spracklen, the great Olympic six-lane specialist would take over the coaching of their rebel crew, then Donald had effectively made certain that that avenue was securely blocked.

Another of our coaches, Jeff Jacobs, also rang Donald after speaking to me. He was rather short on the phone. 'I'm in a bit of a hurry, Donald,' he said. 'But I've just heard from Dan what has happened. *Burn the bastards*.' And he hung up.

That night at a formal dinner in St Edmund Hall, Donald sat next to Duncan Clegg, a former President from the 1960s who now holds the influential position of London Boat Race Representative of the Oxford and Cambridge Boat Clubs. It was just eight hours since the showdown in Oriel Square but Duncan turned to Donald before the main course was over and said quietly: 'I hear the problems of the President are perennial.' The news was travelling like a forest fire, and as it swept through the university. Attitudes were hardening by the minute. 'Of course you must fight it,' Duncan told Donald. 'And the Old Blues will back you all the way.'

Duncan Clegg was an expert on the subject of rowing with Americans, and either pronunciation of the word would suffice. He had rowed at 3 in the winning 1965 crew which contained an all-American stern of Bill Fink, Harry Howell, Duncan Spencer, and Ed Trippe at stroke. They were all from Yale and had had more fun at Oxford than this current group would have in their whole lives.

The following year Duncan was President, and he told Donald how he had walked up and down the towpath with Michael Barry a week before the Boat Race agonizing over whether to sack Christian Albert, a very talented but in his view troublesome American. Finally he did so, and Oxford went on to win. 'These things tend to be cyclical,' said Duncan. 'They occur at regular intervals, and after them, we always win.' I remembered the occasion well, for Christian insisted on rowing in that year's Isis crew against Goldie. I was in it too and we won, covering the course in a faster time than the Cambridge Boat Race crew.

Michael Pelham, Hugh's father, was host of the dinner that evening at his old college, St Edmund Hall, and he too had heard of the day's events. He took Donald aside afterwards and told him quietly: 'Do your groundwork thoroughly. Close all the gaps, make sure of your support, and don't make your move until you are quite certain you can win.'

He spoke with a large smile, and the confidence of a man who had been through it all before, as indeed he had. Mike had been in the thick of that earlier 'mutiny' in 1959 led by the American Reed Rubin, and now his son was Secretary of the OUBC in the middle of another, even worse crisis. At the conclusion of the dinner Hugh himself walked up to Donald, his sworn rival in the sculling boats for all of those months, and he said: 'Donald I just want you to be sure where my loyalties are, and they are with you a hundred per cent. I won't let you down.' He explained that in the afternoon he had told the rebel crew that he supported the President and that what they were doing was wrong.

The only other support in the boat for Donald was from Dr Tom Cadoux-Hudson, who tried to distance himself from the fray. He was extremely unhappy with the 'putsch', particularly with the methods of the mutineers. At first Donald had felt that Tom had 'nailed his colours firmly to the fence', a judgement which he subsequently acknowledged had been hasty when Tom loyally continued to row in a Pair with the President full in the face of Donald's sworn enemies for some vital morale-boosting outings during the following couple of weeks. In a stern retraction of his earlier doubts, Donald felt obliged to say: 'In the end Tom voted with his feet.'

Before the diners dispersed that evening a strategy was drawn up. Hugh would report back to the others to reassure the squad that 'Macdonald had taken his medicine like a man', and had no further plans. He might just decide to carry on as executive non-racing President, or he might decide to resign altogether.

As Donald fell exhausted into bed that night, he had a checklist beside him that would have made General Eisenhower look relaxed in the hours before the Normandy Landings. He had made a note to call every one of the coaches separately. He must call the members of the Oxford University Boat Club Trust Fund, to ensure full establishment support, especially from Ronnie Howard, who had put down the 1959 mutiny. He also had to call Steve Peel, the Cambridge President, to block any possibility of the Light Blues accepting a challenge from a rebel Oxford crew.

Above all though, he wanted to call the number 5 and number 7 men from the old London Rowing Club crew who had fought with him throughout that wonderful season of 1978 when he had pulled the 6 oar with such rare fanaticism. The 5 man was Simon Barker, a barrister who would, he knew, tell him his rights as laid down by the constitution of the OUBC and would allow *no one* to hoodwink him over what he could and could not do.

The other crew mate was crucial, because Donald envisaged a savage instant coup to put down the mutiny in one fell, unanswerable swoop. And the man who had held down that 7 seat right in front of him was just the man to guide him – his devoted brother, Captain Hugh Macdonald, of the elite Ninth Parachute Squadron, Royal Engineers.

This is one of the most dedicated regiments of fighting soldiers in the British Army, and contains many of the heroes who fought their way across the frozen Falkland Islands in 1982. The Paras lost one of their bravest commanding officers, Colonel 'H' Jones, killed in fierce fighting, before they smashed their way to victory in the Battle of Goose Green, outnumbered by the Argentinians three to one. Indeed it was the blood-stained battle-worn men of the Parachute Regiment who strode triumphantly into Port Stanley on 14 June to accept the Argentinian surrender.

By the time Donald had finished pouring out his tortured soul to his brother Hugh, as he could never do to me, there was a ready group of Falklands veterans asking their officer: 'Look Sir, if you think Mr Donald is having a bit of trouble up there, with all them awkward students, well, do you think we ought to provide him with a bit of ... well ... support, back-up – you know, help him sort it out ... know what I mean ...?'

The prospect of the tattered banner of the Parachute Regiment being hoisted above the Oxford University boathouse, as it had been above the racecourse on the outskirts of Port Stanley, was too much even for Hugh. He spoke carefully to Donald about the tactics

Donald Macdonald and family

"It'll soon be
"3 MEN in a
BOAT..."

Clark (Centre) training with
the Oriel College crew
and guest Huntingdon (far right)

Tom Cadoux-Hudson

Chris Clark

Rob Clay

Jon Fish

Peter Gish

Paul Gleeson

Richard Hull

Chris Huntingdon

Rob Leach

Dan Lyons

Chris Penny

Hugh Pelham

Gavin Screaton

Gavin Stewart

Tony Ward

Bruce Philp

Michael Suarez

The crew that never was: Fish, Huntingdon, Hull, Penny, Lyons, Stewart, Cadoux-Hudson, Macdonald, Pelham

'In my day it wouldn't have come up — the whole boat would have been chosen from Eton, Radley and Oundle'

Little and large:
Lobbenberg and Stewart

Trials clash: Fish cuts in front of Lobbenberg moments before

the first punch is thrown

Oxford with Gleeson at stroke two weeks before the Boat Race

I want to sit next to my friend

OXFORD UNIVERSITY BOAT CLUB

BOAT RACE WALK-OUT

"Finally they wanted it re-named the America's Cup!"

The final line-up

'AT LEAST THEY'RE UNLIKELY TO REPLACE HIM WITH A LARGE AMERICAN READING SOCIAL STUDIES...'

The finish: Macdonald's triumphant salute

he should use when dealing with tough and volatile men, especially the kind who believed they were very firmly in control of a situation, as Lyons and his men now did.

There was a routine captains' meeting scheduled for the Wednesday night of that week at which Donald decided he would report to the heads of the thirty-six college boat clubs what was going on. He did not wish to alarm anyone, neither did he wish to serve notice that he was gathering his forces for a counter-action. He regarded it as vital that the American group should have no idea what he was planning. He instructed the loyal Hugh Pelham to tell anyone who was interested, in a non-committal tone, that Donald was going to attend the meeting and that he still planned to carry out the normal administrative functions of his Presidency.

This meant that Donald would be in the chair. It also meant that the earliest he could convene a meeting of his own with his university rowing squad would be on the following day, Thursday. He called the steward at Vincent's Club and booked the upstairs room for a meeting of the OUBC at one o'clock on Thursday. He spent the whole of Tuesday, most of Tuesday night and all day Wednesday on the phone, much of the time to me, to Steve Royle and to his brother.

He broke for just a couple of hours late in the afternoon, in response to an invitation from Ronnie Howard. The powerfully-built scourge of the 1959 mutineers had answered Donald's request for advice, with a typically understated mild phrase.

'Oh dear, Donald. Why don't you come round to tea?'

Although he greeted Donald with tea, sympathy, and some quite exquisite chocolate cake and buttered scones, Ronnie had some hard opinions to voice to the battered President. 'First of all,' he said, 'it was a grave mistake to have allowed them to continue rowing, because each day is a further confirmation of their credibility as the official Oxford crew.' In his opinion the entire thing had to be stamped on as quickly as possible. He considered that our situation was worse than his had been, because his had occurred much earlier in the Michaelmas term. Ronnie is a powerful presence, and Donald felt better for a problem shared. And now here he was face-to-face, over strawberry jam, with the living, legendary, tangible proof that a situation like this could be dealt with and overcome. And he did not forget the cheerful words of the ex-President as they parted: 'Remember, Donald, big hearts win Boat Races, not big reputations. And certainly not big mouths.'

Donald spent the remainder of that evening, and all the following day, Wednesday, on the telephone planning his Thursday offensive, which would explode shortly after one p.m. By the end of the afternoon on Wednesday, his throat ached with the effort of hours of constant talking.

The captains' meeting was to be held at New College, the fourteenth-century place of learning I had myself attended as an undergraduate twenty years before. Donald had two major objectives: the first to inform but not alarm the college captains of the University, and the second to dispel all suspicion that he might be planning a counter-attack. He wanted the gathering to accept that he was attending to the Boat Club's problems in the quiet easy administrative way which on the surface sits so easily with him. Above all, he did not wish to alert Gavin Stewart, who would be one of the few people in the room who was not a college captain.

Stewart's personal position was something of a dichotomy, for he was there as Donald's Vice President, a position defined in the constitution as one 'whose sole duty it shall be to assist the President.' And here he was ensconced in the rebel camp.

Meanwhile, until the very last minute, Donald maintained practically an open line to the headquarters of the Parachute Regiment in Aldershot, where Captain Hugh Macdonald, and one or two other officers, were helping to draft a plan to sweep the betrayed President of the OUBC back to his democratically elected position.

Early in the evening Donald drove to New College in the old family Volkswagen. There he met Steve Royle and me and explained what he wished to do. He had asked us, unusually since we did not normally attend such administrative gatherings, to come and lend moral support, he explained that we would report to the lecture room on the ground floor and he would chair a routine and unexciting meeting. During the course of it he would be grateful for a few words of support from us, but that he hoped to be in and out as quickly as possible.

We all walked in together. The captains were in a group at the back of the room. Donald's VP ambled in, his eyes fixed firmly to the floor, his purpose was clearly to inform his fellow conspirators of the general demeanour of the 'deposed' President, his state of mind and his plans.

Hugh Pelham read the minutes of the last meeting. And Donald took over immediately, saying mildly that one or two of the captains might have heard rumours about some problems with crew selection for the Oxford crew. It was he hoped a temporary affair, nothing too serious, and he would be sure to keep them fully informed of any developing news.

He outlined the main events of the last few days, carefully defusing the scandalous nature of the rebel action, and he assured his audience that he did have the fullest support of the coaches, two of whom were here this evening to speak briefly. He then read a short note from the respected treasurer of the OUBC Trust Fund, Dr Michael Barry, himself a coach and winning Old Blue from 1946, which concluded: 'I am fully confident of the ability of you and your coaches to make the correct selection of this year's Oxford crew, and to enable it to win the Boat Race.'

I stood up and said that Donald was an honourable President, and in my opinion one of the best we had had during the last ten or fifteen years. I told them I had every confidence in him and that I was sure he would not let anybody down. But most of all I stressed Donald's integrity, that as a man he would never behave dishonourably. Neither, I said, would he hesitate to stand down from the crew if the coaches felt that he was not worth his place.

Steve spoke along similar lines and we all left soon after. We gathered outside and Donald went over, once again, his battle plan for the meeting next day. When he had first outlined it to me over the telephone I had been filled with the gravest doubts. As I stood on the pavement outside my old college, chilled by the north wind, I grew more and more concerned. As Steve did.

The operation, said Donald, had to be swift. Brutal. And without mercy. Its victims must never know what had hit them. Donald was utterly uncompromising in his approach. I had rarely seen such steely resolve and intensity of purpose and I found myself thinking of how he had once been a raw Isis hopeful: 'Dan, do you think I could really make it . . .?'

The events of the past week had changed him, I suspect for ever. And the loss of a couple of those men whom he had thought were, at the very least, well-meaning colleagues, if not friends, had provided a short and brutish education. Disillusionment had now been replaced by the historic Scottish steel of the Macdonalds. Tomorrow he would request no conciliation, and he would offer none either. As we parted, he said quietly, 'Dan, tomorrow I will be fighting for the survival of the Boat Club, for its constitution and for its Presidency. As far as I'm concerned, it's them or me.'

CHAPTER EIGHT

RECAPTURE OF THE BOAT CLUB

Donald positioned himself behind the desk, flanked by Steve and myself, the adrenalin pumping through his system. He sat with his forearms hard on the desk top lest an inadvertent movement betray the emotion he felt. There was sweat on his forehead as he looked up to face them – Fish, Lyons, Clark, Huntington and Penny.

The early morning of Thursday, 22 January, saw Donald hard at work in the library of Mansfield College applying final revisions to his long essay on Shakespeare's *Richard II*, the last of England's Plantaganet rulers and one of the great political negotiators of the fourteenth century. Noting, with a sense of deep irony, that Richard ended up being murdered in Pontefract Castle as a result of his conciliatory nature, Donald prepared with renewed vigour to begin his treatise on Henry V, who, by contrast, tended to put his enemies to the sword and remains a towering hero to this day.

Emerging from the scholarly hush of the library, Donald headed home, phoned his only lieutenant, Hugh Pelham, and asked him to collect the keys to the OUBC van from the rebel driver Richard Hull. It was important, he said, that none of them should leave Oriel Square at the appointed time. Then he called Eric, the steward at Vincent's Club, to check that the clubroom on the second floor was still available for the one o'clock meeting.

Next he touched base with me, confirming once more the details

148

of his strategy for the meeting and insisting that it was vital that I say nothing for that strategy to succeed. He believed passionately that should we be drawn into any form of discussion or 'woolly' argument at this stage we would be sunk. 'We have tried that with them,' he said. 'And it has proved to be utterly futile.' He urged me not to go to Marlow to talk to them and reluctantly I agreed.

He then made his call to his opposite number Stephen Peel, the Cambridge President and international oarsman at Downing College. He explained his difficulties and obtained the promise of his Light Blue rival that he would never deal with the rebel boat. Donald finished with a typical flourish: 'There will be a vast mushroom cloud right above Oxford this lunchtime,' he said. 'I am personally going to detonate it in Vincent's Club at exactly 1300 hours.'

Finally he put in a call to the Parachute Regiment, checked his final list with his brother Hugh and sat down to perfect the draft of his speech for that afternoon. There was much he had to remember. Hugh had stressed the advantage of catching them by surprise. It was also important that having delivered his offensive, there should be no room for any debate. It must, said Hugh, be a cold, flat *fait accompli*, an execution, with no question of redress.

There was also the aspect of complete psychological domination from the very start. You must be there a good half-an-hour in advance in order to lay undisputed claim to the territory. You must be at a desk, with formal documents in front of you, an expensive pen, your wristwatch propped up in front of you – the symbols of authority, of organization, of assumed command. If you can arrange for your opponents to be dressed in training gear, so much the better. You will appear in a smart suit, or dark jacket with a tie.

Do not, said Hugh, be afraid to use notes to read from, prepared words from which there will be no deviation or ad-libbing. When you have a message to impart, say it swiftly, without hesitation and without pause for further thought or digression. Polish the work, deliver it with assurance, and make no mistakes. There must be a well-thought out ultimatum in conclusion, which you also deliver without breaking stride. At the end of it you say: 'That will be all for now. Thank you gentlemen. Good afternoon.'

And with that, you gather your documents, pen and wristwatch, and leave the room instantly, closing the door behind you with sufficient force to let everyone know it is shut for good. 'And with that,' said Hugh, momentarily dropping the guise of Field Marshal Viscount Montgomery, on whose manner he undoubtedly based all of the above, 'You will get the hell out of that building and stay out.'

Donald had rehearsed it all very carefully. However Steve Royle and I still had serious misgivings about what he was intending to do; but then neither of us had been subjected to that brutalizing experience he had undergone in what we all now referred to as 'The Lyons Den'.

We both feared that Donald was playing a dangerous game, and all of my instincts told me that we should abandon these hammer blows, however justified they might be, and try some diplomacy, some persuasion or plain old-fashioned reason. But Donald was quite adamant, unbending in his determination to end the mutiny, decisively now, and continued to urge that I say 'absolutely nothing'.

I had tried to counsel caution. But it was to no avail. Donald had just smiled grimly and said: 'Dan, if you had been in Dan Lyons' room with me you would not be talking like that. The course of action I propose to take is the only one which makes any sense. If I do not strike now, it will happen again later. I don't trust this bloody gang, and they have shown themselves to be highly determined and totally unscrupulous.

'I respect your view that they should be given some sort of formula to save face. But they would interpret that as a sign of weakness. I now know them better than you do, and I cannot reveal even a hint of uncertainty. I have to shatter them with a single, unexpected and devastating blow. Then we shall see how the pieces reform.'

Donald and I did however agree on one fundamental point, and that was Clark, whom we both considered to be of no danger to anyone on his own. Although he seemed to have gone to war with me, on the grounds he did not want to follow the training programme, his real problem was one of commitment. He loves a high profile when everything is going well, but when things go wrong – whoosh! Where's Chris? Disappeared.

He was, however, Huntington's favourite, the 'hothouse plant that needed nurturing.' And, as Donald wrote, in his journal: 'The real danger is Clark in tandem with Lyons. It is the perfect symbiosis. In Lyons, Clark has the standard bearer he needs. In Clark, Lyons has the cause, the sense of mission, essential for such a personality to thrive.'

In the previous dozen years I had come to be regarded by most Presidents and probably by most of the oarsmen too, as the leader of Oxford's expeditions, both at home and abroad. And as we had won, time and time again, I suppose they had come to rely more and more heavily on me as some sort of mentor with the ability to sort out all their problems. Now this role had been taken from me; and by one of the most unlikely people. Donald Macdonald had emerged as an iron-hard leader, steely and stubborn, and right now I was having to trot along to keep up. Because he knew precisely what he was going to do, while I was still trying to play it by ear, searching for a way to compromise and regain the loyalty and goodwill of the squad without this unstoppable uproar. Hell! I still wanted to beat Cambridge.

I had not seen the squad men to speak to since last Friday, six days earlier, when we had rowed the seat races. I had left the Leander boathouse with Chris Clark's promise that he would row where I wanted him and that he would settle down to training. Next thing I knew, he and his mates had hijacked the Boat Club.

I left London for Oxford at mid-morning, my heart pounding, my whole body tense and anxious. I drove quickly out through the western suburbs and found myself racing along the M.40, willing the Marlow turn-off to loom up to my left. When it did, I swung the car in the direction of the little riverside town and down into the Thames valley, with a strange feeling of desperation, that I must divest myself of a note I had written to Spracklen. It informed him that there would be no outing today, that I was sorry and would explain later. It was as if the delivery of this simple note signalled the first shot fired in the campaign to save Donald Macdonald's Presidency. Now there would be no turning back.

I placed the note on the boat and drove quickly back to the motorway and thence to Oxford, subconsciously bracing myself for what was to come. There was an inexorable quality about the confrontation ahead which I was now powerless to prevent. Donald was not to be diverted from his chosen path. He was determined that by 1.30 that afternoon, he would be back in control of the Oxford University Boat Club.

I parked my car and walked alone into the club where lurks the history of Oxford's greatest sporting moments since the last century. I climbed the two flights of stairs to the big clubroom, with its deep sofas and chairs, its magazines and newspapers, and the aging permanence that dwells in such rooms. On days like this, when matters of great moment are to be decided, the spirits of past glories seem strangely close, as if the ghosts of other sportsmen, from other times, who have also experienced turbulence and anger, are near.

The world's first four-minute-mile was planned in here by Roger Bannister, Chris Chataway and Chris Brasher before they cracked it on the university running track thirty-three years ago. C.B. Fry, that most gifted of Oxford and England batsmen, held his meetings in this room, as did England cricket Captains Colin Cowdrey and M.J.K. Smith. 'Tiger' Pataudi, the Captain of India, was a member here, as was Dr Tuppy Owen Smith, the legendary Oxford and South African batsman who went on to captain the England Rugby team.

Oxford's greatest Rugby Blues, men who went on to play for England, attended team gatherings in this room: John Kendall-Carpenter, R.A.W. Sharp, the fighter-pilot and wing three-quarter Prince Obelenski, the full-back John Willcox, the Welsh internationals Onllwyn Brace and Vivian Jenkins; the West Point cadet Pete Dawkins, who thrilled huge English audiences with his power running in the Dark Blue Rugby shirt of Oxford. Ronnie Poulton, the wing three-quarter, dined here on the night before he scored a record *five* touchdowns in the 1909 Varsity Match against Cambridge.

American Senator and basketball immortal Bill Bradley was a frequent visitor here during his time at Oxford. The British Prime Minister, Sir Alec Douglas Home, a seam-bowler of the highest quality during his days at Christ Church, dined here on the night the Oxford captain dropped him from the XI to face Cambridge at Lords. Poor Sir Alec had been hit for three consecutive and towering sixes by Percy Perrin of Essex in the final game before the 1926 Varsity Match and this was regarded in much the same light as I saw Oxford's twenty-eighth position in the Fours Head of the River, earlier in the winter.

Another Prime Minister, Harold Macmillan, was a member here, as was the King of Norway. All of the rowing legends belonged to Vincent's: Davidge, Burnell, 'Jumbo' Edwards, Duncan Spencer and Ronnie Howard, and they had all sat in this room wrestling with the intricate problems of team selection, and the downfall of the traditional enemy one hundred and thirty miles away in Cambridge. None of them, however, had ever dealt with a more serious sporting quarrel than the one which now faced Donald and me.

Donald arrived on time at 12.30 p.m., Steve Royle right behind him. The President was understandably tense as I poured some coffee. Thirty minutes from now he would meet the rebels for the first time since he had left them in the van four days before. I wondered whether another night's sleep had mellowed him, whether he would still insist on his hard line. The truth was he had not slept much and he had mellowed not one bit.

It was clear he was extremely keyed up and although I still wanted to alter two important details in his planned assault, I knew I could not put any more pressure on him.

He said for the last time, 'Please, Dan, promise me you will not get drawn into an argument. Say nothing. And when I leave, follow me.' We checked once more his statement and once more Steve and I agreed to abide by its content.

The clock ticked on towards one o'clock, and at ten minutes to the hour Hugh Pelham pulled on his coat and left the club, heading towards Oriel Square where the whole squad was awaiting the arrival of the van to take them to the river for their fourth day in succession of rowing without the President. The group he met was in high confidence, sure of their positions, certain of their ground. All they lacked right now was the van and its keys, both of which were under the control of Pelham who now walked across the square and said firmly: 'Okay guys, there's a meeting right now at Vincent's. Very, very serious. Better come with me. Everyone.'

They picked up their rowing bags and trooped after the Secretary. Back in the clubroom, Donald positioned himself behind the desk, flanked by Steve and myself, the adrenalin pumping through his system. He sat with his forearms hard on the desk top lest an inadvertent movement betray the emotions he felt. There was sweat on his forehead, as he looked up to face them – Lyons, Fish, Huntington, Clark, Penny, Stewart, Hull, Ward, and all of the Isis boys, about twenty in all.

The atmosphere in the room was atomic. No one was smiling, unless you count the sardonic look of Dan Lyons, or the rather bored grin on the face of Chris Clark. Generally they looked rather startled and tense, because none of them had any idea of what to expect. Nor could they anticipate what the next move would be from the President they had forced out of the boat, and to all intents and purposes out of office.

'Right,' said Donald, his voice just breaking, but not betraying the turmoil that raged within him. 'Now settle down.' The room went silent.

He looked at them steadily once, as if to concentrate the gaze of every pair of eyes in that room, all focussed hard upon him. And then, with his fists again clenched tight on the table, to prevent his hands from shaking, he began to speak. 'I intend,' he said, 'To read a statement; but first I should say that this is not an occasion for debate. However you are welcome to telephone me individually. At the end I and the coaches will leave you to discuss the matter amongst yourselves and to make your own decisions.

'Steve and Dan are here to represent the unanimous voice of the coaches and their presence endorses what I have to say.

'And first I should like to place the matter in context. The President, the coaches and Old Blues are all resolved that while we intend to give every priority to producing the fastest crew, we also believe the future of the Boat Club is as important as this year's Boat Race. And we intend to ensure that future is not jeopardized. As individuals we are all unimportant in the wider context of this event because there is a bigger picture at stake.

'As President of the OUBC I have been entrusted with the right to select and manage all university crews, and I have asked a team of coaches to help select a crew to race against Cambridge. These coaches are highly respected, among the best in the country, and have advised the Oxford President for many years.

'Now they have put forward their selection, and this decision has been challenged. This makes the position of the coaches untenable, and the outlook for this club, bleak.

'The entire coaching team stands by its selection, and by the President. They are appalled at the actions of this crew; they refuse to coach this crew, and all are ready to resign if the President resigns. And this includes Mike Spracklen who has continued to coach this week, only at my request.

'As a result of the events of the past few days, the President and the coaches no longer feel able to create a successful team from the original selection. Therefore a new crew will be invited to race against Cambridge.

'You all have until precisely 12.00 midnight to decide whether or not you wish to row in this crew. If I do not hear from you I will assume you have declined. If you do choose NOT to row, you will not be invited again.

'It is important that you understand the following:

'That you will only be asked once.

'That those we have chosen not to select will under no circumstances be selected later.

'That those who agree to row join the team without reservation, and that any further challenges of this sort will result in their immediate expulsion.

'I ask you all to beware of making your decision while influenced by the pressure of this group. Talk to people outside of rowing and perhaps talk to your parents.

'I would also warn you to beware of sacrificing everything out of a misguided loyalty to those who have shown you and this club, no loyalty whatsoever. (At this point Dan Lyons symbolically groaned the deep sigh of the deeply misunderstood).

'And please be assured that if you do not row, then someone will take your place.

'The two crews invited to row are as follows:

'Boat 'A' – coxswain Lobbenberg, Huntington, Hull, Penny, Cadoux-Hudson, Stewart, Pelham, Macdonald, Ward.

'Boat 'B' – coxswain Gruselle, Gleeson, Baird, Gish, Ridgewell, Cheatle, Hill, Chinn, Race.'

Missing were the names of Christopher Clark, Dan Lyons and Jonathon Fish.

'I should also like to hear from 3rd Eight men Ben Kent and Tim Roberts,' said Donald. 'Meanwhile there will be no outing today. Training resumes tomorrow, and there will be no further discussion from us. Your decisions by phone please, before midnight tonight.'

No one moved. It was like the petrified forest, as if each and every one of them had been turned to stone. I watched the blood drain from the face of Christopher Clark. He went white as he realized that his career as an oarsman at Oxford was finally, irrevocably over. Lyons remained quite expressionless, looking neither to his left nor to his right. But the attitude of frowning responsibility he tends to adopt on these occasions was gone.

Everyone just stood there in stunned, impenetrable silence for almost ten seconds – it seemed like 10 minutes – before Donald, without one word more, pushed his chair back, picked up his papers, and walked right through the middle of them and out the door. Remembering my promise, I too, walked to the door behind

Steve. He went through first. I picked up a file of coaching schedules, and by the time I pushed open the door no more than thirty-five seconds had elapsed since Donald concluded his statement. Not one word had been spoken in that room. They were shell-shocked. A situation, of which they had been so firmly and so incontrovertibly in control just twenty minutes before, had suddenly and ruthlessly been reversed.

My own heart was pounding at close to 180 beats a minute, somewhere very near that of a Boat Race oarsman just before Hammersmith. I could no longer control my pent up frustration and anger and I regret I swung round on them as I left and said 'You assholes. You've ruined everything.'

Now there was only Hugh Pelham left with any authority in the Vincent's clubroom and he had been strongly briefed by Donald as to what his role should be. It was a full five minutes before any of them recovered sufficiently to be able to deal with rational grown-up thoughts. Gavin Stewart, the disloyal VP, uttered the first word: 'Unconscionable,' he muttered. He may have been talking about his own moral position in the plot to overthrow his President, but more likely he was referring to Donald's surprise comeback.

Now Hugh started in, as he had agreed with Donald. 'Rebellions like this are only basically worth a damn,' he said, 'if the coaches don't back the President. Otherwise rebel crews don't stand a chance.'

He pointed out that Donald appeared to have marshalled the support of the entire Oxford establishment. He also pointed out that Duncan Clegg, who organizes the Boat Race would not deal with them. 'He's on Donald's side one hundred per cent,' he told them. 'I was in the room when they had dinner together the other night. So you can forget that.'

It was also obvious, he said, that Donald had spoken to the Cambridge President, Stephen Peel and had his assurance that he would not accept a challenge from a rebel crew. 'As far as Peel is concerned the OUBC is under Donald's jurisdiction,' he told them. 'And he will not permit a Cambridge crew to race any Oxford crew which is not on the water under the auspices of the President. So you can forget that too.'

It left them with one option. They would have to force Donald to resign as President, something he was now most unlikely to do. 'At a guess, guys,' Hugh said, 'I'd say you were stuffed. You have no coaches, no establishment support, no boat, no chance of an alternative challenge. Donald thinks you are a disgrace to the university. And he is still very much President of the OUBC. Doesn't look too hot, does it?'

Put like that they had to agree that things did not look very hot at all for the members of the rebel crew. Donald Macdonald had proved to be as dangerous an opponent in the boardroom as he was in a sculling boat, a rowing boat, or in the gym. Right now it was game, set and match to Stockton-on-Tees. Dan Lyons had proved to be 200lbs behind him in more ways than one. It was the element of surprise which had proved to be decisive. The rebels had had no time in which to gather their arguments or to prepare even a mild intellectual counter-attack. One minute they were standing in a self-congratulatory band of all-powerful Blue Boat oarsmen, the next it was all over. Three of the ringleaders had been exiled from the Boat Race, and the rest of them had the choice of either jumping to the President's command or leaving the squad for good and all. Anyone who chose not to row 'will not be invited again . . . any further challenges of this sort will result in immediate expulsion.'

'Jesus, guys, I don't think he's joking.'

I could definitely have confirmed that to any of them. He certainly was not joking. Outside Vincent's Steve, Donald and I decided to go for a cup of tea, and we walked down The High, the three of us, in stunned amazement at Donald's performance.

I'll admit it was not quite the way I would have done it, because I am a man of words, and I did not much like being 'gagged', unable to speak to my squad. I would have much preferred a full discussion for as long as it took, where we would have worked things out, and allowed everyone to blow off steam. But that line had got us nowhere. Now, with the future of the crew which had tormented me for so long hanging in the balance, I was obliged to concede that the President had shown immense courage and willpower, and whatever Captain Macdonald had advised about blowing opponents clean out of the water, had worked in the most devastating manner. For the first time I was beginning to agree with Donald that his method had probably been correct.

We sipped tea in the Queen's Café. Donald reiterated his view that everything would be fine if we stayed united and hung very tough from now until the Boat Race. He reckoned that we ought to anticipate any future problems but he thought that the major surgery he had just performed should have put a stop to the mutiny.

He said in his opinion it was impossible for us to work with Clark, Lyons and Fish. We discussed the future of the Club and in particular the fact that next year, for the first time, Oxford would have a full-time professional coach and administrator, our own Steve Royle. Today had been a watershed, and the action would clear the air and send a clear signal to everyone in the year before Steve took over.

Donald anticipated that the mutineers, when they had recovered some composure, might try to split the coaches, and we should prevent that from happening at all costs. On the back of his notes he already had possible crews drawn up in the event that Huntington, Penny and Hull pulled out in sympathy with the others. In this circumstance we discussed promoting Paul Gleeson to stroke, putting Ward at 7, followed by Stewart and Cadoux-Hudson, Donald at 4 with Pelham, Julian Richards, a former Isis oarsman, and possibly even Rob Clay, a 1984 Blue back doing graduate work, in the bows. Ben Kent, a quiet ambitious man whom I had coached as a relative novice in the New College Head crew the year before, would be promoted to row in Isis. This made me smile, because Ben had come up to me earlier that morning and said: 'Do I have any chance of making Isis this year?' And I had told him wryly: 'Hang in there Ben. The way things are going, you could be stroking the Blue Boat!'

After a couple of hours we adjourned our meeting and Donald headed home. I went back to London still reeling from the events of the day. I wondered just how long it would be before this unholy row crashed onto the front pages of the papers. Major sports rows at Oxford were always greeted with hysterical glee by popular and heavy newspapers alike – the Boat Race itself occasionally hits the front page of the *New York Times* anyway – and a serious bust-up in the Boat Club tends to be treated like a breakdown in nuclear disarmament talks. They've used the same headline, *Crisis on the Isis*, for half a century.

I was not at all sure how long this could possibly be kept quiet. And that was a problem because in Britain the Press does not restrict itself to just reporting rows of this type; it is inclined to start running them. If the protagonists wanted their viewpoints heard, there would be an army of eager journalists longing to give them space.

Meanwhile back at 14 Lime Road, Donald's phone was humming. Hugh Pelham was on the line reporting what happened after we had left and he had much to say. For there had been three international athletes, who had received, each one of them a numbing blow. I suspect that they had believed that united they were inviolate, that no one in his right mind would dare to get rid of all of them. So if they just stuck together they must ultimately succeed in winning control of the OUBC. It was not that Donald had somehow driven a wedge between them, but that he had demonstrated that he was quite prepared to lose them all. And that was an eventuality they simply had not bargained for.

In its way it was a glaring encapsulation of the big-star syndrome of the 1980s. As John McEnroe once said: 'Can tennis do without me?' Our situation was classic: five American internationals faced essentially by a group of Englishmen in rowing caps, doing their best to be fair. They had run slap up against it with Donald and, as Hugh Pelham was now reporting, they had found it hard to believe. Dan Lyons, who had been so adamant that there should be no more tests and that the crew didn't wish to row with him, lamely now wondered if they might make an appeal for 'more time.'

From where he stood, he did of course have as much time as he needed, since he had just been fired from the crew. Hugh Pelham had been quick to point out that since there was no longer a rebel crew anyone who did not agree with the system should just resign. They pondered their predicament for a long time.

Gavin Stewart decided he should fight on the 'moral' ticket, refusing to compromise his own integrity, and announcing that he could not accept what had happened. In his view it was 'unconscionable' that Clark, Lyons and Fish could be treated thus, particularly Clark, who had just begun to behave himself and was clearly trying so very hard to be a good and productive member of the squad.

Richard Hull suffered what might loosely be described as a crisis of conscience. He pointed out that he had two choices: the first a selfish one – to return to the fold, row in the boat, thus earning an honour which had eluded him at Cambridge and would last him for the rest of his life. The second choice, though not necessarily in that order, was of course to stand resolutely by his friends, and take the view that either Donald relented and reinstated the three Americans or he, Richard, would be compelled to sacrifice his own career in the interest of a higher justice. He had not seen the letter from Chris Clark to Donald in December in which he had referred to Hull as a rower merely trying to 'make the boat' rather than win the race.

Now he was agonized, but he felt he was destined to join an all-out US boycott of the Oxford boat. But Donald harboured no such doubts about his ultimate choice. 'Hull?' said the President to Hugh Pelham. 'In the end he'll row. You can put your savings on that.'

Chris Huntington was thoughtful. He had after all been the only one amongst them who had in his own mind believed their actions on the day of the mutiny had been wrong; and he had suspected that this kind of retribution would probably not be long in coming. He had tried to warn the others, but his intelligence was often rough-ridden by Clark. 'Goddammit, Hunt, you're so *predictably* East Coast.'

Now Huntington's was suddenly the voice of reason which ought to be listened to and he advised the greatest caution; perhaps they could request some more time from the President for tests. He just hoped the door was not completely closed because he believed the only chance for the American group as an entity was to keep talking.

Chris Penny was 'really upset by the way this thing is being handled'. What's more he just 'didn't like the method of delivery,' which Donald had used to such devastating effect. Basically he would settle for a few more tests but he was half-hearted in his support for a further assault on the Oxford Presidency. Indeed it was he who had tried unsuccessfully to stop Clark reneging on his promise in Henley a week earlier to row on the bowside. And although it had seemed for three idyllic days that Clark had been right to make his stand, and the take-over had succeeded, it now did not seem like that at all.

There was however one powerful baritone voice which was missing from all this and it belonged to Dr Tom Cadoux-Hudson. I may have neglected to explain what an impressive oarsman Tom is. To begin with his sheer brute power ranges somewhere between that of Dan Lyons and King Kong. He stands around 6ft 5ins and has the build of a Rugby forward, which indeed he was, as a member of the St Mary's Hospital XV which is only one division below the highest class of Rugby Football in England. He went to Radley School and was coached in the harsh folklore of the Boat

Race by Ronnie Howard. He won a first-class fellowship to the Royal College of Surgeons and also rowed for London University, an outfit which prides itself on training hard enough to rival our own.

As the winner of a bronze medal for Britain in the 'hard-man event', the Coxed Pairs, at the world championships in 1981, he was an experienced international and currently our strongest bowside man despite the presence of a reigning world champion Dan Lyons and the fact that he had changed from strokeside only four months earlier. Tom was, however, a family man with children, and he lived quite a way out of Oxford. This effectively separated him from the squad socially, in the same way it did Donald, with his own, very similar, home situation.

Tom rarely saw any of them except in the gym and in the boat. He came, he massacred the waters of the River Thames with his mighty blade, and then he left. But he commanded enormous respect and not a little fear, for he could be surprisingly volatile, as Hull had discovered when steering in the Fours Head a couple of months before. The wrath of Tom was not a pretty sight. I once saw him rip his oar out of its gate in fury at the end of a race and hurl it like a javelin clean across the river. It could easily have decapitated a passing sculler. 'That's what I think of this f---ing crew,' bellowed Tom. But off the water he was sweetness and light and a damned good surgeon.

It was to him that the battered rebels now turned. Still in Vincent's, still talking to Hugh Pelham, they elected to call Tom and arrange a meeting with him at Oxford's Radcliffe Infirmary early that evening. He was, as ever, impossibly busy but he agreed to see them and for a few hours it gave them hope. Tom had always tended to distance himself from any political in-fighting, taking the view that he was in the squad to row in the Boat Race and anything that got in the way of that was a bloody nuisance and nothing to do with him.

This blinkered view rather irritated Donald because, at this time, he was impatient for declared loyalty: 'You're either with me or against me'.

Tom may not have had the time to join a political struggle, but I could not see him joining in with an assault on the constitution of the OUBC. He had after all co-operated from the very start when he had agreed without a murmur to change sides in the interests of a balanced boat last autumn.

They arrived at the Radcliffe at 7.30 that evening and Tom invited them into his office where he already had installed another doctor, the thrice-winning Oxford Blue, Richard Yonge. Richard was himself a former President and veteran of a few fierce political fights as well. He was President of the Dark Blue boat when Cambridge launched an abortive attempt to have Boris Rankov banned from rowing in his record sixth Boat Race. They actually threatened to pull out of the race if Boris was sighted in the crew. Richard held his corner, Boris rowed and Oxford won their eighth successive race. Richard also rowed with the Evans twins in that 1983 crew and with the Australian Graham Jones, he knew what it took to win a Boat Race, even with big international stars on board and I think he hoped to help calm the troubled waters.

But knowing only a limited amount about the true depth and nature of the rift within the Boat Club, he was at a big disadvantage as a peace maker; especially with a President like Donald who had been beleaguered for so long and now felt as if he had smashed his way into fresh air for the first time.

Richard did however believe that they should see Donald and he tried diplomatically to convince the ringleaders that they should go and apologize for their action. But Dan Lyons was uncompromising. No one should phone Donald by midnight. No one should respond to the ultimatum. No one should co-operate. He believed Donald was putting a gun to their heads. Fish agreed. Penny and Huntington felt they had been given too little time to decide what to do and Stewart thought likewise. Richard tried to get an impartial view from the Isis boys.

Tom Cadoux-Hudson, who had not been consulted about the mutiny in the first place, reckoned that the whole thing had got out of hand. He agreed with Richard that there was only one chance for them and that was to talk to Donald in person.

But it was thought that the sight of the OUBC van pulling up outside Donald's house with Richard Hull at the wheel, a man Donald clearly could not abide, with Gavin Stewart beside him would be so inflammatory that the expedition could only develop into a farce. So Richard volunteered to drive them.

'Maybe I can speak to Donald first,' he suggested, 'and find out if he will see them.'

Most of them were now keen to try and have a conciliatory conversation with the man they had so arbitrarily dismissed, just five days earlier with those crushing brutal words: 'No one wants to row with you.'

They walked out of the hospital, and climbed into the back of the van. Richard Yonge sat behind the wheel and drove west, out beyond the big ring road which circles the city, and up the steep hill to Donald's house. The same steep hill they had careered down so recently with such carefree buccaneering abandon, leaving the President devastated on his own doorstep.

The van pulled up outside the house. It was almost 10.30 in the evening and the lights were on in the front bedroom but the rest of the rooms appeared to be in darkness. Richard got out but the others remained huddled in the back – Hull, Stewart, Penny, Huntington, and Paul Gleeson. He walked up the garden path and tapped lightly on the door.

Donald was still up, reading by a small lamp in the drawing room and when he opened the front door he was surprised to find himself face to face with one of his predecessors as Boat Club President. 'Good evening Richard,' he said, politely, 'What on earth can I do for you at this time of night?'

Richard stammered a bit then said: 'May I come in for a few moments. There is something I would like to talk to you about.'

Donald showed him in and Richard proceeded to tell him that outside was a van load of heartbroken repentant oarsmen who very much wanted to plead with him, on behalf of their friends. 'They were not very inclined to listen to *my* pleas a few days ago,' said Donald coldly. 'I cannot think what purpose could be served by them coming in here. Frankly I do not much want to see any of them, but they are quite welcome to go off somewhere and phone me, as many of the other rowers have already done this evening. I did say midnight, you know. And I mean it. If they don't confirm their availability they are out, all of them. And that's final.'

Richard Yonge had one last try. 'I do think it might perhaps help to talk,' he said. 'Can they come in, just for a while? They'd all be grateful.'

Donald relented. 'Okay,' he said. 'Tell them to come in.'

Yonge retreated to the van outside, and returned followed by Hull, Stewart, Penny, Huntington, and Paul Gleeson who all trooped sheepishly into the house. They had come, they said, to apologize, which they did without reservation. 'We made a terrible mistake,' said Hull. 'It was not the right way for us to have gone about things.'

They reported their long talk with Tom Cadoux-Hudson and said that they now all believed the only thing left for them was to have a constructive talk with Donald.

'Does this mean you want to row in the boat?' asked Donald. 'And that question, as I think I explained earlier today, requires a "yes" or a "no". It's entirely a matter for you to decide.'

Donald is slightly uncertain as to the direction of the conversation at this point because Chris Penny began to go on in an almost inaudible voice about a Roman general who apparently had the opportunity to kill all of his troops after an uprising, but in the end showed mercy and spared them.

'After I had managed to grasp the subtlety of this comparison,' Donald recalls 'the rest of Chris's discourse rather went by me, but I think the Roman Senator Cornelius Tacitus, the greatest historian of the period, came into it somewhere. He seemed to be referring to the reign of the tyrannical Domitian, but quite honestly it had about as much relevance to our situation as Clark's views on philosophy.'

Donald then told them that it was not so much that he was personally aggrieved by their actions but that, as President of the OUBC, he had to take firm action. As far as he was concerned the issues were simple, the first one being that the team of very experienced Oxford coaches considered him worth a place on merit. There never have been any issues of a fight for a strokeside slot between him and Clark, except in the Newport Beach man's imagination. Clark was being considered for a place on the bowside and nowhere else.

Donald then laid out once and for all his position. 'If Chris Clark wants to fight a war with the coaches by inventing a phoney competition, that's his affair. And if you guys want to rally round and support him, that's your affair. Frankly I don't give a damn. Fight it out with the coaches.

'But when you think that gives you some kind of licence to rip up the Oxford Boat Club's constitution, make off with the boat, and take illegal control of the club while I am President, then that's a different matter. And I hope you all now understand that. Christopher Clark, in breaking his promise of co-operation to Dan at Henley, finally went one step too far. His rowing career at the OUBC is over. Our decision to fire Lyons and Fish as well is because I regard them both as big trouble, more trouble than any of us need – and I would rather they went and caused it somewhere else.'

It quickly became apparent that the main issue that the rebels were now pushing was the reinstatement of Lyons and Fish.

By now emotions were running extremely high. Paul Gleeson became almost incoherent as he explained that he knew he might win a Blue now because of all this but he really didn't want to win one like this and he dissolved into tears.

At that moment the phone rang. It was the Isis coach Jeff Jacobs, who had coached some of them the previous year and had become a particular friend of Gavin Stewart. Donald spoke briefly to him before handing the phone over to Stewart. The towering-middle-of-the-boat man walked into the kitchen to take it and soon Donald could hear the words 'unconscionable' and 'just so unfair to Chris,' being used. Then he heard him begin sobbing into the phone . . . 'It's not how it seems, Jeff, it's all just so unfair. . . .' And he returned to the main room, his body wracked with sobs, and collapsed into a chair.

'I remember distractedly thinking,' said Donald later, 'that the only fortunate part was that we were meeting at the end of the room which has a parquet floor which is so much easier to swab up than the end with the carpets.'

There was however one issue here that was worrying Donald, that he should be perceived to be firing people in order to hold secure his own place in the boat. For some of us in the coaching team this was the one strand of his strategy that had caused concern, but one with which we had much sympathy. Because he is a fair man and since he was now back in control of the Club, Donald felt inclined to hand the job of selection back to the coaches. He had overthrown the rebels entirely on moral grounds, because their actions had been outrageous, but he wanted no advantage for himself. The suggestion that he might have acted out of personal motivation to retain his own seat in the crew was as offensive to him as the mutiny itself.

With this in mind and with the small hours of the morning fast approaching, he told his visitors that he would be happy to call a full meeting of the coaches at Leander Club that Sunday afternoon to consider the overall situation. He said he was quite prepared to allow the meeting to decide the selection of all other oarsmen. His words of course signalled a possible reprieve for Lyons and Fish.

It was no climb-down by Donald even though the anxious little delegation may have interpreted it as that. His tactics in the

Vincent's Club meeting had been designed to overthrow a mutiny. Now he was sailing his ship in the much calmer waters of straight selection, and order had been restored. He did not want to, nor indeed feel he should, become involved with selection matters; and if the coaches, in their wisdom, wanted to give Lyons and Fish another shot, reconsider Clark, or indeed deprive Macdonald himself of a place, that was up to them. In the early hours of that Friday morning Donald called the meeting to a close. 'You can all go home now,' he said. 'And I will think about it more. But I am inclined to leave the problem to my coaches.'

The OUBC van set off once more down Botley Hill, but there was no elation in the back this time, no jaunty tyre-squealing as they rounded the steep bends going down to the city. It was a very sedate drive on a day which had seen their mutiny overthrown and by a man they had believed was essentially impotent.

They had however bought themselves time to gather their forces and to try once more to get Chris Clark, Daniel Lyons and Jonathan Fish back into the boat.

CHAPTER NINE

THE COACHES WEAKEN

With agonizing self-control Donald said: 'What they are saying has nothing to do with their real position. They want Clark back in the boat, and if we do not grant them that they will not row. Any of them. You are looking at a hard-nosed bunch of rowing careerists, and they know what they want.'

They pushed the *Daily Telegraph* through the letter box of my London flat early that Friday morning, and to my dismay I saw that the mutiny at Oxford had become public. The headline referred to the midnight deadline stipulated by Donald at the Vincent's Club meeting on the previous afternoon – and it read in a big bold typeface 'Oxford Crew Rift Brings Ultimatum'.

Unwittingly Geoffrey Page, the rowing correspondent of the *Telegraph*, had seized upon the one clear falsehood originating from the mutineers' camp which would haunt us mercilessly during the weeks to come. 'The issue,' he wrote, 'was the competition between Macdonald and Clark for the number two seat in this year's crew.' There it was, baldly in black and white, neither confirmed nor denied by Donald, Steve or me, the only three people in charge of selection, and the only ones qualified to comment on the matter. It was an uncorroborated story based on mischievously-leaked rumour.

My heart sank as I read the words because I knew that this kind of row at Oxford always attracts an army of journalists whose combined lack of knowledge on rowing would fill an Olympic stadium. They would descend on Oxford, all set to thunder into print with a big Oxford Mutiny story, based on the words they had read in the *Telegraph*.

I knew that this marauding army of writers would send that misleading story into every newspaper in Great Britain and then onto the wire services all over the world. The story would become a 'Macdonald v Clark' issue for a seat rather than Pelham v Clark v Ward – enhanced by the further and even equally untrue allegation that Donald had fired Clark in order to protect his own place in the crew. I was right too. That's what they did, over and over again and the more they repeated it the more true it seemed to become in the public eye.

Even as I read those words the Press was on the march from London, marshalling its forces for a westward offensive down the M.40 motorway – first stop Marlow to see if they could catch the Oxford crew in action, second stop the Isis to see if anyone could be found with even a remote working knowledge of what was going on in the OUBC. At first there would be a steady trickle of sports writers, then the television people would come and the feature writers, followed by the national news reporters, and soon the Americans from the London bureaux of the big US newspapers and magazines. Then the American television networks would move in with the US television feature writers close behind and, of course, the omnipotent wire services. All of them would be clamouring for information, any information, just as long as it involved more and more quarrelling. For peace, after all, holds no news value whatsoever.

The entire scenario was grotesquely predictable. Oriel Square would be under siege before many days had passed. I felt sorry for Donald, who would have to face it all at Marlow today when the first boat went out under Mike Spracklen.

As it happened he was able to deal with it more than adequately because the boats went afloat as announced by Donald; no Lyons, no Fish, no Clark. However he felt he must take one further step to answer their suspicions about the sinister intentions of myself and Royle. In the changing room before the outing he confirmed his offer to place selection in the hands of the entire Oxford coaching team and he told them he had convened a meeting at the Leander Club for Sunday. 'We want Fred Smallbone there,' they insisted, 'and Jeff Jacobs.' Donald said that of course they would be there. (Smallbone was to take an uncompromising line against the rebels.) Donald assured them he would play no part in the selection process and would abide by whatever they agreed. 'Will *you?*' he asked them. They refused to answer. Then he left to go for a warm-up run while they finished changing into kit.

There was soon, however, to be an indication of just how deeply this chasm between the two groups had become. And in the centre of it, with one foot in each camp, stood the most celebrated coach in the country, Mike Spracklen. A former Commonwealth Games Champion and Britain's leading Olympic coach, with gold medal success at the Los Angeles Games and three world championships, Mike was a true artist of the sport. He had coached me for two world championships so we knew each other well. Mike was a self-made man in his fifties, tight and wiry in stature. He had a big house on the banks of the Thames at Marlow.

I had recruited him to our Oxford coaching team six years earlier and he provided a valuable two weeks of intensive technique work to the newly-formed Oxford Eights. The boys also derived a great psychological boost from his input, but he always took pains to point out that he preferred not to get involved in Boat Race politics. 'I am only concerned,' he would tell Donald. 'with helping to prepare the crew. I just do what the President and Chief Coach ask me to do.'

It was particularly important from Donald's point of view that his team of coaches should fully support his stand in defence of the OUBC constitution. If any of them should decide to break ranks for whatever motives it would give the rebels space to break back. But with Mike he had felt secure on that score. Mike had after all agreed to go on coaching the rebel crew for the past three days at the President's express request, and Donald had detailed to him the events of the Monday mutiny. But today Mike seemed to have other things on his mind and Donald felt a growing sense of disquiet.

Donald always liked to do a full land warm-up which included a short run; and since it was still brutally cold it was even more important to get the blood circulating and the muscles well loosened up. When he got back from his jog he found that the others had still not emerged from the changing rooms, so he waited by the boat for ten minutes or so talking to Mike. Finally the coach said that he would go inside and find our what was holding them up. He was gone for twenty minutes. Inside were Huntington, Penny, Stewart, Hull, Cadoux-Hudson, Pelham and Ward – and various other members of the Oriel Bar splinter group who rowed with Isis.

It later transpired that in the course of a long discussion Mike Spracklen had posed the question: 'Who would you rather row with in a pair over 2000 metres, Donald Macdonald or Chris Clark?' In the charged atmosphere of such a pointed question Cadoux-Hudson did not wish to be drawn into taking sides. But the coach insisted, trying to prise an answer from the big British international.

Finally Tom replied: 'Well, Clark is not fit, so I'd choose a fit Macdonald.'

'No, no,' insisted the coach, 'If Clark was fit, as fit as Macdonald.'

'Then I suppose I would have to say Clark in that case,' said Tom. 'If you are talking about 2000 metres in a Pair, rather than a Boat Race in an Eight. He is an international, but the question's hypothetical.'

They then went outside to join Donald and went afloat. Nothing was said. After the outing, the van headed back once more to Oriel Square where, rather to Donald's surprise, Dan Lyons was standing talking to Fish. The President jumped out and went straight up to him and shook his hand. Dan was wearing one of his most severe frowns and told Donald that he really could not understand why he had been so unfairly singled out for what had happened last Monday. Donald, although aware that his particular form of oblique wit often fell upon stony ground where his transatlantic colleagues were concerned, nevertheless told him brightly that he should take is as nothing but a compliment, that the sheer force of the Lyons personality had made him the evident ringleader.

Lyons looked puzzled but decided, to Donald's amusement, to accept Donald's interpretation and regard it as flattering. Then the lanky number 7 man asked Donald once again if they could talk for a while. They walked, this time with Fish, and it quickly became apparent that Lyons was mortified by what had happened at the Vincent's meeting and that his ego had been badly battered.

'Don, you've gotta tell me, straight. Why me?'

The President looked him square in the eye. 'Because, Dan,' he said. 'you are trouble. Major trouble. And neither I nor the coaches need any more of it.'

At this Fish almost did a double take, tore open his notebook and began to scribble with a concentrated fury.

'I'm not sure what's worse in this bloody room,' said Donald. 'Hull nodding yesterday, or Fish scribbling today.'

Lyons glowered. And he began then, a monologue, which Donald still regards with a shudder. 'Dan Lyons tried to draw for me a picture in words, of international oarsmen who are a breed apart, like no other mortals. He tried to describe them as men from Valhalla, the mythical Hall of the god Odin, into which heroes slain in battle are traditionally received. His drift was that, at this moment, Odin was beside himself with excitement at the prospect of receiving him – Lyons along with Clark, Penny and Huntington.

'He felt that people like me, ordinary people, could, only with the utmost difficulty, attempt to understand the quality of the men I was dealing with, the pain and suffering they had endured as US internationals, the super élite athletes I had been blessed to meet and might, perhaps, even compete with.

'He told me that I could never really comprehend what they had gone through, what they had done. And even Clark, at his unfittest, was still capable of a performance that none of us poor English guys could ever hope to aspire to including Ward, Stewart, Hull and Pelham. He seemed to regard the English people who were supporting him with something approaching contempt, and I thought what a good thing it was for him that they would never hear a tape of their great hero speaking about them in these terms.

'It took a great effort not to burst into laughter at this glorification on behalf of the men who had finished twenty-eighth in the Fours Head of the River, from Valhalla to Putney.

'Also I knew perfectly well that Lyons was doing his level best to talk me into reinstating Chris Clark. Nothing more. Nothing less. But I did hope very much that he did not actually believe any of the arrant rubbish he was spouting at me. Or that I would believe it.'

Donald finally arrived home, late, and in a rush because he had promised to take Ruth out for the evening – a break they both badly needed. But first he had to call Dick Fishlock, an Old Blue from the 1960 crew, a former Boat Race coach and a member of the President's advisory Trust Fund committee, to remind him of a letter he had written promising to help in any way he could. 'Dick,' he said. 'I need that help right now. I would like you to chair a meeting of the coaches at Leander on Sunday.' Dick agreed, and

Donald told him he would call him the next day, Saturday, to brief him about the agenda.

He then quickly telephoned me to let me know the list of coaches who would be at the Sunday meeting. Mike Spracklen next called him to tell him for the first time about the conversations in the dressing room that afternoon. He reported the discussion and then gave Donald his own personal view: 'If I was wearing my Boat Race hat, I'd pick you. If I was wearing my international hat, I'd pick Clark.' He proceeded to tell Donald that he would normally go for the man with the most potential, even if that meant dropping the nice guy in his place. 'Chris Clark,' he said, 'is likely to be inconsistent in a race like the Boat Race and I know you will not let us down. But however dangerous I may consider it to be to select someone like Chris, I would still have an instinct to do so because he is an oarsman of great potential.'

Donald then called me back, to let me know that he thought Spracklen was on the verge of becoming a spokesman for the rebels, and that he had been well and truly lobbied by them in the dressing room that day. Judging from the conversation he had just had on the phone, he anticipated that Spracklen would be representing their interests at the Leander meeting.

Donald also believed the coach's view of Clark's situation lacked logic, and he added, 'For goodness sake, Mike was discussing the number 2 seat, not the 6 seat or even 5 where big powerful internationals like Penny or Cadoux-Hudson could make a real difference to a boat. Nothing of real significance was going to emanate from the 2 seat, so why in the name of God would anyone even consider putting a man in there who might lose you the race, particularly when he himself had expressed his reservations about the man so emphatically back in May? It just doesn't make sense.'

After all, Spracklen had just made the distinction between his two so-called coaching 'hats' – the Boat Race, and a 2,000-metre international class event. 'He'd just told me he would pick me for the former,' said the President, 'and Clark for the latter. So what on earth does he mean? That he would now back Clark for the Boat Race anyway? I can see that Mike was attempting to convey the impression of subtle balanced thought. But all he was doing was creating complete and utter confusion.'

Equally important of course, was the fact that an important

member of my coaching team seemed to be perpetrating the 'Macdonald v. Clark for the 2 seat' red herring, making it seem real.

Ruth, sensing that this particular evening was already shot to pieces, cancelled the babysitter, and watched distraught as Donald became more and more upset on the phone, the injustices steadily building up on his shoulders. He suddenly appeared so isolated while I, on the other end of the phone, appeared so far away. As he was saying goodbye, I could tell he was terribly distressed at the apparent defection of Spracklen. Then Ruth told him they were no longer going out, something he had badly wanted to do, just to get away. Then his father phoned and Donald tried to explain how hard it was for him to cope with the hostility of so many people.

Suddenly it was all too much. He broke down altogether and wept without shame in front of Ruth and the children, handing the phone to his wife and asking her to please talk to his parents.

On the following day the *Daily Telegraph* ran a front page story, over three columns, headlined: 'Mutiny in Dark Blues' Boat'. It was written by a reporter named Lin Jenkins, and it contained the words 'It is Ward who stands to lose his place in the boat, if Macdonald puts himself in the No.2 seat in place of Clark. . . .'

That is tantamount to a sentence containing the words: 'If the Queen places herself upon the throne of England in place of Princess Michael . . . .' Yet again the facts became secondary in the interests of a good story. No mention that Clark's exclusion was the direct result of his non-training, poor test results and disruptiveness over a long period, plus our technical need for an equally balanced strokeside/bowside line-up for the 1987 Oxford crew. And what made it so much more depressing was that Jenkins appeared to have a supporter in one of my coaching team.

Now, with the possibility of this all-star US-based Dark Blue crew on the verge of disintegration, Mike Spracklen with his influential voice, was beginning to take the political interest in OUBC affairs he had always been determined to shun. He was kept regularly in touch by Clark and Fish from the Oriel phone box.

All through that Friday evening after the outing Donald was on the telephone, sometimes to me, sometimes to members of the crew. The issue was the reinstatement of Lyons and Fish. Donald had no wish to become a one-man selection committee and he stressed that the full meeting of the coaches would be irrevocably decisive. If the coaches wished to reinstate any of the Americans he would not use his position to prevent their comeback. So upon the meeting's outcome the entire dispute, which was by now splitting the University down the middle, would hopefully be resolved.

He made it known that if Lyons and Fish wished to turn up to train at Marlow on Saturday, on probation as it were, there would be no objection from him. Just as long as everyone now understood who was in charge of the Boat Club. As it happened, they both did show up and the outing passed off without much incident. Mike Spracklen appeared to Donald to be very much with the Americans and when Donald returned home he telephoned his friend Michael Suarez at Campion Hall. He poured out his fears that the coaches might simply decide to take the easiest way out, pick Clark for the Boat and suggest to Donald that he withdraw from the crew in the interests of peace and victory.

'My God, Michael, what if they don't pick me?'

'If they don't pick you, Donald, you don't row, you know that. It's the only moral way to act.'

'I know. I agree, and that's why I am afraid. All that work for nothing, maybe. But you're right I'd have to stand down. I knew it, but I just wanted to hear you say it. It's just so difficult to think that in twenty-four hours my rowing career at Oxford might be over.'

The fate of the OUBC was now clearly hanging in the balance. On the following day, the Sunday newspapers again carried the story, as positions began to harden all over the University on that cold winter morning. There was a widening rift among the students as they debated the fallaciously-presented arguments. Should Oxford lose the big American internationals who would crush Cambridge? Or should a Boat Race victory be sacrificed for the sake of a self-seeking President who was risking the honour of the University to save his own seat in the boat?

The distortions and misconceptions were now rife throughout the colleges thanks, in part at least, to the media. Arguments were growing bitter, factions were drawing up battle positions and some of the college captains enquired pointedly about the management of the OUBC.

I could not help recalling the haunting words of the Edwardian poet James Elroy Flecker:

'Noon strikes on England, noon on Oxford town,
– Beauty she was statue cold – there's blood upon her gown'

We trooped into the Leander Club. Dick Fishlock, Fred Small-bone, Ronnie Howard, John Pilgrim-Morris, Mike Spracklen, Mark Lees, Hugh Matheson, Jeff Jacobs, Steve Royle, Donald and myself. All selection processes are difficult because they always involve disappointing, and sometimes hurting people. All athletes go through it and all those in the room had been through it themselves as athletes, coaches and as selectors. But none of us had been required to go through the business on such a formal basis, under the glare of media attention and of course with a mutiny hanging over us which could erupt again at any minute.

Dick Fishlock called the meeting to order and outlined the present situation within the OUBC, pointing out the number of occasions where Chris Clark had failed to respond to the requests of the coaches. Dick outlined the responsibilities of the President, and also the power that he held under the constitution of the club. He further stated that the coaching team had a proven record, but their ability to select a crew was now being challenged.

He then outlined the responsibilities of the coaches, working under a chief coach, and in particular their duty to support the democratically-elected President who had appointed them. He explained that if *any* of them was not prepared to do this he should resign. But no one wanted to and they all reaffirmed their support for the chief coach, in whose hands crew selection rests.

I pointed out that although the President theoretically had the final word on selection, in practice he usually handed this task over to his chief coach and this year was no exception. I also stressed that I, as chief coach, had always worked with my colleagues as a team and that we discussed and agreed about selection on equal terms over a period of months. It was important for us all to know that there was no question of this President attempting to influence our deliberations and I had no doubt that he would abide by our decision. He was an honourable man and would withdraw from the crew if the coaches reckoned he had not earned his place.

Next Dick insisted that the final decision of this meeting would be made democratically and that each coach would have an opportun-ity to express his own viewpoint. But when the majority decision was made it would be loyally and unanimously supported by us all.

There could be no further dissension among us. And if any one of you, he said, is unable to abide by these ground-rules, he should resign forthwith. Again no one wanted to quit.

The records of our training thus far were presented to the meeting and it was agreed that the performance of Chris Clark did not automatically warrant a position in the boat, whether on bowside or strokeside.

At this moment Mike Spracklen spoke out on Chris Clark's behalf. Not knowing of the real depth of those conversations with the crew at Marlow, I was taken a bit by surprise. He began to offer the opinion that the boat had greater potential speed with the big American on board, not specifying which side he might row. He felt that if he could be made to train he could be good. I pointed out that we had no guarantee that he would not continue his disruptive behaviour or even walk out again; that his training left a lot to be desired, and that even last year he had run hot and cold.

I could see Donald growing more tense with every phrase that was uttered. He sat at the table, fists clenched, knuckles white, his mouth a tight line. He was fighting to retain a low profile because he knew he must not become involved with the selection debate, but he believed that what he was hearing was misleading drivel and his exasperation was showing. I was adamant about Clark but one or two of the others needed to talk more, feeling that they should demonstrate that they were prepared to give the Californian once more the benefit of the doubt. Had they shared with me the traumas of the past three months and had they been with Donald in the Lyon's Den last Monday, they might have been less accommodating.

Soon, the coaches who had been less close to the situation began to suggest something which sounded like a sudden death play-off on the ergometer, again at Mike Spracklen's quiet suggestion, bringing the Clark v. Macdonald issue back into sharp focus. He reported the rebel view that I had 'rigged' the selection tests as a part of a personal vendetta against Clark, although he was gracious enough not to offer his own opinion on that.

The ergo test solution is very American in origin, although others use it too, and its basis lies in the propensity of some Americans to run to lawyers at the first sign of dissent. American rowing coaches sometimes get taken to court by disgruntled trialists over selection issues on the grounds of 'unfair dismissal' and the ergometer, the big pulling machine which registers results of strength and endurance, is the device they use to 'watch their backs' as it were. At the first hint of trouble, out come the ergometer charts, and they point out that they picked, without prejudice, the top eight men.

An ergometer test is however only a test of how people perform on that machine, it does not tell you how well a man can perform in a moving boat, rolling around on difficult water, how well he works within a team, how well he follows his crew, and above all the size of the fight within him when the chips are down, in a race. As Fran Reininger (himself a formidable erg puller) once remarked to me: 'Put an erg on the water and it sinks.' It also takes away from the coach his very *raison d'être*, the experience that makes him the man for the job. He succeeds or fails on the strength of his results – that's why he's there – and he takes the rap if he makes a mistake. If his selection is faulty, he is the one who gets the sack, his reputation in tatters. To select only on the ergo is the coward's way out, leaving the decision to a machine, which should only be used as an aid.

That's maybe why the American teams so often fall short of their potential when the big medals are handed out – because their coaches are forced to make decisions which don't allow them to exercise their intuition and judgement. In the fiercely litigious world of the USA they may have to justify their every move. As a point of interest, in the Olympic Games between 1900 and 1964 the American Eight won eleven of the fourteen gold medals. In the quarter of a century since then, they have won none.

The rowing world is always mystified why these US teams seem often to fail in the highest competition. They are no more successful than the British or the Germans and the reason, their coaches tell me, is that they are sidetracked by constantly having to deal with all the bickering and arguing.

I pointed out to my fellow coaches that the people we were dealing with represented the very pinnacle of this kind of arguing. They were men who had raised the business of dissent to a pure art form, and what's more they would do the same thing again when they returned to the USA. I heard later from the coaches there that they had indeed been beset by daily meetings and confrontations of the sort we were experiencing at Oxford.

I tended to resist the one last test option because it would reduce selection to an arbitrary, sudden death choice when our policy had always depended upon months of constant monitoring. To change that policy suddenly in midstream now would simply be appeasement under threat. I also knew how unfair it would be to these men, particularly those who had been training diligently every day since September, working to a known selection process.

This applied especially to Donald, who had for months tried to lead from the front and now found himself shouldering this extraordinary added pressure which was obviously playing havoc with his constitution both mentally and physically. To have asked him at this low ebb, to undergo a complete reselection procedure, would in my view have played right into the hands of the rebels. I was not prepared to do that, to offer Donald up as a sacrificial lamb. It was all too easy to see their strategy. The President had already beaten Clark on three separate ergometer tests. Another test at this particular time would have been completely unjust. Donald was not sleeping; he was trying to deal with the Press from six o'clock every morning until ten at night. The stress on him was enormous and furthermore he had never once missed an outing or an encounter on the river in the past four-and-a-half months.

Clark, on the other hand, whom some of the coaches now seemed prepared to reconsider, had missed well over half of the inter-squad competition which, if anything, made him mentally and physically fresher at that moment than all the other men in the squad. The whole selection procedure which had served us so well all these years would be rendered worthless. I, for one, was not ready to re-open the Oxford University selection process to accommodate someone who had proved himself to be such a dangerously unsettling influence on our squad.

But I needed the full agreement of the coaching team to feel that those sentiments were free of prejudice. Mark Lees suggested seat racing in Pairs but everyone agreed that positions were now so entrenched and antagonisms so violent that no seat race could guarantee a fair result. The athletes would be pulling harder, or less hard, depending on the camp they were in. The situation was now so charged that any further tests of any description could only cloud the issue further.

As darkness fell over Henley, and the street lights began to glint their reflections into the ice-cold waters of the river outside, the meeting moved on into its fourth hour. Most of the coaches were of the firm opinion that Chris Clark had blown his chances, and that given Donald's open-mindedness over the Lyons/Fish issue, they ought to let them both have a further chance.

But Mike Spracklen continued in non-committal mood; while he accepted that Clark had been a thundering nuisance, for as long as most of us could remember, he stayed true to his ingrained instincts which were, unless he was himself in charge as chief coach, to place himself on the side of the athlete against perceived authority. While he kept saying that he wanted to distance himself from the political fray, that he was only operational for two weeks, he had nevertheless become immensely involved. Whether he knew it or not, and whether he liked it or not, Mike Spracklen's verbal probing that afternoon in the changing room had given credence to the mutiny, and driven the grievance deep into the psyche of those most brittle personalities. However he said that he was quite prepared to go along with the majority decision of the assembled coaches.

When finally, after more than five hours we all seemed to be agreeing on our course of action and the statement we would present to the Press waiting downstairs, it was still clear to me that Mike was not really with us.

'Now look,' I said wearily, 'Mike is not happy. We have to make him feel comfortable with this decision. We have to make sure that he feels convinced by what we are saying, otherwise this whole bloody business is going to go on indefinitely.'

I turned to him and I said: 'Isn't that right, Mike?', and he said not really and that he was happy to go along with what we all decided. But I still did not feel that that was good enough and we went on for another hour trying to get Mike to understand what was at the root of our inability to rely on Clark; that we did not believe he would lay down his life if necessary in the cause of helping Oxford to beat Cambridge. That was one of the most compelling reasons for not including him and it seemed crucial that Mike recognize that. In the end he said he agreed with the meeting, and at last I was convinced that he was now an integral part of that decision. Jeff Jacobs too, who had said that Clark should be kept on only if all the coaches felt they could deal with him, accepted the reasons why finally he had to be dropped from the squad.

So the meeting was able to draft a unanimous statement to the Press, which read as follows:

'As a result of recent disagreement over the selection of the Oxford crew for the Boat Race on 28th March, the President called a meeting of his coaches on Sunday 25th January.

'The meeting was chaired by Richard Fishlock (OUBC, 1960) as an independent party. Ronnie Howard (Chairman of the President's Advisory Committee) also attended.

'The President, Donald Macdonald, made it clear that he had invited his team of coaches, under the leadership of Dan Topolski, to select the crew, and this would not be conditional on the President being in the crew or even party to its selection. The meeting fully endorsed this policy today.

'The coaches discussed the merits of those under selection and came to the conclusion that since Chris Clark had failed to honour the demands they had made on him on a number of occasions, he will not be invited to continue training with the OUBC Squad.

'As a result of today's meeting Monday's crew will be as follows: cox Fish, stroke Huntington, Hull, Penny, Lyons, Stewart, Cadoux-Hudson, Macdonald, Ward (bow).'

We gave this to the reporters and headed, thankfully, home. Everyone was wearing a smile except for Donald and me. He was frowning at the prospect of having to go to University College to break the news to Clark, and I just knew, deep down that the battle was not over yet. Not by a long way.

At first Donald had some difficulty in finding Clark but finally they met in the kitchen and Chris, cool and laid back as ever, invited the President into his room. Donald told him that the decision announced at Vincent's had not in his case been overturned and that he was now formally out of the squad. The Californian thought for a moment, and then said quietly, in a statement Donald was becoming accustomed to and which invariably heralded trouble. 'Dan Lyons is not going to like this. He's just not going to let this one rest.'

As he spoke, Donald knew there would probably be a total mutiny, that the Americans would refuse to accept the axing of Clark, despite their affability at his house late on Thursday night, and all their 'gosh, all we want is for Fish and Lyons to have a fair chance.' Donald had known in his heart that they would accept nothing but total capitulation and he phoned me that evening to tell me so.

'It looks, Dan, as though we are going to have to call *another* coaches' meeting, and I suggest it should be a crew meeting because unless I'm misjudging them, this lot have no intention of going on the water tomorrow. Any of them.'

He was right. When Donald arrived in Oriel Square the following day, Monday, the rebels told him they would not row. They wanted a meeting. So Donald wearily went through the motions, saying that was fine with him and they could turn up that evening and see for themselves the united front of the coaches. His view by then was that no matter what the rebels heard, they would abide by no decision until some meeting, somewhere, voted them the result they wanted. And that was to have Christopher Clark reinstated in the crew in place of Donald Macdonald. They believed they would win, for they were unshaken in the belief that they were indispensable as a group and that Oxford would not dare face Cambridge without them.

Once more Donald called all of the coaches, once more he invited Dick Fishlock to chair the meeting, and once more he fixed a room, this time the St Giles House at St John's College.

Donald, exasperated by the whole affair, headed for the river to the peace of his sculling boat and the solitude of the Thames above Oxford. The Press were already well established at the club and as he put his boat on the water away from view, a young woman from the *Daily Express* arrived and asked if he could help her with some background on a story she had been sent to write. Donald told her everything, chapter and verse, every detail, all from the President's point of view. The reporter asked if he was anyone important, and he replied: 'Me? Oh no, I'm nothing to do with it. Just an observer.' And she went off to find an OUBC official, and never printed a word of her world scoop.

The position of the Americans that night was powerfully entrenched – put Clark in the boat or it does not leave the dock. But this time they planned a rather different approach, one which we had not seen before, but which would bring the coaches to the brink of retreat.

We arrived at the 400-year-old college named after St John the Baptist. A blanket of snow lay thick over the lawn and upon the branches of the famous copper beeches. This was the college of Archbishop William Laud, executed for high treason in 1645 and whose body lies in the Chapel here. While imprisoned in the Tower of London, awaiting his impending death for his unfailing loyalty to

King Charles I, he wrote of St John's in his will: 'And God's everlasting blessing be upon that place and that society for ever.' To this day the ghost of the Archbishop is said to walk the library of St John's and on that dark, freezing Monday night I was glad we were in a different room, for this treasonous business would almost certainly have caused the old Prelate to put in a personal appearance.

The effect of the crew refusing to row at Marlow that day had divided Oxford down the middle. By now there was practically no one without an unconsidered opinion. The Clark v. Macdonald issue had become irrefutable fact. People Donald had never even spoken to were suggesting that in the interests of peace and winning the Boat Race he should stand down and give up his seat. The subject exercised not only the students but just about every gathering in the city – in pubs, clubs and restaurants, libraries, common rooms and banqueting halls, there was talk of little else.

Should the President step aside in favour of the giant US international, Chris Clark? How could this callow English nobody be so selfish as to hand the Boat Race to Cambridge because of his own fraudulent claims on a place in the boat? Others demanded that the 'Yankees go home'. Who were these men who wished to take over 'our' Boat Race? That is the way a story grows. No one felt inhibited from airing their views upon a subject of which they were, almost without exception, totally ignorant. It did however make us feel very isolated and under siege.

The effect of all this loose talk served only to widen the great gulf which already existed between the two warring factions inside the Boat Club. When we finally all gathered together at St John's the atmosphere was dreadful. Someone had managed to mislay the keys to the great room in which we were scheduled to air our differences, and we stood, divided and awkward on opposite sides of a corridor, avoiding each other's gaze with studied indifference.

Dick Fishlock was by now beginning to realize the toughness and resolution of Dan Lyons and his friends, and he had prepared meticulous minutes of the Leander meeting to be distributed to everyone in order that nobody should be in any doubt about the hard decisions of the coaching team. I, in turn had brought copies of all of the tests we had been conducting among the squad for the past four months, in order that everyone should see how scrupulously fair the Oxford system was. It also showed, in passing, that the President featured so high in the lists that his exclusion from the crew by any fair assessment would be extremely hard to justify.

When we finally gained entry it was quite late and the mighty notes of Great Tom in the massive bell tower of Christ Church were already tolling out the 101 nightly beats which announce to the city that the hour is past nine o'clock.

The coaches sat at a table in a line, flanking the President and the Chairman, three to their right, four to their left. They were myself, Ronnie Howard and Michael Barry and then Mike Spracklen, Jeff Jacobs, John Pilgrim-Morris, and Steve Royle. By now no one was in any doubt. This was without precedent. It was the most serious, far-reaching row in the history of the Boat Club.

The mutineers sat before us on a semi-circle of chairs. They were so strangely quiet, subdued and polite that some of the coaches wondered whether we were over-reacting against this extremely nice bunch of guys from America. But for we who knew their ruthless side, their present careful meekness was without doubt the harbinger of intensified resolution and a new tactic.

Ronnie Howard made one of the few remarks that passed between the two groups before the meeting began. While Dick Fishlock was organizing the papers, the 1959 President said to the cox Jonathon Fish: 'Do you always treat your coaches in this way?'

'Sure,' replied the New Yorker. 'Last year we got rid of our coach altogether.'

I listened to the exchange, thinking what an unsavoury reputation for sportsmanship this group gave to the name of American rowing, because of course it was not always like that in the States. They have as many chivalrous sportsmen as we do. I knew many of them, had rowed with some and coached others. In David Halberstam's excellent book *The Amateurs*, Tiff Wood, one of the great American oarsmen of the post-war years – a Harvard crewmate of Al Shealy's – is asked, after he fails to be chosen for the boat, if he thought he had been given a fair chance at the US squad's selection camp.

'No,' said an enraged Wood, 'not at all.'

Pressed further, as to whether he would talk to the coach Harry Parker about it, Wood said simply, 'No.'

Why not? 'Because I don't think it's an oarsman's job to complain to the coach,' he answered.

And so we faced each other across the floor. In the front sat Jonathon Fish, with a notebook on his lap, his pen ready, searching for a chink in someone's armour. He wore an eager grin and he was ready to interrupt anybody in order to please Dan Lyons. His voice scarcely stopped all night with its ceaseless monotone of sniping interjections.

Four times Chris Penny and Huntington snarled: 'Shut *up*, Fish' as they fought to maintain their well-rehearsed front of polite reason. And at one point, all pretension of control set aside, I too rounded on him and hissed: 'For God's sake take that bloody smirk off your face you *dreadful, dreadful little man!*'

Later Donald would go home and vent his anger in his diary: 'Tonight I shall probably have a nightmare about Fish's voice – I cannot know how it will present itself to me, but I could easily envisage a dozen flickering images based on Munch's famous oil painting 'The Scream' – with coaches and oarsmen reeling away, stricken, their hands clasping their ears in self-protective horror, at the murderous, endless, shrill monotone, with pause for neither punctuation nor breath.'

It was clear from the very start of the meeting that the Americans felt they had us on the run. Just as Donald had predicted they considered his reasonable compliance towards Lyons and Fish as a sign of weakness. And with this toe-hold they began the fight once more to reinstate their friend Clark. Cleverly, they had decided that a British voice would be preferable to state their case. For this task they selected Gavin Stewart who began his opening speech with his voice slightly cracking, pained, hurt, fighting back the emotion of the moment.

'These men have become my friends,' he said. 'Through all of the months of training I have grown to trust, and in a way to love these guys.' He seemed on the verge of tears as he asked if it would be asking too much just to throw open the selection process once more to allow Chris Clark to have a chance, not a special chance, just a fair chance like everyone else. 'I am only asking for fairness, for my friends,' he said, his head shaking sadly, his eyes cast low towards his gigantic shoes.

Gavin laboured on. 'These very great friends of mine are concerned only with the speed of the boat. We want only for everything to be right. We want the selection to be right – this is the critical issue. This is so terribly fundamental to everything. We only want the fastest boat.'

He said it as if I somehow didn't want the fastest boat. As if I was all out to choose a boat that wasn't the fastest boat. As if I had won twelve of the past thirteen Boat Races *without* putting out the fastest boat.

All they wanted, they said, was some fair testing, some more decisive work on the ergometer, perhaps some seat racing, just to make it fair. 'That's all we want Dan. Nothing more. Just to give everyone a fair chance. Is that too much to ask?'

It was of course a request in startling contrast to Lyons' dismissal of the President in Oriel Square just one week before. 'Donald, we don't want any more tests . . . this is over. . . . The crew will not row with you.' They made it all sound so reasonable, and it may be that some of them had really persuaded themselves that they were indeed fighting a just cause.

As the meeting progressed Fish continued to get out of hand and Penny continued to suppress him. Even Dan Lyons spoke with restraint and made good use of the ploys of the debating chamber. At one point he began to read from my book – *Boat Race: The Oxford Revival* – in which I maintain that I would never want to row in a crew which had been selected on the basis of friendships rather than ability. He read it triumphantly, the oldest debating trick in the world – read your opponent's own words at him. 'You say it yourself, Dan,' he said, delighted with himself. "You only row with proven winners."'

'I believe it,' I snapped back, 'and that's why Macdonald is in the boat.'

If he had read a few lines further he would have seen: 'All you need is one weak link in the crew, for when the pressure really comes on he breaks. For months in training he may get away with it and the coach may well not notice, (or he may know but will hope for the best) but come the big race, if it's a close one that suspect link gives way. . . . Past reputation counts for nothing.'

As the meeting wore on their speeches seemed to be carrying some weight. They were sounding so injured and accommodating that one or two of the 'panel' appeared to be wavering as they heard the American version of the arguments. But of course they were not getting the real avowed position of the other side. They were listening to a completely new position, one neatly constructed so as not to ruffle any feathers. It was an Oscar-winning performance.

Suddenly it was no longer a case of mutineers flinging out the President, hijacking the boat and trying to take over the club and the selection process and rejecting all that the OUBC had stood for.

Now they were a group of misunderstood athletes (Clark's che-quered winter's training conveniently forgotten) trying to appeal against an unfair selection process. And by hiding the true thrust of their intent, their strategy was working most effectively. What Ronnie Howard and Dick and Michael were hearing was a travesty of the real situation.

Their pre-determined line of attack was to isolate the coaches, one by one, and to ask every coach, individually, to state his position over the Clark situation. Under this pressure the previous unity of the coaching team began to crumble. It was as if they had been hypnotized by the opposition. The painful discussions, agreement and joint statement of the day before were cast aside. Jeff Jacobs now changed his vote and said that he had abstained from the decision at Leander. Spracklen said that he felt that Clark should be in, Steve Royle prevaricated and I said I could not and would not work with Clark anymore. I was no longer prepared to gamble on him. His contribution was destructive and I believed now we would lose the Boat Race again with him in the boat.

But now another voice joined the fray, that of John Pilgrim-Morris, a former Royal Airforce officer and coach to Britain's bronze medal Pair at the Moscow Olympics. He was, despite being in his early 50s, still a tremendously powerful sculler and very much a sensible well-ordered military presence in our camp. Also from Marlow, his full-time government job prevented him from devoting as much time as he would have liked to the river, so he tended to find himself sometimes in Mike Spracklen's shadow as a coach. But he was certainly not so as a man, his quiet confidence in himself rendering self-aggrandisement strictly unnecessary.

Well aware of the charade that was being enacted and of the endless problems we had been through, John now intervened. Seeing the President's lonely plight, and concerned at the way Donald was having to fight for control both of his temper and of the meeting, he stepped into the breach. 'It is quite clear that Clark should, and could be very good,' he said. 'He is a good puller. But in this squad he is destructive. And we have to acknowledge that we cannot work with him. I can see exactly why he has to go. I do not think he has what it takes to row for us in the Boat Race. I think he might let you down.'

Finally we asked the crew to wait outside. Most of the coaches' group headed for the men's room. On the way there, an interesting exchange took place when Donald asked Jeff Jacobs what he thought of the proceedings so far. 'It looks rather as if you and Dan are going to have to resign,' he said.

So once more, upon his return, Donald had to rally his troops and pull them back into line.

With an agonizing exhibition of self-control, he began to speak, and all the tension which had built up inside him was there in the tight strained quality of his voice. He summoned every ounce of patience he had left, and, grinding out each word, separately, he said: 'What they are doing and what they are saying has nothing to do with their real intentions. Their position has never changed. Try to understand they want Chris Clark back in the boat, and if we do not grant them that, they will not row. Any of them. You are looking at a gang of hard-nosed rowing careerists. They know what they want. And they think they have found a way to get it. We will not back down.'

There were a few conciliatory noises from the table. But Donald went on, amazed that no one had seen the smirks on the faces of the oarsmen as they had trooped out of the room. He had thought to himself as they left: 'Can no one but me see this, can no one else understand what they are doing?'

He said yet again, 'You have heard nothing new tonight. You have just heard the same complaints, but this time from the squad in a manner which has taken you by surprise. If our decision was correct yesterday it has still to be correct today. We cannot back down, and then go out and tell the Press downstairs that we actually did not mean what we decided at Leander, and that really we would very much like to bring Clark back in. We will look absurd in front of the world.

'Besides, I am still President. And I am not going to do that. You must face the facts. In my opinion it is extremely doubtful if any of these guys, except for Tom and Hugh Pelham, will row in the Boat Race. Either we pick Clark or they will pull out. You have to get used to that. That's our only decision. It's tough but it's true.

'No Clark. No US stars, and if that's the way it has to be, then that's that.'

At that moment, Mike Spracklen made his move. He sprang to his feet, banged the table, and shouted: 'This is *victimization*. And I cannot be a part of it. I think this is absolutely disgraceful. I've had enough – and I don't want to be involved any more.' Upon which he headed for the door.

Donald also jumped up: '*What are you talking about?*' he roared. 'You agreed yesterday and now you are suggesting that we change our minds? Do you have any idea what that will mean?'

That stopped Mike in his tracks. His burst of temper vanished. There was a look of disbelief upon the face of the President, firm in his resolve not to hand the OUBC over to Lyons and Clark and the rest of them. He said again: 'It was clear yesterday, and to me it is still clear today.' But at this moment he seemed completely isolated.

Outside, the college clocks were chiming midnight. I said again that in my mind there was no question that Donald deserved his place in the boat on merit. That I *would not* even consider dropping him from the crew. I did so partly to clarify my own complete support for Donald as an oarsman, and also because I honestly felt that he might very well crumble if I wavered in my assessment of his ability. In my opinion no one in my entire experience of boat racing had ever deserved my unstinting support more than this President.

But the other coaches were still seeking a compromise, and Donald stood up and told them, once and for all, 'You cannot cave in. If you do you will destroy my Presidency and very possibly the Boat Club. You must understand that this is no longer an argument over selection, this is a war.'

Dick Fishlock made one last attempt at tipping a tubful of oil on these troubled waters and he said to Donald in a very quiet voice: 'Donald, you are allowed to change your mind, you know. But in the end you must decide for yourself. We can only advise but the final decision must always be up to you, as President.'

'Right,' snapped Donald. 'Bring 'em in and I *will* tell them.' The crew filed back through the door, eager, confident of victory. And Donald said coldly that in the absence of any further evidence, the decision made at Leander on the previous day must stand. For the second time in four days they stood gawping at the toughness of the OUBC President.

We should perhaps have risen and left right there and then. But somehow this was not possible because everyone needed to speak.

Clark referred back to the Vietnam War. 'Donald, I just want to ask you one thing. For the sake of one objective would you guys really want to blow up the whole village?'

Donald thought very carefully for a moment and then said: 'No Chris, not the whole village. Just the one hut, and I'm afraid that's you. It's you guys who want to blow up the whole village.' I nearly offered a round of applause but thought better of it.

Around that time Dick Fishlock and Michael Barry, himself a fellow of St John's began to panic as they foresaw the entire gathering degenerating into a free-for-all. They took themselves off to the back of the hall and returned ten minutes later saying to the oarsmen: 'Look chaps, we want you to trust us. We will adjourn now. But the members of the OUBC will sort something out for you – hopefully by tomorrow.'

Donald was totally exasperated. He told me later, 'No one would face up to the simple decision. If Clark was out they wouldn't row, so we had better start looking for a new crew. Privately Dan, I thought the coaches turned out to be rather wimpish.'

The meeting broke up at 1 a.m. on the Tuesday morning. The oarsmen went off and made their statements to the Press. We issued formally our confirmation that Sunday's decision stood – no Clark. The Americans left stating that, 'we are just unable to accept this,' and I went to Michael Barry's rooms with Ronnie Howard and Dick Fishlock where we spent a further hour-and-a-half locked in discussion.

I gave them a detailed account of the experiences of the past few months to show the reasons for Donald's and my unyielding stance, yet at the same time vainly trying with them to formulate even now some kind of acceptable compromise. For the four of us, apart from Clark and Macdonald, were the only men who had rowed in the Boat Race, who knew what it meant and how imbued it was deep within our souls. It wounded us deeply to see the thing we loved being fought over and ripped to shreds with what appeared to be such casual carelessness. The Boat Race and Oxford's continued success was uppermost in our minds and we felt a need to explore every avenue for a solution. But the evidence was clear that in the prevailing atmosphere of ill-will nothing would work. It was ironic that our winning streak had begun with a dynamic, constructive American back in 1974 and had ended thirteen years later with a negative, destructive one. But, in truth, the Boat Race was more important than the individuals and that was why we sought a way out of the impasse.

Donald arrived home, battered but not broken. He said to Ruth, more in despair than anything else, 'This is just terrible. The coaches just about fell apart, and with the exception of Dan and

John, no one stood up for me. I'm afraid I have had enough. I have nothing more to give them.'

Ruth Macdonald, unlike her exhausted husband, did not sleep that night while she wrestled with the problem. Her conclusion as the dawn broke was that her husband *should not row in the Boat Race* – the race for which he had been preparing ever since that glorious morning in the car-park in faraway Stockton-on-Tees.

CHAPTER TEN

A PRESIDENTIAL SACRIFICE

The sheer injustice of it was like a knife in my gut, but I was powerless to change his mind. The apparition of the mutineers, coming back, again and again, listening to nothing, just arguing their point, doggedly, mindlessly, until the opposition broke down.

The announcement in the small hours of that Tuesday morning that Chris Clark was not to be reinstated came too late for England's big national daily newspapers. But they all carried major stories of the mounting crisis – 'Scot must quell Oxford Mutiny' – 'Boat Race Could Be in Jeopardy'. However the most serious item from our point of view was the statement of Mike Spracklen in a full-column story in *The Times*.

He was quoted as saying: 'The unhappiness of the whole crew is not just confined to the Americans. It appears that the Americans are leading, but there are other members of the squad who are not happy with the selection. The great worry is that the majority of the crew will pull out.'

Did he already know before last night's meeting in St John's that the crew would refuse to row unless Clark was put back into the squad? His public comments, made the day before, indicated that the unanimous statement issued after those hours of discussion on the Sunday in Leander had counted for nothing. Yet all the coaches there had been invited to resign if they did not feel able to support the democratic decision of the meeting.

Fortunately, most of the 'heavy' London papers had realized by now that the Clark v. Macdonald angle was a red herring. But Christopher Dodd continued in the *Guardian* to run the story for months afterwards, never checking with the chief coach for accuracy. He wondered 'whether the inclusion of the President, Donald Macdonald, or the sacked Californian would make the boat go faster', and he added: 'It became apparent that Clark was competing for the last place in the boat with the club's President .... When the Californian was left out of the Trial boat and the quiet Scot was put in, there were accusations that Clark's tests had been better – and that justice was not being done.'

If Donald had walked out of the squad at that point, and Clark had been returned, I would still not have been able to use him on the strokeside, since it would have left me with the four biggest men all sitting on the same side and weighing between them almost an extra man again more than the bowside. They were, for the most part, stronger and far taller than the men on the other side. Even the non-rowing journalists could hardly fail to notice the imbalance.

Although it was irritating to read, I could easily dismiss it as shoddy journalism, but back in Oxford Donald had finally reached the end of his tether. He awoke to face another enormous academic work-load and almost certainly another hopeless struggle with the coaches. Endless vacillation was pointless at this stage. What was required was major surgery. Donald decided that all the absurd speculation that he had thrown Clark out in order to award himself the seat would have to end, once and for all.

Ruth's suggestion fulfilled these criteria. The more Donald thought about it, the more appropriate it became. His resignation from the crew gave the Americans the most complete face-saver, blood would have been let on both sides. The demise of Clark, counter-balanced by the sacrifice of the President. In the eyes of the world it would be seen as the ultimate gesture, which, if rejected, would reveal the true motives of his tormentors. Motives which, Donald believed, were still unrecognized by most of his coaching team.

Such a resignation would of course have to be tendered by Donald the OUBC President with cool executive detachment. For Donald the oarsman, however, the decision would be one of pure torture. He spoke at length to Ruth over breakfast. She had not changed her views, and she thought he should give up his seat but continue on as President of the Club, and to fulfill his duties until the end of the academic year. In her view there was no reason for him to continue to fight for a place. The truth was that he had already earned it. But sadly truth had become the first casualty of this conflict.

However, it was not the prospect of resigning his seat in the boat that Donald found the most distressing part, although goodness knows it was bad enough. It was that he was experiencing his first taste of personal vilification, of widespread unreasoned hatred directed at him and, as far as he could see, through no fault of his own.

'That was the most difficult part for me to deal with,' he told me later. 'Suddenly realizing that this sports issue had been converted into a personal attack. It was terribly hard for me to cope with that. I don't know why. Just because I had never felt it before I suppose. And I think the loneliness also had a lot to do with it. At times I just felt as if I had no one to turn to. Except my family and you. Just about everyone else seemed to be an enemy. I was emotionally under siege from all sides.'

Ruth's view remained solid. Leave the crew, but stay on in office. Donald accepted the advice and telephoned his father later to tell him of the events at St John's. His father was also inclined to agree with Ruth, recognizing the wisdom of a resignation from the crew. His father's independent opinion was important confirmation in Donald's mind that this was indeed the correct decision.

Donald then telephoned me and tried to explain his position. I too was more than a little upset and, although I hated to see what they were doing to Donald, I accepted that it was an honourable solution and that he had had enough. Yet it was troubling to think that they had succeeded in driving him out. The sheer injustice of it was like a knife in my gut. The apparition of that gang coming back, again and again, listening to nothing, just arguing their point, doggedly, mindlessly, until the opposition broke down.

Donald's mind was made up. He drove down to Oriel Square where he met Fish and Hull and gave them the message to be relayed to the rest of the crew. It was that the original decision made at Leander on Sunday afternoon would stand. Clark was out. But that he, Donald, would also stand down, in the cause of unity and in the interests of peace. This would require a new man in the 2 seat in place of Donald and we would be promoting Paul Gleeson from stroke of the 'B' crew Isis up to the 'A' crew.

'I hope this is a clear signal,' he said, 'that I have never acted for personal reasons. You have lost Clark. Topolski has lost me. So go and deal with Clark, and tell him this is the fairest way for everyone. Let me know of the crew's acceptance, formally by four o'clock this afternoon.'

Hull thought deeply and sucked in his breath. Then he said: 'Dan Lyons is not going to like this.' Then Donald drove to the river to keep an appointment for a training outing with Tom Cadoux-Hudson in a Pair. Donald had made it clear to me that as President he was, of course, prepared to help the OUBC in any way he could, and that included rowing in the reserve boat if I thought he should.

Late that afternoon the crew rejected Donald's offer. Ruth heard it on a radio programme – and the crew did not make contact. The radio reported a crew spokesman as saying that Donald's proposal was 'not in the best interests of boat speed.' What was really meant was they were *never* going to agree to anything that omitted Clark from the crew.

The President took the news thoughtfully and deep inside him, some of that old Macdonald spirit began to return. He had made what he considered the supreme sacrifice of his life. He had offered to give up his priceless place in the Blue Boat, never to row against Cambridge as President of Oxford. And he had done it to ensure that his crew could get on with the nitty-gritty preparation for their date with the Light Blues on 28 March. Yet they had dismissed his gesture of conciliation so painfully made. Christ! He had just about thrown himself on his sword.

What was he now to think? What was he supposed to do? They were at a total impasse. The crew would not row. They would do nothing which did not include Clark's return. The story was now blazing daily around the world. Journalists were spilling out of trains and cars onto the university campus. Television crews were on permanent location in Oxford and the Americans were giving more interviews than Joan Collins. Every television news programme, whether national or local, was carrying progress reports from the embattled University Boat Club.

The Americans remained on strike, as did their British brothers-in-arms. And from where we were standing, Donald and I, it looked very much as if the boys in the reserve crew Isis were behind them too.

Contact between the two sides was now virtually impossible with each learning of the other's latest position through news reports or from eager-to-help journalists like the man from AP, who maintained a constant phone link throughout the fortnight. Of course there was no way of checking the veracity of their information and it took a day or two, naïvely responding to their 'helpful' liaising, to realize that more often than not they were fabricating conversations to elicit a quotable response. 'They say, Mr Topolski, that you . . . .' 'They what? Well that's rubbish . . . etc, etc.' Scoop.

Donald's phone and mine virtually never stopped ringing, and we began to leave the receiver off the hook from 2 a.m. to 7 a.m. in order to catch some sleep. Donald after all had a family and in my home we were expecting our first child at any time. During the rest of the time both phones rang, and rang, and rang. Journalists were beginning to call from all over the world.

'When is all this going to be resolved, Mr Topolski?' 'What's the latest Mr Topolski?' 'What should I tell my readers, Mr Topolski?' 'Is it true the Boat Race has been cancelled, Mr Topolski?' 'Why are you being so unfair to the Americans, Mr Topolski?' 'Why doesn't the President resign, Mr Topolski?'

The people I wanted and needed to speak to could never get through.

It was finally two o'clock on that Wednesday morning when Donald broke through to report the fact that his offer had been turned down on 'moral' grounds, in the 'interests of boat speed' – 'boat-speed' being a euphemism for 'Chris Clark'.

This now added a new dimension to the conflict, for Donald was still President, with a loyal Secretary in Hugh Pelham, a loyal bowside international in Tom Cadoux-Hudson, and a loyal chief coach in me. Between us we had to do something, although Donald felt he could no longer rely on all his coaches for proper support. We both now had good reason to regard Mike Spracklen as a member of the other camp.

In Donald's opinion the rebels had made a big mistake in rejecting his offer to resign from the crew. 'My offer,' he said, 'was made out of regard for the reputation of the OUBC, and in an effort to solve the crisis and produce our best possible crew for the race. Their rejection was made in the tiresome self-interest of certain members of their group. I think that's the end of it now.' It represented the critical turning point in the battle for control.

However we did face one unfortunate little reality. We did not actually have a crew to race against Cambridge, since nearly all of our men were apparently on strike. We agreed that we would call upon the members of the New College third Eight if necessary to do the honours if nobody else would row for Oxford, but that further efforts at compromise with the mutineers were over.

In our hearts we knew that our chances of defeating Cambridge this year were fast evaporating, but we believed too that the integrity of the OUBC and its elected President were well worth defending. Donald said that in the morning he would go down to Marlow to see Isis, who were training for an important London fixture on Saturday against the Thames Rowing Club. He would sound them out and then, if they too rejected him, well . . . he might well have to put in a call to the New College captain. The College squad would of course be bolstered by the inclusion of Donald, Pelham and Cadoux-Hudson and any other loyalists remaining in the squad, but we were serious about our course of action.

We awoke to Wednesday, Day Three of the strike. *The Times* had a huge six-column headline over their sports page which read: 'Macdonald Quits Boat Race Squad'. The *Independent* announced: 'Oxford Skipper Offers To Sit It Out'. Chris Dodd in the *Guardian* persisted with his Clark v. Macdonald theme for the same place in the boat. However he did suggest a mind-boggling compromise: 'The way . . . would be for Macdonald to put himself on the bank and give Clark a bow-side seat "on probation".'

Now there was someone we could use on the selection panel! There had clearly been some serious thought involved except that his solution ignored a couple of awkward facts: namely that Macdonald would not need to be on the bank if Clark was on bowside since the President rows strokeside; and it was also my original suggestion, on the evening of the seat races, to put Clark 'on probation' on bowside, which had caused the entire uproar in the first place. Now Mr Dodd saw fit to present the cause as the solution.

The *Daily Mail* devoted its entire feature page, arguably the most important page in the paper, to the story of the Oxford Mutiny. The strap along the top of the story ran for four columns and read: 'Behind the Gentlemanly Façade of a British Legend . . . .' And the headline in huge black letters: 'Mutiny Of The Oxford Yanks'. It called them 'mollycoddled mutineers' and accused the Americans of 'insufferable arrogance'.

Meanwhile, as promised, Donald went to Marlow to see Isis and attempt to raise some sort of crew. They were training under the tuition of two redoubtable characters: the reigning Olympic champion Steve Redgrave, and Fred Smallbone, the London Eastender who rowed in the British Eight which won a silver medal in the Montreal Olympics.

They both liked Donald, and they were both good friends of mine. They talked to Donald for a while and listened carefully to his proposal to use the Isis crew for the Boat Race if he had to. Donald told them that he thought it was possible that they might decide to be loyal to the American group and refuse. Fred dismissed this with 'What a load of bollocks.'

The crew gathered on the bank. With Hugh Pelham were Paul Gleeson, Matthew Ridgewell, Justin Cheatle, Christopher Chinn, Tom Race and the Oriel bar men Peter Baird and Peter Gish, a decent bunch of oarsmen, though not of course in the same class as the men in the 'A' crew. Donald explained the position to them; that it was very possible the Americans and their British sidekicks would not row in the Boat Race. They were on strike and now looked like remaining on strike. He told them he might need to call upon almost their entire crew to represent Oxford. What were their views?

A few of them were not sure how to respond, how much loyalty they were expected to show towards the rebels. They hesitated, they looked uncomfortable. Finally this was too much for Smallbone and he waded into the discussion. 'Right,' said Fred, 'now listen. You blokes are faced with a chance to row in the Blue Boat for Oxford University and you are actually wondering whether to take it? I can't believe this. This is the chance of a lifetime. If I was you, I'd be in that boat now. Nothing would stop me, I'm telling you.'

Redgrave himself now spoke with the authority that goes with being an Olympic gold medallist, an MBE and the best-known rower in Britain. 'In twenty years time,' he said, 'no one will care a damn whether Lyons and Clark and their pals rowed or not. They will only know whether Oxford won or lost, and who rowed, and how good they were. You guys would be mad not to take your chance. Fred and I never had the opportunity to go to university but if somebody offered *me* a chance to row in the Boat Race I'd take it like a shot. I'll be very disappointed if any of you fail to make yourselves available to Donald and Dan.'

That did it. The boys went off to have a chat and after a short while Hugh Pelham came back and said that they had agreed to have nothing more to do with the mutiny, that they would be available as a crew to row for Donald as the Blue Boat, and they also understood that not everyone would get in, because of the President and Tom Cadoux-Hudson. Donald smiled, and recalls Fred saying: 'Blimey, sweet f - - - ing reason. Thought I'd never 'ear it again!'

The only stipulations the Isis boys made were understandable. They wanted to complete their race against Thames on Saturday, and they wanted to know, one way or another, whether they would be required for the Boat Race by Sunday night. If not, they would like to carry on together as a crew, to race the Cambridge second boat on Boat Race day and then perhaps go on to Henley.

Donald agreed to their terms with a growing sense of relief. In fact he positively welcomed them. At last the tide seemed to be turning in his favour. It was the first break we had had in what seemed like months. He walked over to the platoon of journalists packed along the river bank and told them he was now planning to use the Isis crew in the Boat Race and that the striking members of the Oxford crew had until Sunday night to make up their mind if they wanted to be considered for selection.

Then he and Tom went for a row together in a Pair, in front of them all, a clear signal that the President was once again very much alive. In Donald's eyes the end of the mutiny was in sight. If the Americans would not row, then at least he had a crew, and not a bad one at that. We would probably not win the Boat Race, but at least Oxford could now compete with dignity.

The news of the Isis crew's support for the President beat Donald back to Oxford. By the time he arrived everyone seemed to know, and there was a message for him to the effect that the Americans had now decided to accept his offer of yesterday to stand down. For the first time they agreed to the dropping of Chris Clark. Forgotten now was the issue of 'boat speed'. They were moving the goalposts at an alarming rate.

It was, in Donald's view, a desperate last ditch attempt on their part to head off the fact that if they did not row someone else would.

Donald called to tell me the latest developments: 'They must be out of their minds. Yesterday was yesterday. I gave them until the late afternoon to accept or decline. They declined. Now that I have made another move and got us a crew they suddenly decide to accept yesterday's terms. Which, I am pleased to say, are now no bloody longer available. Because they are just no longer needed. Those laddies are, I am afraid, going to have to grow up.'

'I have told them,' he said, 'that they have until midnight on Sunday to let me know whether they will row for this university or not. If they decline, we proceed without them.'

As for me it was going to take a lot of skill to transform these raw kids into a Blue Boat. I could not yet be sure how many of them we would need because the positions of Stewart, Hull and Ward would not be known until after Sunday night should the US brigade stage a total walkout.

Besides Hugh Pelham, the Oxford Secretary, who was most likely to end up in the bow seat of the first boat whether the American rebels – minus Clark – returned or not, the first strokeside man for promotion would be Paul Gleeson, the twenty-one-year-old Isis strokeman, an engineering student at Hertford College who had been captain of a Cherwell Eight (Oxford's Third crew) I had briefly coached the previous summer for Henley. He was a man who had clearly caught the rowing bug, and that August had taken himself off down to the River Lea in the East End of London, to row with the hard club oarsmen who every year produce high quality crews at Henley.

They always claim the scalps of many of the 'Toff' clubs, and I have many friends among their members including Steve Simpole, who rowed behind me at 6 in the World Lightweight Gold Medal Eight of 1977, a man Donald says is the toughest person he ever trained with. The River Lea bears little resemblance to the upper reaches of the Thames. It rises in Bedfordshire and flows out into the pool of London near Limehouse. It has its share of dead rats, like all industrial waterways, and it does not have much of a straight on which to race. But somehow they manage and those boys taught Paul Gleeson what real rowing is all about.

He rowed with them week after week, racing in round after round of hard competitive regatta events. They taught him the hurly burly of the inside bends, how to power round the outside, how to grab a quick half length at the start. He experienced the excitement and the rivalries, and when he returned to Oxford he was a changed man. His body still lacked the teak-hard quality all oarsmen develop after many years in the sport, but he was quite solid for a guy who had only been at it for a year and a half. In truth, the physical strength of this virtual novice was some way behind his competitive edge and technique, but he was pretty determined and getting better all the time.

The way things looked at present, I was going to have to throw this 'rookie' right in at the deep end, into the fabled stroke seat of the Oxford Blue Boat, a position occupied by men of Dark Blue folklore – Davidge, Mike Davis, Spencer, Ed Trippe, Saltmarsh, Sawyier, Michelmore, Diserens, and Bland. For Donald was convinced that, in the end, the Americans would not row.

Peter Baird, the Isis 7 man, was another I would probably need. He was 6ft 4ins and over 200lbs, studying chemistry at Oriel. He was very powerful, but clumsy, and having gone to school at Henley knew something about the subject of rowing. He tended to rush forward on his slide a bit, out of control, but that was a technique problem that could be cured. What I also hoped could be cured was his tendency to be rather morose and negative.

Peter Gish was another man we might need after Sunday, he was also a relative novice with less than two years rowing experience behind him. An American from Dartmouth College, he told me once that he was the grandson of Lillian Gish the actress. The fact that he had been a karate expert at Dartmouth rather belied his appearance for I never thought he looked hard enough for the sport; but he was fit and liked to keep himself looking good both on and off the water. He was at Oriel College (home of the mutiny) reading law and to begin with appeared to keep himself just a little bit apart from all the political shenanigans. In races he did not yet have the technique to completely pull his weight, and always looked to be working below full power. But he was prepared to learn and had a lot of self-belief. He featured in the middle of the pack on individual strength tests.

Then there was Matthew Ridgewell, a twenty-two-year-old former pupil of Rugby School, 6ft 4ins, 200lbs, and a fine athlete with great endurance, courage and tenacity. He currently lacked subtlety in a boat and some crewmen found him uncomfortable to row with for he could be a bit of a bull in a china shop with an oar in his hand. But he was terrifically strong and I thought we could iron out his technique in a month or so. He was a delightful guy, and a loyal supporter of Donald throughout the affair.

In addition we had Justin Cheatle, a twenty-year-old member of Clark's College, University. He was reading Classics and had learned to row at Oundle. Very determined and a bit of a character with a slightly off-beat sense of humour. In the Boat Race programme biographical notes he described how he played the piano for a Newcastle Dixieland Jazz Group, called Fatcat (£200 a night o.n.o.).

Tom Race from Abingdon would also now come into contention. He was a good lightweight having rowed for England as a junior. I did not recognize him at first as a member of that same Henley Cherwell Eight, because last summer he had worn his hair long and curly; this year he had contrived to look more like a convict. But he was a tough and effective oarsman and I was glad to have him around.

Chris Chinn too, though light, had a good junior record behind him. He produced excellent sculling results but lacked brute power.

And there was of course the Isis cox who had done such a good steering job in the reserve race the year before. Andy Lobbenberg from Shrewsbury school was probably a better cox than Fish for the Tideway.

So Donald told the rebels his offer to stand down had expired with their rejection of it and that, as a result of the Isis stipulation, they had until precisely midnight on Sunday to decide what they wished to do. The following morning, Thursday, the papers ran splash stories: *The Times* had one on the front page – 'Oxford Threaten To Use Reserves As Crew Mutiny'. Inside the paper half their main sports page was devoted to the crisis with a big picture of Cadoux-Hudson and Donald at the top of the page. There were interviews with Donald and with Clark who said: 'No way is this a US rebellion and there is nothing that should indicate that it is US incited or led.'

By now *The Times* had dropped the misleading Clark v. Macdonald angle to the story, as had the *Telegraph* and the *Sunday Times*. Jim Railton, Geoffrey Page and Richard Burnell had pretty well sorted out the facts and only Christopher Dodd in the *Guardian* persisted: 'Macdonald calls cabals of coaches and Oxford rowing heavies to investigate the data of ergometer readings and individual contests to determine whether he or the Californian Blue, Chris Clark, is the best man to sit in the sharp end of the boat.'

After these bruising months, I had to admit that my own confidence had suffered quite a battering. If enough people swear to you that black is white, or wrong is right, you actually begin to wonder whether you might be losing your grip altogether. And I know that Donald was feeling much the same.

I began to doubt all of my intuition about the Boat Race, about the athletes, about rowers, about rowing, and people and Oxford and Cambridge. I did not really know where I stood even in my own mind. In fact I was not altogether sure what I believed in any more. It had just worn me down, all my natural combative instincts had dried up. I was just dragging myself around, from argument to argument and I was punch drunk.

At times during the past weeks I had, in quiet moments, tried to go over it all, write it down in sequence, to understand better how it had all come to this but I always came to the same conclusions. There was a basic injustice that was irrefutable. Either that, or I was losing my mind. The squad was in revolt against a perfectly well-meaning diligent President who had done more than enough to prove he was worth his place in the boat, and half the world seemed to be telling me I was in the wrong and never really knew much about winning the race anyway. Now I turned on the television and had to watch the Americans talking about the Boat Race. 'Well, it's all about honesty and fairness', they were saying. 'We have been just so shocked by how dishonest it is here. We had come to Oxford believing this was the very home of amateur sport. We had such admiration for it. And now we are just so disappointed.'

And broadcasting faces, wearing heavy responsible frowns were nodding wisely in agreement – and other people implying the most shocking dishonesty in the character of one of the most decent Presidents I have met.

And the phone went right on ringing. 'What AM I to tell my readers about this unprecedented situation, Mr Topolski?' I am proud to say I retained my cool and never once informed any of them precisely what they could tell their readers.

It was a very bad time for me, because I had not experienced a mental battering like that before, and upon reflection I am not at all sure how well I stood up to it. The one thing I remember most is that I felt Donald might cave in altogether unless he had my full support. I tried to give it to him, but I think in the end he managed to rally me, more than I managed to rally him.

Donald now believed the mutiny would end in a few days

because we finally had a crew, so I decided to see if I could salvage Stewart and Hull from the wreckage.

I contacted Stewart first and braced myself for an emotional outpouring against the 'unconscionable' behaviour of Donald and myself. I asked him what he was doing mixed up in all this mess, for it was still only five weeks since we had returned from our successful Spanish tour, the best of friends. He had wanted Clark out of the squad then. Now he said I was treating Clark unfairly. He dragged up every little rowing grievance which had befallen him during his time at Oxford in a disjointed grumble. He was clear on one thing though. Clark had won a seat race, so he should be in. I ran through all the evidence yet again, explained the great range of considerations that go into selecting a Boat Race crew.

When he had got all these confused thoughts off his chest, he confided that he was under some pressure from his parents to forget about the mutiny and concentrate on rowing for Oxford.

He was wavering. I told him that I had spent two-and-a-half years preparing him for this race against Cambridge. I reminded him of the times I had been there to help and comfort him, particularly on the occasions when he had broken down sobbing in the changing rooms at the murderous training, swearing that he could not go on. I reminded him of the many occasions when he had felt he had nothing more to give and that it was I who had got him up to fight again. I growled down the phone at the giant of Wadham: 'Goddammit Gavin. I have spent years helping to get you to this point in your career. And you just want to go out and throw it all up. I'm quite sure your parents are not pleased with you, I'm not pleased with you, and if I know anything about you, deep down you're not too pleased with yourself either. Come on, get yourself out of this bloody stew, and get back on the river.'

There was silence for a moment. Then his voice came down the phone faintly, cracking slightly, saying he'd have to think more about it. And I knew I had him. At that moment I reckoned Gavin Stewart would be rowing for the Dark Blues on 28 March. One down. One to go. Then I called Richard Hull.

It was clear from the very start of our conversation that Richard wanted to row in the Blue Boat, and somehow extricate himself from the quagmire of this mutiny. He wanted of course to do it with some vestige of pride, and without looking like a traitor to the rebel movement. In broad terms, Mr Hull wanted to feel good about himself.

I read him a mild riot act, and told him that what he and the others had done was appalling, and that it was something he was going to have to live with. However, if he could put it all behind him and make himself available to row, I was sure he would soon feel better about the entire business and at having ultimately made the right decision.

We had a long conversation during which I sensed he was probing for a sign of weakness, a chink which might be exploited before the Sunday deadline. But by the end I could tell that Richard was back on board, and in his own mind at least, determined to rejoin us. Donald's earlier assessment about him had been right. Now we had Macdonald, Pelham, Cadoux-Hudson, Hull and Stewart. Just give me three more fighters, I thought, just three more racers, and we might yet give Cambridge a run for their money with or without the Americans.

Even as I was speaking to Hull, Donald was fielding a rather unusual call from an unlikely but insistent source. The caller must see him, something very important, a first-class idea, which would put everything back into order. 'Let's meet in a bar where no one will recognize us,' said the voice. 'No, I'm afraid this is too serious to discuss on the phone. We have to meet.'

With resignation Donald agreed to the East Gate Hotel for a secret rendezvous with Christopher Clark. There were probably over 100 journalists of various descriptions wandering in packs around Oxford that night in search of the principals in this melodrama. But none of them turned up at the East Gate, when the President faced once more the man who had brought the OUBC to its knees for the first time since its foundation in 1839.

They sat in the bar with their backs to the door and Clark began the discussion with the news that he had abandoned plans to return to the crew. He realized that he no longer had any future with the Oxford squad but that right now he only wanted 'to put the other guys back on the water.' What's more he had a plan to do just that with as little pain to anyone as possible.

'I'm all ears,' said Donald.

'OK, Don, here it is,' said Chris. 'First of all, you continue rowing in the crew. OK? But what you do is, you resign the Presidency and hand over to Gavin Stewart. The guys would feel happier that way. They all think you should be in the boat, but after all the trouble, they would just feel a little better if they had Gavin as President. But you could row and everything would be fine.'

Donald sat with that cool, rather amused half-smile of his. 'Sometimes, Chris,' he said. 'You guys make me feel about a thousand years old. And once more you assume this extraordinary position where you think you can not only pick the crew, but also name Presidents with not one single thought for the ordinary democratic process of the college captains which has survived here since the Duke of Wellington was Prime Minister of England. You just cannot do things here in this way. I *am* the President. I am the only person in this university who may challenge Cambridge. I am the only person from whom Cambridge may accept a challenge. Your proposal is pure nonsense because, basically there is no apparatus here for the removal of a President, except in the event that his very existence threatens the welfare of the Boat Club. And I doubt that even my worst enemies would suggest that of me.'

That was what Donald said. What he thought was that they would attempt to get Gavin into the Presidency, have him fire me, and then get the coaches to fire him, Donald, from the crew, thus permitting them eventually to recall Clark. 'I might be a bit slow-witted,' said Donald. 'But I am not f - - - ing crazy.' And with that he stood up and wished the ex-Oxford number 6-man 'Goodnight', and left.

'The naïvety of their tactics was a bloody insult to my intelligence,' he told me later. 'But every step they took, betrayed a near fanatical resolve to get Chris Clark back into the crew.'

That night Donald slept the sleep of the righteous, while I rushed Suzy to hospital to have our baby. Except that she did not quite do so – and when finally I drove home in the early morning, I picked up the newspapers to find Clark's resignation offer to Donald all over the place in big letters, complete with its proviso that Macdonald resign his Presidency.

Well, I was getting used now to this sort of political leaking but I was quite surprised when I turned to the serious leader page of the *Daily Telegraph*, an editorial column which has been known to turn the knees of Prime Ministers to jelly.

They ran two leaders on that Friday morning. The bigger one commented on the 'resignation' of Alasdair Milne as Director General of the British Broadcasting Corporation, a story as highly charged politically as any you could hope to read at a time when the Tory Government was determined to force the BBC to toe the party line.

The second leader began: 'Not since the Owl and the Pussycat went to sea in a beautiful pea-green boat has there been an odder occurrence in rowing circles than the quarrel which engulfs Oxford's preparations for the Boat Race.

'There lurks,' it said, 'an issue which has divided humankind since the days of Ancient Greece. Is the Oxford crew in times like these to be autocratically selected by the coaches and the President? Or is it to be democratically elected?'

In conclusion the newspaper declared: 'The fact remains that the sum of this (the crew's) experience, however recruited, believes that it outweighs the combined experience of President and coaches.

'It is a turn of events which even in well-founded democracies like our own, wise daughters of Oxford, like Mrs Thatcher, are at pains to avoid.'

It was a droll and thoughtful piece of writing. But the extraordinary thing was not *that* it was, but *where* it was. And emblazoned over the top of the most august page in British journalism was the largest possible cartoon, showing the unfortunate Alasdair Milne, swimming for his life, with a rowing Eight in the background labelled BBC. The strokeman was saying: 'At least they are unlikely to replace him with a large American reading Social Studies.'

Chris Clark had made the bigtime.

Donald called early in the morning and told me about the meeting at the East Gate Hotel. He was certain that the rebel group would now attempt some sort of political manoeuvre. 'Dan, these guys, they really will stop at nothing, believe me. I hear from the Oriel Bar that they are busy lobbying all the college captains they can find. They may try to use the OUBC constitution to get me out.'

Donald was not far off the mark. In his mail box at Mansfield College that morning was a note from a six-man group of captains calling for an extraordinary meeting of all the captains of boats, 'as allowed under the OUBC Constitution' to be held as soon as possible. It was signed by the captains of Balliol, Oriel, St Benet's Hall, St Peter's College, Corpus Christi, and Wadham.

They wanted the meeting on Sunday night, which gave Donald what they must have thought was the absolute minimum time for him to prepare. It was a worrying development on two counts: it would fall before the midnight deadline for one thing, but more seriously he was not really completely sure of the details of the constitution, nor what his rights were.

He headed home instantly and telephoned Simon Barker, his old London Rowing Club crewmate, by now a barrister in London. Donald told him that he badly needed help. Could his friend guide him through these most dangerous waters? The lawyer gave Donald the number of the fax machine at his chambers at Lincoln's Inn, and told him to wire the entire document of the constitution into his office immediately. Donald grabbed the sheets of paper, and since Ruth had taken the children out in the car, he leapt aboard his bike and sped down to an office on the outskirts of Oxford to avail himself of this modern method of transmission.

Simon was back on the line in twenty minutes just as Donald came steaming up Botley Hill on his bike and into the house, breathing hard, both from the effort and from the high tension he was feeling. 'Nothing to worry about,' said the lawyer. 'You are in charge. They cannot even hold a constitutional meeting without you. And it is you who carries the responsibility of naming the date.'

'You mean I could make it 2 April – *after* the Boat Race?' asked Donald half jokingly. 'Yes, if you so wish,' said Simon. 'As a matter of fact you can do almost anything you like.'

With a huge sigh of relief, he thanked Simon and headed back down to Mansfield College, to the common room where he began to draft a reply to the captains, explaining that their meeting had been improperly called. He was about half-an-hour into this exercise, when the door opened and in strode the huge figure of Christopher Penny with an envelope in his hand. 'Oh, hi, Chris,' said Donald, 'just bringing me a copy of the letter from the captains, are you? Just to make sure I couldn't ever say I didn't receive it.'

'Well, sort of,' muttered Penny, handing Donald the envelope.

'Well, that was an excellent delivery, if I might say so,' said the President. 'Very professional. You could probably get a job as a bailiff if you worked at it. Actually,' he added 'I'm glad you popped in, because you can now go and tell your friends that you can't have the meeting. It's unconstitutional. I call the meetings around here. Tell them all how sorry I am, won't you?'

'Aw, c'mon Don,' said Penny. 'You can't do that. You're just playing politics as usual.' And he shook his head, slowly, and a trifle sadly, at the sheer lack of fair play being demonstrated by the President of the OUBC. That did it. That really got to Donald, the sheer unmitigated hypocrisy of it, and he fired directly back, barely controlling his anger.

'Christopher, your little group has scheduled this meeting, which you have presumably prepared for, at forty-eight hours notice, in order that I should have no time to prepare my defence. How is it that you can all, any time you like, make serious plans to chop off my head, but if I, all alone, try to protect myself, you treat me as some Machiavellian monster? All you can really accuse me of is not putting my head on the block properly, and this seems to have surprised you. Chris, I am not so much upset by your actions – those I suppose have something to do with the fortunes of war. However, I am becoming increasingly irritated by your propensity to treat me as if I were a fool.'

In the face of this statement, Penny retreated, still shaking his head in sadness at Donald's unreasonable attitude; he frowned heavily, perhaps in anticipation of the inescapable fact that once again Dan Lyons was not going to like this.

Donald completed his letter, and it was an absolute little legal treasure. It was stuffed with expressions like 'Further to the Document', 'May I refer you to Sections C.0. C.3. C.7 and C.8', 'Propose a resolution to repeal, amend or add', and 'ensued to subvert the proper process . . .' etc, etc. It must have taken an element of genius on the part of Donald's crewmate Simon Barker to make that read like an Act of Parliament. It concluded by letting them know that he would be sending a detailed report of the selection process, and that he would call a correctly constituted meeting of all the captains for 8 p.m. on the following Tuesday, under an agenda, and properly chaired by himself. Their proposed Sunday meeting? They could forget that. No officers of the University Boat Club would attend.

On the Saturday morning *The Times* and the *Telegraph* and a brand new dark-haired daughter, as beautiful as her mother, burst into my life. Emma, aged 12 hours, had tipped the scales at 6lb 9ozs, while the two newspapers sent yet another shudder around Oxford as the second week of this sustained rancour drew to a close.

The Telegraph announced that the captains were seeking to find the truth of the matter, and that they might try to call for a vote of no-confidence in the President which would require a two-thirds majority. Jim Railton in *The Times* formally announced this latest stage of the rebellion and offered the following speculation: 'Quite clearly this request for an extraordinary meeting is hardly to pat Macdonald on the back or acknowledge the intolerable strain on the President and his family but rather a move for a vote of "no confidence" in him.

Would this ghastly business never end? I had no idea how well we were equipped to deal with this new line of attack, nor what the level of support was within the rest of Oxford's rowing community. Student friends assured me that the undergraduate body were all behind us, but somehow the noisy barrage of antagonism seemed to belie such support. Where, I wondered, would the majority of the unbiased college captains stand on the issue?

Ignorant of the fact that Donald was by now in full cry preparing his defences, I left for the Tideway, having been up all night for the second time in a row, in sombre mood. I should have been brimming with elation at having just become a father. How I was coming to resent these shrewd opportunists! My objective was to see and talk to the Isis boys before they raced Thames Rowing Club. I also had to do an interview for the BBC's *Grandstand*, with its fourteen million viewers. The British public, longtime aficionados of what they considered their very own National Institution, deserved to know what was going on. I looked horrible, and the latest developments at Oxford were making me feel sicker by the minute. I decided therefore to honour my commitments in London, and hope that Donald could hold the fort in Oxford for the rest of the day.

Little did I know that he was doing better than that. He was already getting positive reactions. For the combination of Donald's superb legal letter and the implied wrath of the rowing correspondent of *The Times* had slightly unnerved some of the captains. A letter from Adrian Davis, Captain of Boats at Corpus Christi, one of those six challenging signatories, was already on its way to Donald, stressing that he had no intention of supporting any move to force Donald to resign, asking him to ignore *The Times* speculation, and sincerely apologizing 'if our actions have caused further anguish for you and your family.'

Meanwhile the Isis boys and I had a long and serious chat about the future which enabled us to clear the air. They then went out onto the water and thrashed a slightly weakened Thames crew by four lengths in a seven-minute race. Thames changed strokes, but were no more effective. Isis tore them up at the start and stayed in front. They showed a lot of grit in spite of the traumatic events that had overshadowed their training for the past two weeks. I was very pleased with them, though you would never have known it if you had caught a sight of my glum harrassed face on the television that afternoon. But at least baby Emma's arrival was announced to a breathlessly expectant world.

Back at home, Donald and Ruth, surrounded by a towering mountain of documents for the captains' meeting, fought in turn on their aged typewriter for hour after hour, night and day throughout this long weekend, preparing the most meticulous case against the rebels which we hoped would bring the Oxford Mutiny of 1987, finally and irrevocably to a close.

CHAPTER ELEVEN

A POET TO THE RESCUE

'And yet these events bring us together tonight to question the integrity of Donald Macdonald'. And his voice rang around the room as he demanded: 'How can that possibly be fair?'

On Sunday morning, 1 February, the most powerful voice in British rowing thundered forth in the *Sunday Times*. Richard Burnell, the official Boat Race historian, an Oxford Blue of 1939 and an Olympic gold medallist in 1948, was finally fed up to the teeth with the American mutiny – and he thumped the table in metaphoric anger. His headline read: 'The Worst Dispute in my 50 Years of the Boat Race'. And what followed was a damning indictment of all that Chris Clark and his friends were doing at Oxford. 'The Yank comes to Oxford,' wrote Burnell, 'Not . . . to rescue the crew from defeat but to invite the President of the University Boat Club to step aside to allow the outsider to row in his preferred position in the crew.'

He pointed out that like all stout-hearted mutineers and strikers, they are 'in no way challenging the establishment but just request-ing reasonable negotiations. Translated out of doublespeak,' he added, 'that means "This dispute can end if you back down".'

He had taken the trouble to phone the US National coach, Kris Korzeniowski, who said of Clark: 'A difficult kid, who can be quite disruptive.'

Of the forthcoming captains' meeting he wrote: 'I do not believe that a captains' meeting has ever dismissed a President. And it would be unthinkable that this should happen now simply because a disruptive element in the university squad has seen fit to challenge his authority.'

His words gave heart to Donald as he wrote diligently on in Lime Road. Britain's newspaper readers waited expectantly for news of Sunday's midnight deadline: would the giant American stars fall into line and row for Oxford in the Boat Race? Or would the tight loyalty of the mutineers hold them together in defiance of tradition? In addition to the influential voice of Richard Burnell, Donald and I were now discovering new allies, as letters poured in from Old Blues, imploring us not to back down, to stick to our guns, and to be guided by our consciences.

Ex-President Richard Yonge copied out Kipling's moving poem 'IF – ' in its entirety and ended it with the lines: 'And – what is more – you'll be a Man, my son! And a fine President too.'

But for Donald the first lines were the most poignant:

'If you can keep your head when all about you
Are losing theirs and blaming it on you,
If you can trust yourself when all men doubt you,
But make allowance for their doubting too;
If you can wait and not be tired by waiting,
Or being lied about, don't deal in lies,
Or being hated, don't give way to hating,
And yet don't look too good, nor talk too wise:'

There were also letters of encouragement from last year's stroke Matt Thomas, from Angus Robertson bringing support for Donald from the US rowing establishment – 'I wish their fellow countrymen at present at OUBC could have heard their views,' he wrote after attending the annual dinner of the world-renowned Power-Ten Club in New York. Two other old rowing colleagues wrote to him in support, world gold medallist, Paul Stewart-Bennett and the stroke-man of his London RC crew, Andrew Gamble. Tony Morton-Maskell, who rowed in the Blue Boat in 1962 and 1963, wrote: 'Anyone and everyone who undermines this private race between the two Presidents should be sacked – even if it means losing one race.'

Toby Tennant, the 1963 President who dropped himself from the crew, wrote: 'A note of encouragement and support. I am sure you

have taken the correct stand – keep it up and the best of luck.'
M. L. Thomas, the 5 man who rowed so heroically behind Davidge in
that desperate victory by a canvas in 1952, also sent a note of
encouragement.

From all over the world letters arrived, many of them openly
hostile to the rebels. Clark actually began to receive hate mail but still
the Americans pushed forward with their campaign. On that Sunday
however, the phone calls from other squad men promising to row
for the university began to come in. One by one the rebels said they
would be back on the water for Oxford. Huntington and Penny both
called. Even Dan Lyons, who could not bring himself to call the
President personally, had someone call for him to say he would row
on the Monday morning. They all knew the penalty Donald would
bring in the recently victorious Isis crew to replace them.

But Hugh Pelham's reports from behind the enemy lines were not
encouraging. He said that although they were promising to row, they
were planning secretly to do so only for two days, for they were quite
certain they would have sufficient support at the Tuesday night
captains' meeting to throw Donald out of office once and for all, and
sweep Gavin Stewart to power.

'The fact is Donald,' he said, 'They want you *out*. And they will do
anything to achieve their end. But you know that already.'

The cynicism behind such a plan shocked me and I did not really
believe it. It seemed so dishonourable, to give such an important
undertaking in the knowledge that they would renege *en-masse* if
things did not go their way. However I would have badly misjudged
the situation if I had gone to meet them in the hope that sheer force
of persuasion could win the day. But then I had always underesti-
mated the reality of their motives. Donald had no illusions on that
score. He was to impress me greatly with the thoroughness of his
preparations.

Armed with the irrefutable backing of the rowing establishment on
both sides of the Atlantic, Donald drove to the headquarters of the
Henley Royal Regatta on that Sunday morning. Simon Barker had
arranged a meeting with the London QC and Chairman of the Regatta,
Peter Coni, who was most anxious to help. They were joined by Mike
Pelham, a non-legal layman familiar with the background to both the
mutiny and to the OUBC constitution; and so Donald was flanked on
either side by some of the most incisive minds ever to pull an oar.

They spent three hours perfecting the document that Donald

would use to fight off the onslaught of the hostile captains two days hence. This amount of brainpower was usually only found in the boardrooms of the big City multinationals. The old King of the Overkill had struck again. But Donald knew as he headed home in the afternoon that defeat on Tuesday would be the end for both of us. He could afford to take no chances – or prisoners.

He and Ruth typed the huge pile of painstakingly-drafted pages long into the evening, and they waited anxiously for the phone to ring with the news of the unofficial captains' meeting which was taking place at Balliol College. Finally the doorbell rang. It was Rob Clay, the history graduate from Eton, who had stroked Oxford in 1982 with his twin brother rowing behind him at 3, and who was the bowman in the record-breaking 1984 crew. With him were Louise Ainsworth, the college captains' Secretary, and Peter Sudbury, a crewmate of Donald's from Isis '85. They had come hot-foot from the unofficial meeting.

The news from the front was bad and the three of them had come up to offer advice. 'It was bloody ugly down there,' said Clay. 'It's mob rule and they are baying for blood. They want you out of the Presidency and there's a damn lot of them ganged together. You and Dan are in real danger. And we are just not sure what you should do, because they are determined to force a vote of "no confidence".'

Rob said that he had thought from the start it could spell trouble. But not on such a scale. 'You should have heard them down there,' he said. 'Most of them have no idea what they are talking about, but when you get a rabble roused like that they seem to lose all sense of reason and judgement. There was a lot of sniping at Dan – and if they can get you out, the new President will just fire him. I'm telling you Donald, the situation is bloody desperate.'

It was now obvious that if Donald had wandered naïvely down to that meeting unprepared he may by now have been an ex-President. As things stood he had forty-eight hours to finish getting his act together, and save himself from what now looked like certain destruction.

By the time Rob, Louise and Peter had left it was almost midnight, and Donald sat alone downstairs, writing, rather touchingly in his journal: 'I am getting hellishly tired now. I have been essentially, on my own since Monday, nearly a week. The crew have not rowed for that week either. But it has been rather a lonely time. I have been relying greatly on old friends from past crews. Their loyalty has meant a lot to me.

'What seems important to me now, is that I go on doing what I believe to be right. I cannot deviate from that. And as long as I continue on that path, it ought not to matter whether in the end they vote me out or not. Nonetheless I still feel very vulnerable.'

First thing on Monday morning Donald rang Simon Barker and explained how badly things were going for him among the college captains, and how penetrating the American lobby had become. Simon pointed out that one of the key things at the meeting the following evening was that Donald should make no mistakes in matters of procedure, and that he dominate all issues on what the captains could and could not do. He said he would take care of much of that detail and that he would be back in touch.

As Simon put down the telephone Donald felt once again uncomfortably isolated in Oxford, and he wracked his brains for an experienced friend, someone mature and reassuring he could turn to for assistance and advice. He turned to the man who had been so clear-cut in his thinking two weeks before, on the very night of the mutiny, at dinner in St Edmund Hall – Mike Pelham, father of Hugh, a businessman of considerable personal stature, and a true Dark Blue loyalist. He could not think of a sophisticated way of explaining the problem to Mr Pelham, a way to show he had control and merely sought refinement. When the great man picked up the call in his office he heard a voice say very simply: 'Mike, it's Donald. I've been going for a long time now, and I'm running out of steam. I need some help. Badly.'

Mike Pelham cancelled his day's meetings, strode out of his office, jumped into his Ferrari and headed out on the fast lane towards Oxford. He arrived at Donald's house, having picked up Hugh on the car telephone, and assured the President that there would soon be three of them to fight this particular battle.

'It's time to regain the initiative,' he said, 'and tell your side of the story.'

Hugh arrived shortly and together they drew up a list of all the colleges whose captains would be at the meeting. Mike suggested they first put a check against the names of those who were definitely in the pockets of the Americans like Oriel, Balliol, and St Benet's.

The rest they divided up into groups. There were those where Mike had friends, those where Hugh had friends, and those likely to be naturally loyal to Donald. Mike drew up a master chart on which there were three columns. They were headed in turn: 'Support', 'No Support', 'Don't Know', the latter group being critical. Mike informed Donald that he must galvanize his support, preferably through the Old Blues. Responsibility should be split up between the three of them for contacting every person on the list who might command a vote at the meeting.

The two ex-Presidents still in residence, Bruce Philp and Graham Jones must be asked if they would be ready to speak on Donald's behalf at the meeting. They should both be told that the dispute was bringing the OUBC into disrepute and the Vice Chancellor of the University, Sir Patrick Neill, had let it be known, in no uncertain terms, that he wanted it rapidly concluded.

Whenever the question of selection came up, Mike suggested that it be stressed that the process can never be absolutely clear-cut on paper because there are three major factors involved with each oarsman – 1) Technique, 2) Fitness, 3) Psychological make-up. There was a major question mark against Chris Clark in the latter two areas. There was no question mark against Donald in any of them.

Mike felt the Old Blues should be motivated to pump out the message by asking the question: 'Why should Oxford rowing be hijacked by a bunch of mercenaries?'

Mike also insisted that the Isis crew be kept informed of all developments – firstly to keep their goodwill, but secondly in order that the two Oriel members communicate the firm resolve of the President.

They began the task of gathering the loyalists behind the President. They assumed they could count on historic Christ Church, the palatial college founded by the Lord Chancellor of England, Cardinal Wolsey, and currently occupied by Hugh Pelham. In the 450 years between these two loyal courtiers to their respective Crowns, Christ Church had been home to eighteen British Prime Ministers as well as to the great men of letters, W. H. Auden, Lewis Carroll and John Ruskin.

Donald thought, with wry unreasonableness, that Christ Church should have at least ten votes at the captains' meeting, rather than one single voice, like St Benet's, the college of Benedictine monks, with its tiny student body. Why, in the form of one Robin Geffen, they should suddenly agree to align themselves in open hostility against the President of the OUBC was something of a mystery, especially since, at the time, St Benet's did not even have a Boat Club and Geffen had indeed never rowed for them.

And yet here was this name 'Robin Geffen, St Benet's Hall', written clearly beneath those of the captains of Balliol and Oriel, and above those of the colleges of St Peter's, Corpus Christi and Wadham. They were all demanding, with only marginal politeness, that the President, who was struggling to retain the traditional rights and dignity of his office on their behalf, should turn up to explain himself forthwith. And in the months to come three of them would apologize profusely for their part in it all, though Robin Geffen would not be one of them.

Donald, a religious man, was upset by the position adopted by St Benet's. However, he also was to have the support of a religious college, and in addition he would have the benefit of an independent American voice speaking on his behalf in the shape of his friend Michael Suarez, godfather to Donald's youngest son Alasdair, who was incensed by the mutiny of his countrymen. He was in the process of completing the fourteen-year qualification period it takes to become a Jesuit priest, and he was currently reading English at Campion Hall.

This is the college established by the Society of Jesus in 1896 in the Lutyens-designed building in Brewer Street. Michael Suarez and Donald, both reading literature, met frequently at lectures. Both combined a love of prose and poetry with a passion for competitive sports. Michael Suarez, a twenty-seven-year-old American from Long Island, was in the process not only of gaining First Class Honours in English Language and Literature, but also of winning the Newdigate Prize for English Poetry. This is England's oldest poetry prize and had been previously won by Oscar Wilde, Matthew Arnold, John Ruskin, Julian Huxley and C. S. Lewis. He also became the first student ever to win, in the same year, the Chancellor's English Essay Prize. As if to ensure these achievements were not lightly dismissed as flukes Mr Suarez also won the university's Kirkcaldy Prize for his essay on The History of Science.

Michael Suarez was infuriated by the way Donald was being treated and outraged at the injustice of the rebels' action. He called a meeting of the whole faculty of Campion Hall to explain in that clear and resonant English of which he is a master, the appalling circumstances which were besetting the Oxford President. He told them it was a matter of decency and justice affecting everyone at the university, and that every community should take the responsibility of being represented on such an issue.

'We are entitled to a voice,' he told them. 'And I ask you to appoint me Captain of our Boat Club, so that I may have that voice.'

There was no dissent in Campion Hall, and the American prepared to speak on behalf of his friend. In Oxford, it was unusual to find the Jesuits pitched against the Benedictines. But the stance taken by Robin Geffen would now make that possible.

Also lined up on Donald's side would be, they hoped, Lady Margaret Hall, with its Boat Club captained by Tom Race; Lincoln; St Annes, the college of Matthew Ridgewell; St Edmund Hall, the domain of Mike Pelham; and Mansfield, Donald's own college.

Plainly against the President, were the colleges of Balliol, represented by Will Landale; Oriel, home of the mutiny; St Peter's represented by Julian Beck; and Wadham, the college of both Christopher Wren, the architect of St Paul's Cathedral, and of Gavin Stewart who was almost as tall. Donald, who has a rather penetrating eye for such detail always said it was fitting that in the charming old yard of Wadham, there should be growing a rare and shady Judas tree.

The rest were essentially up for grabs, with the President using all of his powers of persuasion to win vocal support of the Blues in residence, Graham Jones, Bruce Philp, Rob Clay, Gavin Screaton and Mark Dunstan who, as former participants in the Boat Race, were also eligible to attend the meeting.

All through that Monday morning Donald made what calls he could, but at a quarter to one he had to leave for Oriel Square to pick up the crew, all of whom had now promised to be there as selected. And there they all were – Huntington, Penny, Lyons and Fish, as well as Stewart, Hull and Ward. Clark of course was not there.

The crew now came under the control of Hugh Matheson, a wealthy Nottinghamshire landowner who took up his spell on the Oxford coaching roster. Matheson is a tall, blond articulate man, an old Etonian and Olympic silver medallist who rowed in the same Montreal Eight as Fred Smallbone. He is also a close friend of mine who worked with me in the early coaching days of the Oxford revival back in the mid-seventies. He rowed in the Blue Boat in 1969 and has been trying to make up for the defeat ever since; he is a superb oarsman, and finished sixth in the single sculls final at the Moscow Olympics. This would be his first Oxford coaching stint for some years, but he was always an inspirational teacher.

On this particular day he wanted peace and quiet for the crew on their first outing for a week, and he proceeded to lay a couple of false trails for the Press, sending them on wild goose chases to Wallingford and Marlow. But after a car chase around the outside of Oxford they finally all ended up at Henley. Hugh was not best pleased at the intrusion of the journalists as they stood on the bank at Henley, but he did not get much sympathy from Donald or me. We had suffered them in the front garden all day, and on the phone half the night for weeks.

When the crew took to the water Oxford was stroked by Huntington, with Hull at 7, Penny at 6, Lyons at 5, Stewart at 4, Cadoux-Hudson at 3, Donald at 2 and Ward at bow. I told Hugh that in my opinion the bow seat might possibly necessitate a change because, before the mutiny, I had on balance, preferred Clark to Ward for 3 with Hull, Pelham or Ward at bow.

Nonetheless the outing went well, and none of the Americans alluded in any way to the assault on the constitution they were coordinating for the following night.

On this particular Monday evening Donald himself would be busy at a meeting which I, too, was due to attend. It was a gathering of the innermost sanctum of rowing at the university – the OUBC Trust Fund, and among those present would be Bill Parry, a maths tutor and don at Oriel, the Treasurer Michael Barry, Richard Burnell, the cigar smoking Churchillian figure of the ex-President and 1960 Olympic oarsman Ian Elliott, Dick Fishlock, Ronnie Howard, and Mike Pelham.

On the previous evening Bill Parry had called Donald to let him know that he had declined a request to take the chair at the captains' meeting because he was too strongly in favour of the President even to pretend at impartiality. This was an important sign of the attitude of the senior members of Oxford's academic body and with Dick Burnell sitting alongside as well, it gave Donald heart, if not confidence.

We gathered at one of the most beautiful rooms in the medieval college of St John's with its walls trimmed with perfect Wedgwood-blue mouldings. The silver tankard from which Donald sipped a pint of ale was casually dated 1605. St John's is considered by many to be, secretly, the wealthiest college in Oxford, and the room bore this out. Michael Barry brought out a very decent 1947 port, worth about £150 a bottle, and handed the decanter to Ian Elliott, master of Wolverton Hall, Worcestershire, and 5-man in the winning 1960 Blue Boat. 'Well, Ian,' said Michael, 'What do you think?'

Ian sipped boldly. Then he drew luxuriously on his monstrous Cuban cigar, raised his fist, and crashed it down hard on the big oval table. '*I'll tell you what I think*', he roared. '*I think he should tell them all to f - - - off!*'

Donald smiled in appreciation of the sentiment, and said, 'Well, Ian, I'm not sure I ought to do that. I think it likely that that would lose us the vote . . . .'

'Well, so what if you do?' yelled Elliott. 'Who the devil wants to be president of a club that doesn't let you tell everyone to f - - - off from time to time! Just walk into the room and tell 'em all to bugger off home and have done with it.'

But dearly as Donald would have loved to implement Ian Elliott's strategy, he knew it could not work tomorrow night. And he said quietly, 'Tomorrow I have to survive. They may be able to force a vote of "no confidence", and if they do I could be beaten. I could probably block it on a technicality, and if you want me to, then that is what I will do.'

There was much experience in this room, and the Old Blues decided that it had to be fought out to the end. 'Let them vote, if they must,' said Michael Barry. 'Because if the madness has gone so deep that they do not want you, then spare yourself the agony, and let them have it.'

The meeting sipped a little more port. Then everyone wished Donald good luck and shook his hand and he walked through the silent college and out onto the wintery night expanse of St Giles, knowing that he might be in the final hours of his Presidency, perhaps the first Oxford President ever to be ousted by the captains during his term of office.

The next day, Tuesday, the national newspapers declared that peace had finally broken out on the upper Thames. 'Oxford Paddle Into Calmer Waters At Last,' claimed the *Independent*. 'Oxford Rebels Are Glad To Be Back On The Water' announced *The Times*. 'Crew Bury The Hatchet For Now' said The *Telegraph*.

The real truth however eluded them all. Which was as well,

because it was both sinister, and bitterly entrenched. Donald was convinced that if the big meeting at New College this evening ended with a vote for the President, none of the Americans would row again for the university. They would come out in support of Chris Clark, as they had always done, and they would totally renege on their promises of Sunday night to make themselves available for the 1987 Dark Blue Boat.

If however the rebels should manage to force a vote of 'no confidence' in the President, Donald was certain he would be instantly driven from office with Gavin Stewart elected in his place. Before the ink on his signature was dry Gavin would fire me; except that I would have quit as the vote against Donald was announced. But, either way, the climax of the long and bloody battle for control of the Oxford University Boat Club would be concluded tonight one way or another. Press rumours of peace were woefully premature. This one was strictly a fight to the finish. None of us was saying so, but all of us knew it to be true.

Donald read the papers and sighed wistfully at the general lack of insight. Then he began his usual round of telephone calls. He got to Graham Jones, still a voice of authority in Oxford rowing and a man I counted as a friend; but he was late. Dan Lyons had got to him first. The Australian said quietly that no, Donald could not count on his vote, that he was inclined to think the Americans had right on their side. The President asked if Graham would at least listen to him. And for half-an-hour he explained the entire story, until Graham finally said, 'I see. That does rather put a different light on things.' But he would not commit to speak for the President though he did say he would not speak against him.

For hour after hour Donald stayed on the phone until at last he could wait no more, and without lunch, he sped down to Oriel Square to pick up the crew for the afternoon outing. 'Whichever way this meeting goes,' he thought, 'This is the last time I go on the water with the Americans. If I win tonight they'll quit. If I lose they will throw me out.'

The outing, coached again by Hugh Matheson, went off smoothly, the boat running extremely well through the cool Henley waters. It began to look precisely what it was, a good big international-class Eight, with the three US national squad men demonstrating their world and Olympic pedigrees backed by a British world medallist Cadoux-Hudson and the experienced Old Blue Macdonald. There

221

was no question that this had the makings of a great Boat Race crew and Donald thought with some sadness, as they paddled along the Henley reach, that it was a shame they would probably never row again like this after today.

But this was no time for sentiment, and certainly not for friendship, for he knew that six of the nine men in that shell were set hard against him. Two hours from now they would collectively try to smash his life, and he simply could not let them do that. At the conclusion of the outing he helped put the boat away, but declined the invitation of Fish, the cox, to join them all in the weights-room at the Leander Club.

'There was only one thing in their minds,' recalled Donald later. 'They just wanted to keep me busy until the very last minute in order that I should have no time to prepare to avoid the execution they had in store for me that evening.'

With Fish still standing there, there was a sudden crunch of tyres on the gravel outside the club, and the biggest limousine Donald had ever seen swung off Remenham Hill into the drive and turned round with its engine ticking over. The electric window slid silently down, and from behind the wheel Simon Barker said cheerfully: 'Jump in Donald. We're going straight back to Oxford.'

Donald, who at this particular time would have been pressed to afford a bus fare to Oxford, said 'Goodbye for now,' to the perplexed Fish. And shutting the door gently behind him, he slid thankfully into the back seat as Simon gunned the limo hard over Henley Bridge in a truly outrageous display of intimidating power politics. They sped through the deep hills of Buckinghamshire and over the border to Oxford, approaching the town from the south. They snaked through the early evening traffic in The High and turned down to Brewer Street, parking quietly outside Campion Hall, the only building in all of Oxford where no one would dream of looking for them. Michael Suarez was waiting for them, and he brought them tea as Donald, tense with anticipation of the fight ahead, laid out his battle plan in the finely-proportioned ecclesiastical chamber surrounded by twelfth-century icons.

Carefully they went over Simon Barker's procedural notes until Donald was quite certain that he knew precisely what he would NOT allow to take place. They discussed the psychology of the unstructured attack that Donald might face, and in this Michael was a particular help.

Before coming to Oxford, Mike Suarez had spent some years 'on location' in the toughest areas that the Jesuit hierarchy could find. Not for nothing is this strict, intellectual Order known as the Green Berets of Catholicism. They had sent him to the notorious Barios in Santiago in the Dominican Republic, then out onto the Campos to help build pig-sties with the poorest 'campesinos'. He had worked in a home for unwed teenage mothers as a 'labour partner', in New York's most shocking ghetto, the South Bronx. Then they had appointed him Chaplain for four months to the terrifying Rikers Island prison across the East River from Manhattan, holding 13,500 inmates, some of them the most dangerous criminals in the United States. On one chilling occasion Michael had found himself trapped in a bloody race-riot inside one of the 'cages'; and with the armed guards massing around the outside with cannisters of tear-gas, Michael had gently placed his arms around the enraged black ringleader and walked him to safety. Tonight the Jesuit poet would attempt to subdue the challenge of Christopher Clark of Long Beach, California.

The three men went thoughtfully over their documents. A report to the captains had already been circulated by Donald, and it spelt out in great detail the precise, and considerable, powers of the President, in particular his supreme authority in the selection of all Oxford University crews. It detailed the qualifications and enormous success rate of the Oxford coaches, and it confirmed that every one of the oarsmen in the squad understood fully these traditions, 'enshrined in the constitution of the Boat Club'. To suggest that somehow he and his coaches had all suddenly decided to select an inferior crew was, said the report, ridiculous.

A file dossier was produced to counteract every argument that claimed a place in the boat for Christopher Clark. Michael Suarez, an outsider to the selection process, had compiled a well-researched statistical performance chart that showed that Clark's results against Huntington, Penny, Stewart and Macdonald not only rendered him clearly ill-qualified for a place in the boat on strokeside, but that he was also in fifth position on the weaker bowside behind Lyons, Cadoux-Hudson, Hull and Ward. My test result sheets were prepared as well. They also drew up a plan to outline general conduct for the meeting and for the opening addresses. The President intended to use the occasion mainly to inform the captains, and to explain to them the selection process.

Shortly after 7.30 p.m. Donald and Simon left Campion Hall in the limousine and headed for New College, the handsome 14th century building set just inside the old City Wall to the north east of the town, a place which had been eulogised by Henry James a hundred years before: 'of nightingales and memories – a sort of chorus of tradition'.

But on this bleak February night the nightingales had long departed, and the silver-grey battlements of the great wall loomed eerily in the pale moonlight, the frost already hardening below onto the long cold barren flower beds which have been tended by members of this college for more than six centuries. The Bell Tower which loomed above the big car as it stopped in New College Lane had, 350 years earlier, been converted into an army magazine as another Civil War erupted in Oxford. At that time the Royalist Warden of the College drilled loyal volunteers in the front quadrangle but there were none on duty tonight to help Donald Macdonald. On arrival Donald nodded goodbye to Simon Barker and turned and walked through the gateway, glancing at the guardian statues of the Virgin Mary and the Archangel Gabriel as he passed. Shielding his eyes from the glare of the television arc lights and dozens of exploding flashbulbs, he said tersely, 'Nothing to say right now,' and shouldered his way forward.

The room which had been selected for the meeting was already becoming crowded, and gathered around Donald on the podium were Dr Michael Barry, Dave Foster of Balliol, the secretary Hugh Pelham and Louise Ainsworth. Dick Fishlock and I, as guests specially invited to report on selection procedures and the recent coaches' meetings, sat in the front row. The test and analysis charts were circulated, but it was clear from the start that the prevailing mood was hostile.

Hugh Pelham conducted a roll-call, and Donald asked all of those not entitled to be in the room to kindly leave. It was, he said a meeting for captains of colleges or their representatives, and for Old Blues in residence.

It was not, he said, for the Press, nor for anyone else from the outside. Landale of Balliol was instantly on his feet pointing out that the captains' meeting on Sunday had been open to all members of the current squad. Someone else shouted to enquire why Donald was allowed to invite people to speak when no one else was. Donald replied, 'You have asked for a complete selection report.

How can you have one without the chief coach and chairman of the coaches' meeting being present?' Derek Hayward of Wadham immediately asked for another squad member to be invited. Donald refused, pointing out that Stewart and Clark were already present.

The minutes were then read for the captains' meeting which Donald had chaired ten days before, and which had given him a motion of confidence. And once more Hayward was on the attack, demanding to know whether a 'murmur of approval' was considered then to have been a vote of confidence. This was allowed and formally deleted from the record. It was obvious that we would have our backs to the wall on every point raised or answered during this evening.

Donald then went through the chain of events that had brought them to this point, and asked Dick Fishlock, who had chaired the crucial coaches' meeting at Leander, to confirm the accuracy of the President's account of the mutiny, which he did without reservation.

He stated that as an Old Blue, and an Olympic oarsman, he believed that Oxford had the best set of coaches in the country, and that he had known the President for three years. It was he said outrageous to suggest that he would conspire to lie and cheat and that he had acted honourably and with good conduct throughout his entire Presidency. The OUBC was fortunate, said Dick glaring out at the meeting, to have such a man for President and such a team of coaches.

Donald briefly explained his responsibilities, and the duties of the coaches against whom, he added rather acidly, there had never been any such allegations of dishonesty in previous years.

I then outlined to them the process of selecting a Boat Race crew, of the disagreements and grudges which are bound to crop up now and again when people are so strung out and under pressure. I also spoke about the impossibility of always appearing completely fair to everyone all the time, for athletes invariably believed they were better than the next man. I also described the fine lines of merit against which we must work. Selection depended on a coach's experience, intuition and constant monitoring. It's never cut and dried. I explained the strength imbalance we had this year between our strokeside and bowside, and how difficult people always ran the risk of being dropped, because of the over-riding need for tight team spirit. The Oxford selection system was considered to be one of the fairest because it was so exhaustive and thorough.

I told them how the Boat Race is different from any other rowing race because of the severe endurance aspect, the very challenging course and the high pressure publicity it attracts. I let the captains know that it had been especially difficult this year to convince the oarsmen that this was so, and that specific training was needed. I said that the whole programme had been resisted on the very first day, and many times since by a small cabal of oarsmen. If there was one thing I had learnt coaching Oxford, it was that you cannot, must not, compromise on the training. For that way lay complacency and ultimately defeat.

'One member of this squad was the core of this disruption,' I said, 'and he has been dropped because of it. The dispute has proved to be the most damaging ever to Oxford rowing and if it continues I really don't have much further wish to go on coaching here.'

The chair was then handed over to Dr Michael Barry, who formally expressed his support for Donald. Instantly a voice shouted from the floor that since he was in the chair he should not express opinions. Dr Barry ignored this and read out a crucial statement relayed through Steve Royle from Mike Spracklen, in which he made four points:

1. He confirmed his support for the selection decision.
2. He would have been happy to go ahead and coach the crew in the line-up announced.
3. He confirmed his support for that crew being under the direction of the President and current Chief Coach.
4. He would not be available to coach any other crew than the one under that directorship.

While I listened to its contents gratefully, I could not help comparing it with his previous public position.

Then questions were invited from the floor and we sat forward to take the anticipated barrage head-on. And we were not disappointed. Wadham was up demanding to know whether Donald felt that I should have the task of ultimately selecting the crew. Brasenose College accused us of a massive communications breakdown, and a lack of trust between the rowers and the coaches. What about a compromise, he asked?

I stepped in and told them of the compromises already made, of all the American promises after each confrontation that it would never happen again. Of the 'hothouse plant' who now sat in the meeting, and his refusal to train or row where he was asked. As for the charge of a lack of communications, I said that the squad were issued with a detailed weekly programme and I had specifically gone through the whole year programme with them at their request on a number of occasions. They were the best-informed Oxford squad I had ever dealt with. The problem was they chose not to hear.

Up jumped St Benet's, voice of the Benedictines, demanding to know why Clark 'was acceptable on Saturday one week, and then a week later not acceptable.' 'Simple,' I replied; 'he refused to row in the seat he'd been picked for.'

Then Clark stepped in mentioning the case of Tony Ward. Donald hit back, but now his Vice-President was on his feet. Gavin Stewart began to talk about the seat racing issue, about promises made to Ward in Spain that he would be seat raced against Clark, how badly managed it all was, how appallingly the OUBC had treated people over the years. Donald tried to answer. Gavin interrupted, accusing him of doing things in a 'morally unconscionable way.' Donald snapped back 'My apologies . . .' at his Vice-President, the man who was allowed to be in this room only by virtue of his acceptance of a role 'to assist the President.'

For one nerve-wracking moment I thought Donald was going to actually lambast him, 'Judas', right in front of everyone, and he told me later he had given the matter serious consideration.

I remembered Ian Elliott's straightforward solution of the night before and thought how appropriate it would be.

But now someone else was shouting out: 'Since the crew now seems to have taken over, does this not point to a lack of expertise?'

And someone else called out: 'If boat speed is more important than personality, why are you all talking about Chris Clark's personality?'

I explained that it was all about compatibility and reliability not personality.

'Then surely if Chris Clark was incompatible, the crew would not be objecting to his omission, as they are now?'

'We have been told the coaches lie to the oarsmen. Is this true?'

Donald vainly insisted that the coaches did not lie. But the tide was threatening to engulf him. Graham Jones stood up, and caused a temporary calm, but he spoke in platitudes, with no firm statement for any of us. He left half-way through the meeting. I was bitterly disappointed in him.

Now Landale, one of the ringleaders, joined the torrent of accusations: 'Surely if the crew felt strong enough to walk out there must be some truth in their allegations.'

I tried to describe the extent of the influence of this strong vociferous group we had this year, how used to political in-fighting they were. But it was pretty futile because no one was really interested in hearing the answers. They were out for blood. Now they were going at it all together, shouting questions from compiled notes about the ergometer tests. Had Donald re-done one to make himself look better? Why was Clark's test done later than the others? Clark himself was proclaiming the crew were not willing to row without Ward. 'Why should he be dropped?' he asked.

I joined the fray once more, shouting back at Clark: 'Why should someone like you be fighting for a marginal seat? You should be in the stern four if you had done the training like everybody else. Ward is very marginal, and you made yourself marginal too. This is all idiotic and you know it. Donald is way ahead of both of you – just look at the evidence.'

But now someone was demanding to know 'Why was there no further testing after the marginal seat racing at Henley?' 'Something has clearly gone badly wrong!' 'The crew want further testing for Clark'. 'The coaches cannot be certain in their judgement.'

However many times we tried to answer, they just kept coming back. It was a bombardment technique which swamped our answers and made any objective assessment by the uncommitted captains impossible. If someone could have forced a 'no confidence' vote right now, we would have lost for certain. The one crash-barrier currently holding us back from extinction was that Donald had made it clear from the beginning that he would accept no motions from the floor. As President he had the right to dictate the format of the meeting. They had asked for a report on selection and that was all they would be allowed to seek. But we could find no independent voice to speak up for us, and the tide of opinion was now running swiftly as the Radley current, in favour of the mutineers.

Our words were falling upon ears that would not hear. But suddenly there was a momentary hush in the hall as a resonant, but unfamiliar American voice asked permission to speak on behalf of the Boat Club of Campion Hall. And every eye in that room turned towards Michael Suarez.

'There has been much talk tonight,' he said, 'about the principles of just government and the manner in which communication breakdowns can destroy team unity. But now perhaps we might get down to the facts. The true question before us this evening, the question each and every captain must ask himself, or indeed herself, is this – has Donald Macdonald discharged his duties as President of the OUBC with competence and integrity?

'I refer you to the training sheets which give a statistical summary of the many tests undergone by the Blue Boat candidates. And I would like to remind the meeting, if I may, of three relatively simple facts.

'Number one – in the overall placings Macdonald finishes first. Easily. Clark finishes ninth. Fifth among the weaker bowside men.

'Number two – in sculling boats, which the coaches value so highly, Macdonald is first by miles. Clark is nowhere near him.

'Number three, all of Clark's results are DOWN on his performances last year. All of Macdonald's are UP.

'Is there anyone in this room who would select Clark over Macdonald? Because if there is, I suggest with the greatest of respect that you may be leaving yourself open to ridicule.'

The silence was practically deafening. 'Ladies and gentlemen,' he continued. 'These results clearly prove Macdonald to be both a highly competent oarsman, and the kind of President who leads his team by example, by being the best. Again and again he has produced winning results'. And his voice rose as he demanded: '*Is there anyone in this room who is prepared to say the same of Christopher Clark?*'

No one spoke. No one uttered a sound – though I very nearly stood up and cheered. He continued relentlessly: 'That Mr Clark has not achieved a standard of fitness comparable to that of his team-mates, is self-evident from these figures taken from Mr Topolski's record book. That Mr Clark is divisive should be readily apparent from the very existence of this meeting.

'But whether the cause of his substandard performance, both on and off the water, was injury, inability or attitude, does not concern us here. And certainly it was *only fair* that Clark and his gang should appeal Macdonald's decision to drop him from the boat, since there was a potential conflict of interest.

'But who are we to contest the considered opinion not merely of Macdonald himself, but of the overwhelming majority of Oxford's coaches? *Would that too be fair?*

'The rebels pledged they would abide by the coaches' decision. Now they threaten to walk out – *is that also fair?*

'And yet, these events bring us together tonight to question the integrity of Donald Macdonald'. And his voice rang around the room as he demanded: *'How can that possibly be fair?'*

At this particular moment no one felt like taking on Michael Suarez, though for the first time I began to hear some murmurs of agreement. The Jesuit's next words were a major surprise for those who had not met him. 'When I captained the England regional lacrosse team,' he said, 'we were competing for places on the lacrosse World Cup squad. I realize that in this country lacrosse is only a minor sport, but my coaches and selectors would never have tolerated Clark's behaviour. *Never*. By what right, then, can Christopher Clark expect to wear the Dark Blue of Oxford in the greatest boat race in the world?

'I ask you not to be taken in by the rebels' references to the way things are done in America. I assure you nobody over there would have endured the activities of Mr Clark for as long as Macdonald and Topolski have. And he knows it, as well as I do.

'Indeed, if the competence of our President is to be challenged, then I myself challenge him, not for excluding Clark, but for *keeping* him on the squad for so long, when he was neither fit, nor contributing to the morale of the team.

'Christopher Clark,' said Michael Suarez. 'You and your friends have done serious damage to the OUBC because of your own selfishness. You are an *embarrassment to this university – you are an embarrassment to your sport – and you are an embarrassment to the United States of America*. I suggest that you accept your failure like a man.'

He paused, for perhaps ten seconds, and everyone exhaled. It was as if we had all been holding our breath while his words slammed around the room. He spoke again, quietly now, but his audience was helpless.

'Fellow captains,' he said. 'This is not the time to be fighting among ourselves. While we argue, Cambridge is preparing to defeat us again. Now is the time to give our full support to Donald Macdonald and his coaches. Now is the hour for us to set aside our differences, and set our sights on victory over Cambridge.'

As he concluded his remarks the lady sitting next to him waded into the attack – Zaza Horne, the 5ft 9ins blonde most coaches regarded as one of the best woman rowers in Oxford and an Olympic trialist. She glared at Clark and scoffed at his stand on the twin principles of Tony Ward and boat speed. 'Where were his principles last year,' she asked, 'when Tony Ward was thrown out for Graham Jones? Clark has said at this meeting that he only rows in boat races for fun, and I for one think that is an example of his wrong attitude.'

Clark swung round on her. 'This is just a bloody boat race,' he said. 'Not the game of life. I have to enjoy what I am doing. Why should I feel guilty about what happened to Tony Ward last year?'

Zaza, inspired by Michael Suarez, now warmed to her task and she retorted: 'Look, I row for Oxford University Women's Boat Club. I have been out there. I know what it takes too you know. But I would never have you in my crew because I wonder whether you have the balls for it.'

Once more the room went absolutely silent. Zaza seemed uplifted by her own success, and she added: 'I don't know why you're so big on this moral stand . . . and . . . this claim that the race is just for fun. It is not for fun, and I just don't think you have any idea what this race means to all of us. You have the wrong attitude.'

Now Gavin Stewart stepped forward to try and save the day for his American friends, but the words of Suarez and Zaza had been devastatingly effective. The big Wadham College man strove manfully to recount his life as a rower, told the meeting he was doing it for his parents, but then made the mistake of admitting that he did not really believe in it any more. I had told him that in three years I had helped him virtually to reach international level and now he was saying that none of it was of any consequence.

Right at this moment another powerful independent voice was raised on our behalf as the distinctive figure of Bruce Philp, last year's President, began to speak. 'We can sit here and argue till kingdom come,' he said. 'But it won't get us anywhere. Neither will arguing every one of the coaches' decisions. Look, I have rowed for both Cambridge, and Oxford. I have been picked, dropped, rowed for the reserves. I've won and I've lost. In this game you just accept it. If you get dropped, for whatever reason, you just accept it. If they pick you, you row. That's all there is to it. And if some of you guys could get that through your heads, you'd find life a whole lot simpler.'

Then Rob Clay added his own typically uncompromising remarks in defence of the President and the training programme that he said had worked so well for Oxford over the years. For another hour-and-a-half the arguments went back and forth. And bit-by-bit the vituperative attacks of the hardcore of antagonists became counter-productive as they began to alienate the meeting. Slowly but surely the mood of the meeting swung as the combined reasoning of Suarez, Zaza and Bruce took hold.

Finally Julian Beck, the big Rugby-playing captain of St Peter's climbed to his feet and declared: 'I was one of the original signatories to the letter demanding we should have this meeting. But I have sat for a long time listening carefully to all that has been said and I have changed my mind completely. In fact if I were Dan Topolski, sitting up there being attacked on all sides for winning ten out of the last eleven Boat Races, I would gather up my stuff and walk right out of here now, and I'd never come back.

'How can we possibly sit here and risk losing him? We cannot allow this lunacy to go on a moment longer. It is obvious after three hours of discussion that Dan and his team are completely in the right. Anyone can see that. And I suggest that we do something very quickly to stop them all from leaving us. And I would like to propose a motion which endorses the work of both Donald and Dan.' The President nodded his assent.

Immediately there was an objection from the floor. 'You said you would take no motion from the floor.'

Donald snapped back: 'Correct. I'll take it from the podium. Perhaps Dave Foster will propose it'. The Balliol man did so instantly, proposing that the meeting pass a vote of confidence in the President of the Oxford University Boat Club. The St Peter's captain loudly seconded it. And a ballot was taken.

The Chairman and the President did not vote. And within a few minutes Dr Barry read out the result. 'Those in favour of the President twenty-eight, those against the motion, eleven.'

Christopher Clark stood up and stormed out of the room. He had lost and for him it was all over. There really was no more that his friends could do for him now.

Donald was back in full command of the Boat Club, and this time it was for keeps. As we walked out through the ancient halls of my old college, I felt it was suitably appropriate that Jacob Epstein's statue of Lazarus, returning from the dead, should be standing eerily just a few yards away in the college chapel. Somehow we had done it, and the only remaining hurdle left for us to overcome, apart from Cambridge, was whether the Americans would once again rally around Clark and renege on their promises to row which they made so reluctantly on Sunday night.

The answer was not long in coming. When Donald drove the van into Oriel Square at one o'clock the next day, he was met by Dan Lyons, who told him with regret that he was suffering from a rare disease which affects Americans over 6ft 4ins living near to Oriel Square. In short he, in company with Huntington, Penny and Fish (he was at least 6ft 5ins in his own mind) would not be rowing today. Donald replied that he was sorry to hear that, and left for the river. Events had turned out as he had forecast, either they all rowed or none of them would.

So that was the end of them. After all the trouble they had caused for so long, it was now to be finished at last. One of the great Boat Race crews would never be, and now we were left to pick up the pieces with a crew that was bitterly and irrevocably divided. The Americans would not of course be going home. They trained in a Four in Oxford for the US trials and irony of ironies there was Chris Clark happily installed on the bowside at 3. They would stay here still lobbying, keeping the poison flowing. But Donald no longer had to take any notice of them, or of anyone outside his own team. He was immovably in the driving seat. But our morale was crushed – all of us were shell-shocked, and the Boat Race was only seven weeks away.

Could we recover and win? Not a chance. But maybe we could recover enough to put up some kind of a show. It would depend on how quickly the crew could revive their spirit and blend into a fighting unit. We needed to go out and beat some crews quickly. But in all honesty we did not have the personnel. For the 1987 race we would field a boatload of rookies, and while victory was almost certainly out of the question, it was my task to see that Oxford was not humiliated.

Donald went home, a flat sense of relief mixed with sadness upon him. His vision of leading one of the greatest boat crews to victory was shattered. He had won the battle, but the war was not yet over. The residents of Lime Road heard an unfamiliar sound as the hour approached midnight. It was the sound of Scotland, as Donald took up his bagpipes, with their green tartan of Macdonald of the Isles, and played that most haunting lament, the Dark Isle, in memory of his broken dreams.

CHAPTER TWELVE

ARRIVAL OF THE NO-HOPERS

As a fighting unit Oxford were unreceptive, bloody-minded, resentful and unfriendly. For the first time ever I could not bring myself to stay in the crew house, with its deadly pall of defeat. And each night, after dinner, I took myself thankfully home.

We had lost the heart of the crew – the stern three of Huntington, Lyons and Penny. In their place would be three vastly less experienced men. We summoned Paul Gleeson to stroke the boat, Hull we put to 7 and Stewart sat at 6. Behind him were the two most seasoned oarsmen, Cadoux-Hudson at 5 and Macdonald at 4. Ward and Pelham at 3 and bow would now be included and the only American, the novice Peter Gish would complete the line-up at 2. Andy Lobbenberg was promoted to cox the boat.

It was not the worst crew in the world by any means. I had probably coached two or three other Oxford crews of the same standard in the past fifteen years and had got them to the finishing line first against ostensibly better Light Blue boats. But this year Cambridge had a top-class Eight, and I had not faced such a gaping discrepancy between the two university boats before.

What was perhaps worse, was that we were also labouring under an atmosphere of total discontent. The ugly ungracious sniping continued, as if to ensure that the wounds should not be allowed to heal. After our first outing together, Hull felt obliged to remark to the Press that it was like driving a mini-car, after a Rolls-Royce. The same individual was also quoted in the Oxford University newspaper *Cherwell*, which had uncritically supported the rebel cause throughout, without once contacting the President or myself, for the other side of the story: 'Everybody who took part in the seat race felt very, very strongly that it had been rigged. There is a lack of trust in Topolski, and a lack of confidence in Macdonald. It is inadvisable to have a President who is marginal for the Boat.'

In the same article Ward was quoted as saying: 'Macdonald and Clark are not in the same class. You cannot compare a good club oarsman with an international. Morale has taken a tremendous blow. If we already had our Blues, we would not be rowing at all. Our boat is nothing like the same – it is perhaps eight lengths slower.'

Mike Spracklen was quoted too: 'The only way to get the Americans back is if the President is forced to resign. Topolski and Macdonald see honour and respect for the OUBC as more important than picking the best team.' In the *Sunday Times*, Richard Burnell picked up the Spracklen quote and added: 'I fancy more loyal Oxford supporters than Spracklen will be echoing the words: "Me too".'

As a result the crew, still under Hugh Matheson, were required to give an undertaking not to speak to the Press any more. If they could not behave with dignity they would have to be treated accordingly. It was a hopeless situation.

Meanwhile Robin Geffen, the representative of St Benet's, signed a further proposal, seconded by Will Landale of Balliol, to convene *another* captains' meeting. They demanded a motion to change the constitution of the Boat Club, allowing a secret ballot to be used for a vote of 'no confidence' against 'any officer or member of the committee who must then "resign immediately".'

Fish went into print with an exclusive signed article over two-feet long in *The Times*, resplendant under the headline: 'Ideals of the Boat Race Just A Myth.' In this little epic he confirmed that the mystique of the Boat Race representing honesty, fairness and sportsmanship, had been found by him and his friends 'not to be true.'

He pointed out how proud his parents would be of his decision not to participate, 'because only they know how much I really wanted to beat Cambridge and earn my Blue.'

And of course, having castigated Donald and me, he made the cry of all strikers: 'All we have ever asked for is Clark be included in a fair selection process.' He did not mention anything about Clark's activities over the four months when everyone else WAS involved in a fair selection process. But that was water under the keel. The Americans had gone. His article earned him a flood of stinging rebukes in the letter columns of the newspaper.

So the divisiveness remained. Gavin Stewart's 'conscience' was finally focussed upon himself and he resigned as Vice-President. Duncan Clegg, the London representative of the Boat Race and a past President wrote to congratulate Donald on his victory at the meeting and said that 'public opinion is almost totally on your side.'

Richard Burnell wrote: 'I am delighted that you got your vote of confidence without having to ask for it. Please tell Ruth we all owe her a debt of gratitude. You have both had a very rough ride.'

Ronnie Howard's letter confirmed how worried the rowing establishment had been that Donald would be overthrown and he added: 'Last night's meeting was your triumph and made all the dreadful occasions of the last two weeks worth enduring. I am delighted with the outcome and thoroughly humbled by my inability to offer worthwhile advice.'

The Press of course went wild with excitement: 'Rebels No To Oxford' – 'Reserves Step Up As Yanks Snub President Again' – 'Walkout Scuppers Oxford' – 'Unseemly Waste Of A Good Crew' – 'Oxford's Rebels Sacked' – 'The Cruel Cost Of Mutiny' – 'Boat Race Rebels Ditched By Macdonald' – 'The Great American Disaster – And The Great British Institution' (this on the top of the sports page of *The Times*).

Burnell took Spracklen to task in the *Sunday Times*. *Newsweek* ran a half-page article entitled 'Mutiny on the Thames'. And Landale of Balliol wrote again to Macdonald, still demanding a re-match at a captains' meeting and insisting that a motion be included: 'That this meeting deplores the Anti-American sentiments expressed by the President and his coaches, and affirms that the OUBC is for all members of the University to row together regardless of colour, creed or nationality.'

Donald wrote back angrily: 'Your statement is neither proposed, nor seconded, and furthermore it is defamatory. Were I to put your charge before a captains' meeting I would be publishing a defamatory statement which I am not prepared to do. I invite you to

withdraw it or particularize the allegation.' This elicited an immediate retraction full of abject apologies. Another captain wrote to
explain how they had been constantly lobbied by the rebels: 'we
were a bit awestruck by them at the time,' he said.

And so it went on. Reed Rubin, the 'yankee' rebel leader in
Ronnie Howard's year phoned to say he wanted to fly the Atlantic
next day with Charlie Grimes the American Olympian who was
dropped by coach 'Jumbo' Edwards for wearing a cap in the boat in
1959. They wanted to mediate. 'We'll take you and Huntington to
lunch in Leander and we'll thrash this out.' I said I appreciated his
concern but that sadly it was too late now. 'It's hopeless,' I told him.
'We'd all sit there with me and Hunt in tears wishing it could all be
different.' We spoke for half-an-hour and I wished he had made his
offer a month earlier. Jim Rodgers, the American cox of the 1966
crew, also sent messages of support.

Mark Evans, one of the Canadian gold medal twins at the Los
Angeles Olympics, who rowed for Oxford in 1983 and 1984, also
now got in touch and spent over an hour looking for ways in which
to reinstate two of the Americans who were rumoured to have
reconsidered their position. His interest as an Oxford man was to
win the Boat Race. 'Dan you can't do it with this crew.' 'Probably
true,' I replied, 'but it's the only crew I've got.' I explained at length
the trauma we had been through and why it was just not possible to
re-open the affair. We had come too far. It would simply all begin
again: 'Don't underestimate them. They really cannot be trusted.' I
told him too that his intervention would have been constructive and
very welcome a few weeks earlier, he acknowledged that there was
little else we could do now but go with what we had. 'It's going to
be lengths and lengths,' he said as he rang off.

But now the Oxford Union, the private debating society of the
University, was recruited as a final attempt to rally support. They
decided to get involved and tabled a motion that 'This House
believes the Oxford University Boat Club has mishandled the
organization of the Boat Race crew.' Both Donald and I declined an
invitation to attend. It would be another trial by the mob, and we
were not inclined to fight the battle again. We now had to
concentrate all our energies on the imminent Boat Race.

Christopher Dodd of the *Guardian* wrote a major story on the
day of the debate, using the occasion to rekindle the old issue of the
Clark–Macdonald battle for the 2-seat. 'Clark came out of the test

(the seat race) better than Macdonald'. He also printed a quote from Spracklen which contradicted his statement to the captains' meeting. As a newspaperman, and a non-oarsman, his interests were obviously best served by fanning these flames. But if he had been in my place he would have been praying they would finally flicker and die, leaving Macdonald and me to carry the coffin of Oxford's hopes to the Tideway.

The debate at the Union was addressed by Chris Penny who told the assembled gathering that he and his colleagues were 'rocket fuel'. And he added: 'Donald Macdonald is a nice guy but he is not the rocket scientist that's needed to control this stuff.' The motion was virtually unopposed save by a group of witty debating regulars who knew even less about the issues under debate than the assembled throng. Someone phoned me later that night to confirm that the Union had passed, by an overwhelming majority of 153–10, the motion that the organization of the Boat Race crew had been mishandled. They also told me about Chris Penny's remarks.

'Yeah,' I sighed, 'the same rocket fuel that finished twenty f - - - ing eighth in the Fours Head of the River.' The barrage of words which the Union now levelled at the Boat Club, just served to cause more trouble, more argument and more divisiveness.

Back on the freezing Henley Reach we fought to put the crew into some sort of shape. It was not easy. The returned rebels were preoccupied with their regrets at losing the crew of their dreams. Stewart, Hull, and Ward seemed to hate nearly everyone. They did though forge friendships with Gish and Gleeson while ostentatiously ostracizing Donald. This internal hatred, mixed with guilt and anger at the failure of the mutiny, was tearing at them day and night. They appeared to hate themselves too for wanting their Blues so much that they had, in their view, betrayed their American friends. The Americans had however 'absolved' them of responsibility and were now, they claimed, encouraging them to go ahead and row.

On the river Hugh Matheson was in charge, and his was the most thankless task. First of all he hardly knew the crew and he was now, during this difficult time, trying to build bridges, mend mangled egos and give courage to this totally divided group. Apart from his obvious urbanity and sophistication he had been one hell of an oarsman. At Henley in 1978 he beat the West German, World

Champion Peter-Michael Kolbe, one of the two great scullers who have dominated the world stage these past twelve years.

Hugh possessed unlimited enthusiasm, self-confidence and even a touch of arrogance. In my view he was just the man for this job, but the task was proving monumental. Most of the crew did not believe for a moment that we could win, though Hugh Pelham would never admit to such a thought and the indomitable Cadoux-Hudson never accepted defeat. Donald was concerned mainly with recovering and I told him to forget about rowing hard for a while. He had been through a lot and did not need any additional pressure. I wanted to give him time to get his strength back.

There were still minor political machinations going on, and some of the captains used the Union debate as a springboard to call for yet more meetings. The name Geffen was still high on the list of objectors but Landale had grown tired of the fray and faded from the picture.

Donald gave them very short shrift and concentrated on getting back into shape.

Hugh's heavily-interrupted two week stint of coaching was due to end at the weekend with a series of races against our big rivals, the University of London. We had beaten them by around a length-and-a-half in a similar fixture a month earlier, but we were a very different Oxford line-up now. UL were a powerful crew of youth and senior internationals. We had missed ten days of training and were bedding down a new crew. We were demoralized and ill-prepared. A chief coach more sensible than I would have cancelled the whole thing; but I have always believed in going out and dealing with whatever is thrown at you, whatever the handi-caps. No mercy asked or given. You had to be prepared for anything in the Boat Race because it was so unpredictable and my Oxford crews had learned the lessons well in the past. 'I don't want any excuses,' I would tell them. 'Remember there is no shame in defeat, only in the manner of the defeat. My intention is to turn you lot into hard, aggressive bastards.'

The day of the race was cold and we were scheduled to row a series of three-minute pieces up by Barnes Bridge and along to Kew Gardens. Ward was out sick and Hugh Matheson himself had to row for us in his place. We lost the first race by half-a-length, but dropped nearly two lengths in the second. There was a bellow of fury from the middle of the boat and I heard Hugh giving them a round of abuse. He accused them of being pathetic and wet, and showing no fight. It worked, and on the next piece we finished level, with Hugh pulling in the 5 seat for all he was worth. But then we lost the last two races and Hugh came off the water shaking his head in frustration. 'It's a bit gutless,' was all he would say. The following day London University were dominant, beating us by around one-and-a-half lengths on each of three seven-minute rows.

Everyone was very despondent. But I was encouraged for I had expected worse. On this evidence we were about three lengths slower than the Oxford crew that had beaten London the previous month. That would be hard but not impossible to make up; it was, though, nothing like as bad as the eight lengths the defeatist Ward had suggested in *Cherwell*.

Now the crew came under the care of John Pilgrim-Morris, the former Olympic coach who had spoken so authoritatively and supportively at the St John's crew meeting. JPM (as everyone knew him) was still a hard man in a sculling boat, but his value to us was in the field of refinement, for he is a wise technician. His tasks with this crew were many. He had to work on Pelham's rough but aggressive technique, try to get the stiff-backed Hull to become more flexible, to get Stewart to move more athletically and more explosively in the boat, and try to put a lifetime's experience into Gish and Gleeson in two weeks.

He met with some success for they looked a much smoother unit when they next arrived on the Tideway for our regular twice-monthly fixture.

This time we were scheduled to race Bedford Star, one of the best provincial crews. These informal weekend training races against good club and national squad crews have been the bedrock of Oxford's success in the past because they gave us much-needed racing experience and they also helped the boys to get used to the treacherous water of the London Tideway. They learnt to respect it, to handle it, and not to fear it.

It does have an intimidating effect with its swift currents and heavy swells, and in my view you can never get enough of it. One of my main jobs is to help the guys overcome their anxieties on this water, to teach them how to deal with the fierce little eddies that throw a crew around, especially near the Bridges. I show them how to change gear when they come out of calm water and into sudden rough conditions; that is where I always call for a power-twenty, driving them into it, hard and vicious.

John Bertrand, who captained *Australia II* to victory in the 1983 America's Cup, says something very similar about the sea. 'Dan,' he said, 'when the water's calm we sail like cats, very stealthy, very cunning. When it comes up rough, we sail like tigers, splitting the waves, driving forward into the spray, total aggression.'

The theory is the same, you smash your way forward when the others might hang back, intimidated by the conditions. Most crews go soft when they hit rough water. Mine never do. You can usually steal a few quick feet for free from an unsuspecting crew.

On the Saturday, a month before the Boat Race, the boys rowed well against the gutsy Bedford Eight, stroked by the World Junior silver medallist Jonathan Singfield. We matched them in short sprints, and in the last race we beat them by a couple of lengths. On the Sunday we raced them again, this time for seven minutes and they beat us by a length. Oxford went well for the first minute matching the club crew nicely, but when the Bedford crew began to increase the pressure, it all fell apart. Gish put his shoulder out, and Hull and Stewart said they were not feeling well.

On this rather downbeat note Steve Royle, the civil engineer who had been helping Oxford for a decade, took over the crew for the penultimate fortnight. They would train on the long broad stretch of the Thames above the little town of Pangbourne, some fifteen miles upstream from Henley. Here the Oxford crew would begin to hone their speed, and Steve had permanent 500 and 1,000 metre marks placed along the river banks. This gave him an accurate guide to the current speed of the crew compared with those of the past six years.

He raced them hard in a series of carefully-timed sprints and found that they were travelling surprisingly fast, though you would not have known it from their downcast demeanour. They had no belief in themselves and seemed to be just going through the motions. Although they were a couple of seconds down on the very good crews of 1981, '83 and '84, they were faster than '82, and on a par with the boys of '85, who had lacked real talent but had fought Cambridge like tigers.

Halfway through Steve's fortnight we entered them for the Reading Head of the River, traditionally an important race for us. Back in 1968 when I was rowing in my second Oxford crew we lost at Reading by *one* second to the University of London, and our coach, the famous ex-pilot 'Jumbo' Edwards, went berserk at the sheer indignity of it. He made the most sweeping panic changes in the boat which scared the life out of us because we had thought we were great; and we lost the Boat Race by three-and-a-half lengths. London University, our conquerors, went on to represent Great Britain in the Mexico Olympics, which showed that we had not been that slow after all. Without the panic things might have been different.

We usually won this competition, although on a couple of occasions we had been pushed down to second place by a national squad group rowing as Leander. In 1987 there were some good crews competing and we knew we would have to beat London University and Leander to win over the winding and difficult three-mile course.

They raced in a blizzard and seemed to be moving the boat well enough. Afterwards, as I waited alone for the results to come up, I was feeling reasonably confident. As predicted, Leander won it and London University were second. But I had not expected to get beaten by Imperial College and Reading University who finished in joint third place. We finished fifth. I nearly jumped off Reading Bridge. 'Jumbo' would have shot himself.

This was the crew that in one week's time would be reporting to the Tideway for the final ten days of practice before the battle with Cambridge. Right now we'd just been beaten by Reading University. And I felt as if someone had finally signed our death warrant. Our main trouble was undoubtedly morale. There was a round-shouldered look to this crew. They were still at loggerheads with each other and every day the newspapers told them they were no good.

Their peers at the university and in rival crews looked at us all with pity. There was much smirking and regular cries of 'Poor old Oxford'. We had to push them through the training, but their hearts were not in it. They simply all believed they were going to lose. As a matter of fact so did I, but I never let on. I was not hypocritical enough to tell them they would win, but I never said they *could not* win.

Like most races this one was most likely, in the end, to come down to sheer guts but at this moment that sort of raw courage and self-belief were commodities we were tragically lacking. It was something I had only really encountered before in individuals and they did not stay around for long. But here it affected most of the crew and I did not yet know how to cope with it. The oarsmen were just too divided. The rift in there was too great, the hatreds too ingrained. It would for instance, be hard for Donald to forgive Hull and Stewart for their campaign against him. And his feelings towards that other political in-fighter from Oriel, Tony Ward, were hardly much different. In turn these three had taken a position which stood them firmly against me, the man who, in their eyes, had blighted the careers of their American friends, and against Donald, for fighting back.

Pelham and Cadoux-Hudson each quietly supported Donald and wanted to get on with the business of winning the Boat Race. But Gleeson, of Hertford, and Gish, of Oriel, were both inclined to find friendship in the sniping atmosphere of the Oriel bar, and were in any event too inexperienced to have much effect on crew morale.

The crew returned to Pangbourne; and every day they rowed along the silent wooded stretch of water between the rolling hills, with Steve in the bows of the launch coaxing and rallying, trying his best to reconcile the warring parties in his crew. But he met with scant success.

I suspected that Cambridge must have been greatly enjoying the spectacle of our self-destruction; but in fact they were suffering some minor setbacks of their own. Jim Pew, their American Old Blue and the new British international Jim Garman had both come down with chicken pox while Paddy Broughton, another Blue and member of the British Eight, and Nick Grundy and Richard Spink had also been out of the boat for a few days through sickness or injury. But those problems apart, they had spent a productive winter on one of the most brutal stretches of river in England, the River Ouse near Ely, going through their usual relentless long distance work under the eagle eye of their visiting Canadian coach, Neil Campbell. This inspirational coach had masterminded the Canadian Olympic Eight's victory in Los Angeles with the two Oxford Blues, the Evans twins, on board, and he had helped Cambridge last year to their first Boat Race victory in eleven years. He was back again for 1987.

The rivers up there in the Fens are bleak and lonely, for they have high sides, like big deep ditches, and the weather, when the wind is out of the East, comes straight from the Urals. Cambridge think of themselves as the 'Hard Men' of the Fens after what they endure, and they always arrived on the Tideway believing themselves tougher than us. That suited me fine because it seemed to instil in them a mood of over-confidence.

That mood must have been reaching a high point at this time as they read about us in the papers, day after day, losing races, having rows and losing our best oarsmen. If I had been coaching them, I would have taken much care to guard against creeping complacency. My own problems were of course the precise opposite, and how very depressing it all was, as I began to make my final arrangements for Oxford's arrival on the Tideway.

As usual, I acquired a house from friends, where the crew would live for our final two weeks of preparation in London. Number 9 Ranelagh Avenue, overlooking Barnes Common, was a big house south of the river, well carpeted and with central heating. But there was one problem. It was completely empty – no furniture, no refrigerator, no nothing. But since my friends were charging us nothing, it seemed worth supplying all we needed ourselves. Before the crew arrived I ran myself ragged all over London – borrowing chairs, tables, sofas, fridges, plates, cutlery and all the rest of the kit a boat crew in hard-training would need.

I hired Cordon Bleu cook Louise Cutner who had helped us in the past; and Hugh Pelham borrowed a dozen beds from his old school in Oxford, and ferried them down to the house in the OUBC van. The only things the crew had to find were bed linen and blankets, which they all did reluctantly with much griping and moaning. As usual Donald, Hugh and I worked flat out to get things ready while Tom Cadoux-Hudson was busy at the hospital. But the rest made virtually no contribution at all. A sullen work-to-rule mood prevailed in which they were able to satisfy their bitterness with petty boorishness. It was sad to see what they had become for they saw these displays of truculent discourtesy as more important than beating Cambridge. They would sit in the van in sulking connivance while Hugh and Donald loaded the trailer and tied down the boat. It's your boat, your race, so you do it, they seemed to be saying; nothing to do with us. It was perhaps the only matter on which Clark and Macdonald would have agreed: 'This lot of freeloaders aren't here to win the race,' observed Donald in frustration, 'they're here simply to collect their Blues.'

Our budget for the two weeks in Putney was running low but Louise was adept at making the most of what she had and she bought in mountains of food. Like all rowing crews of relatively hard-up undergrads, they went crazy at the sight of so much free nourishment and ate far too much during the first three days. But the tiresome insolence continued and morale remained at rock bottom. The performance at Reading ranked easily as one of the worst by a Dark Blue crew in living memory. But it was further augmented by another beating on the Tideway, this time at the hands of the talented national lightweight squad from Nottingham on the day before we moved in to the house. It was Saturday 14 March, just two weeks to the Boat Race.

The men from the Midlands hit us four times, in three-minute pieces, matching Oxford off the start and then drawing clear. Between pieces Stewart, over whom the blackest cloud always seemed to hang, would hang his head and shake it gloomily from side to side. 'For Christ's sake, Gavin,' shouted Tom from the seat immediately behind him. He was getting exasperated with these displays of despair. 'Stop shaking your bloody head. Wake up and get a grip.'

The fact was we were utterly screwed up and whichever way I chose to tackle the conundrum things looked unlikely to change. We had no hope of beating Cambridge. Everyone knew it – the newspapers, the bookmakers (some of them were quoting Cambridge at 1–5) and the other coaches.

As a fighting unit Oxford were unreceptive, bloody-minded, resentful and unfriendly. They simply did not want to be here. They wanted to get their Blues two Saturdays from now, and get away as fast as they could. I could tell by the extraordinary amount of time they spent on the phone, in constant contact with the outside world, that they had no wish to be closeted here as a team. They were in residence in Putney under sufferance. They would give nothing extra, and acted like men working out their penance for having been on the losing side in a political war. Which of course they were.

Some nights a group of them would take off after dinner without saying anything, presumably to the pub. Not, I suspect, to drink very much, but just to get away from their team-mates.

One of the little Oxford rituals we had become accustomed to over the years, was a weekend by the sea halfway through the Putney training camp. John Wolfenden, an ex-Isis oarsman from my time at Oxford, invited us each year to his fine country hotel,

Peacock Vane in Ventnor on the Isle of Wight. He and his family looked after us for two days without ever charging us a nickel. The food was superb, nothing was too much trouble, and Wolfy enjoyed it all tremendously. He had never won a Blue, but he had rowed with great success for Isis and for his college, St Edmund Hall. His proudest moment had come when the 'B' Four he was rowing in beat its own college first boat, with the Oxford President Duncan Clegg on board, in the final of the University Fours. The weekend for Oxford was his way of contributing to our victories.

It was a very important contribution, because we walked along the beach and the cliff-tops as a team in splendid isolation from the world it seemed to weld us together, and for years the oarsmen loved it. Shealy, Rankov and the Evans twins always had a great time on the Isle of Wight, eating like kings, and revving the others up. I considered it a vital element in building our fighting spirit, and I was delighted to receive a letter from Wolfy to say that, although he had finally sold the hotel, he was keeping it open especially for us, for our annual weekend before the race.

Donald, Tom and Hugh Pelham felt it would be just the tonic to improve the atmosphere. But halfway through that first week, the others said they did not want to go. It was almost as if they were trying to divorce themselves from anything that represented the years of Oxford success that had preceded them. Or perhaps it was because they knew it was something I considered important. When Mark Evans came for an Old Blues dinner early in that first week he asked whether we would be going to Peacock Vane. Donald explained that the crew did not want to go. 'What?' cried Mark incredulously. Stewart sitting opposite looked a bit sheepish and said that they preferred to go and watch the womens' Boat Races in Henley. 'You guys must be crazy,' snorted Mark. 'That weekend with Wolfy is the main reason I rowed in the Boat Race!'

Half of them clearly resented themselves for being a part of this crew, and since the telephone was right outside my bedroom door, I became something of an expert on their various states of mind, as I heard them whingeing and whining down the phone to parents and friends.

I had to telephone Wolfy and cancel his generous offer, and it was around this time that I began to get royally fed up with the whole gang of them. They were, in their own wet way, nearly as bad as their mentors back in Oxford. I told Donald I was not planning to take much more of this rubbish without killing one of them. Occasionally, I would catch his eye and detect a sardonic amusement at the infantile charades of his crewmates.

Donald was now back at full strength and, despite so many of his crew refusing to speak to him at meals and refusing to have anything to do with him, I detected a return of that old spring in his step. The fact was Donald believed that somehow I could pull it off for them. I had done it before from an underdog position and he thought it could be done again.

Deep down there still glimmered for him that competitiveness, that hope which burns so strongly in all fighters. He spent hours by himself, churning over in his mind the awful sniping, and personal consequences he believed he would have to endure if we finally lost the Boat Race next week. 'The President who ruined one of the greatest Oxford crews, and then rowed to one of the most humiliating defeats in the history of the Boat Race.' He could hear it all, vividly. So could I.

But Donald would never give up. Tom Cadoux-Hudson also felt we had a chance even in the face of the growing mountain of evidence to the contrary. He was one of those men who never quits no matter what the odds, and he believed that no one could beat him in a close fight to the finish. Hugh Pelham's philosophy was that of a born scrapper. Cambridge might be good, but they were going to have to get past him first; and he was not going to let them do that.

Whatever fighting spirit that the others possessed had deserted them for there was little spark. Yet in the past they had shown spirit; they had won races, survived the early tribulations of selection. So how could I rekindle that fire? Was there time? Could I find the right buttons to press, the right words to inspire them? How best to concentrate their frustrations on the Light Blue enemy? Or were they just too far gone?

For the first four days of Tideway training I was on hot coals. It was a bad time, the worst ever. There was no response from them and I was virtually pleading with them to try harder. All I got in return were cold blank looks. For the first time ever I could not bring myself to stay in the crew house, with its deadly pall of defeat. And each night, after dinner, I took myself thankfully home.

Their arrival on the very first day had been the precursor of their prevailing attitude, because half of them had not bothered to put on their special-issue Blues' kit. For the last two weeks the crew usually liked to dress uniformly to stress their unity and I encouraged it, because they were now very much in the public eye. 'Jumbo' Edwards would have had a heart attack if he had seen them, some without their ties, not all wearing their Dark Blue scarves and big white initialled sweaters. It should be borne in mind though, that 'Jumbo' was a little eccentric on this issue. He threw Charlie Grimes, the great American oarsman and Olympic gold medallist, out of the Oxford crew altogether because he wanted to wear a striped flat cap while he rowed. 'It is quite impossisble to represent Oxford University properly,' he said, 'unless you *look* as if you are going to represent Oxford University properly.'

The Press were naturally out in full force reporting the arrival of the two crews, the Light and Dark Blues, in London. My launch driver Bert Green, a true London waterman, who was taught to row by the late great Ted Phelps, took one look at the crew when they set off on their first outing, and said: 'Yes . . . well, Dan, we've got a lot of work to do here, I'd say.'

For Bert that constituted something of a soliloquy, because he tends to be fairly economical with his words. But he and I understand each other well, and have known each other since I was a boy. Ted Phelps taught me to scull too and had taught Jumbo about the Tideway, and now that both were gone, Bert and I always felt that we were the main inheritors of that traditional relationship between some of rowing's most enduring families.

Bert was my right hand during this critical two weeks. He watches the Oxford crew like a marsh-hawk. He works as a boatman on the Thames when we are not here and he knows every ripple on these waters. Also he can tell me more about an oarsman by casting his eyes heavenwards at a crucial moment than most coaches can communicate on two sides of foolscap.

'Yes,' he added, 'a lot of work here, I'd say.'

In roughish water the crew paddled on up-river all the way to Chiswick. Every four or five minutes I gave them short bursts of speed work. On the way back they sprinted at Chiswick Steps, St Paul's School, Hammersmith and the Mile Post. Later we flung a rope out to the cox and practised a few starts off the launch, with Bert easing back in reverse to give them the feel of taking the strain against the running stream they would meet on the stake-boat on Boat Race day.

Generally speaking, at the end of that day Bert did not consider the 1987 Oxford crew would be in any danger of breaking the course record when they finally lined up against Cambridge.

There was however plenty of muscle in the boat. Indeed we were heavier per man than Cambridge, thanks largely to Gavin Stewart who was on schedule to become the heaviest man ever to row in the Boat Race. However, as a crew, we simply did not punch our weight, as they say in the fight game. We had all the power but not enough explosion.

I had hoped that the sense of occasion, which is always present on the Tideway once both crews are here, might put some fire into these Oxford bellies. But the only men who showed fire were the men who always showed fire, Donald, Hugh and Tom. However the Tideway was arousing in me all the old desires for battle. I kept looking at these big tough Dark Blue oarsmen, ambling around, moaning, and sullen, and I began to think to myself that there must be young men all over this country who would give their eye teeth to be in this position – ten days away from rowing in the Boat Race for Oxford.

The more I thought about it the angrier I grew with this bunch of ingrates. I decided that we would fulfil our racing fixtures against Imperial College on Wednesday, and against the crack Tideway Scullers on the Thursday, and if the results were anything like as bad as I knew they would be, I would make some major changes that would, I hoped, shock them into action.

As it happened I was about to embark on two of the most hideous days of my life as coach.

On Tuesday morning, 17 March, Donald left for the Tideway immediately after breakfast and formally challenged Cambridge University to a Boat Race. In the words of the ceremony he said: 'In accordance with the University Boat Race Charter, I, Donald Macdonald hereby challenge you, Stephen Peel, to select nine good men and true from the University of Cambridge to row against nine good men and true from the University of Oxford over four-and-a-quarter miles on the River Thames, London, from the University Boat Race Stone in Putney to Mortlake, on the championship course.

'On acceptance of my challenge we shall meet on the aforesaid River Thames at 12.15 p.m. on Saturday, the 28th day of March, when our skills and endurance will be put to the test, to see who will be victor. Do you accept my challenge?'

Stephen Peel replied: 'On behalf of the University of Cambridge I accept your challenge. And may the best crew win.'

Shortly after that rather poignant piece of tradition Oxford went out in rough water and put on one of their more moderate performances yet, constantly burying their lightweight reinforced plastic oars too deep, and lacking the rhythm that is critical for a big crew racing in these conditions.

I watched them glumly. It looked so fundamentally pedestrian. I could not even think of the adequate words with which to admonish them. Bert said: 'Yes, well, Dan I'd say they're not getting any better. There's no run to the boat.' I ordered them back to Putney, because as I looked at the Tideway that morning I began to harden up a plan that had been formulating in my mind for some days.

A major part of our trouble, I had concluded, were our American-made Dreissagacker plastic oars. They were grey in colour and stiffer and lighter than traditional wooden blades. I had grave doubts about their usefulness in rough, windy conditions; and so now I had the crew swap over to the wooden oars from the Isis crew before going out again. And to my eye there was an instant improvement. The boys felt it too.

The boat moved better, and the backswing of the blades seemed more definite. The catch was more positive and the oars were not plunging in quite so deep now. I was on to something here, of that I was certain. As soon as we docked I was back on the phone to Jerry Sutton, the oarmaker from upriver at Staines. I had touched base with him four days earlier to alert him of a potentially drastic decision.

Jerry is a very old friend of mine, despite the fact that I have disappointed him badly on two occasions in my life. The first was in a Tideway Scullers crew at Henley back in 1971. Jerry was rowing at 2 between Steve Royle and me, and in a neck-and-neck battle with Leander, he had collapsed and had to be carried out of the boat after the race, which of course we lost. They had to give Jerry oxygen on the bank and in the heat of the moment some of us behaved disgracefully, instinctively blaming him for our defeat, and turning away from him as he lay stricken on the bank. It was appalling, really, and I remain embarrassed about it to this day. But oarsmen who have fought that closely together understand each other, and Jerry and I have remained friends ever since.

The second time I disappointed him was in September of 1986 when I called to inform him that Oxford would probably not be using Sutton oars as usual in the Boat Race. 'I'm switching to the plastic Dreissigackers, Concept II,' I told him. 'I have a lot of Americans here, and they all think the plastic ones are lighter and more sensitive. Remember Cambridge beat us with them last year.'

Jerry was quite put out and he said to me, 'Dan, I honestly think you are making a mistake.'

And now I knew I had made it. And here I was, phoning him just ten days before the race to plead with him to make us a set of English wooden oars, best sitka spruce, with a strip of carbon down the middle to give stiffness. Somehow I had to have them by this weekend, and I was nearly out of money, so I could not even promise to pay for them.

'Bloody typical. Crawling back to your old friends now we've unloaded the Yanks are we? That's very nice, that is. He only wants a bloody free set of the best oars in the world. Mind you, you're right. I'm just surprised it took you so long.'

But Jerry's cheerful indignation shielded a passionate desire to see Donald and me win this race. He ended our conversation with the words: 'I don't know for the bloody life of me how I'm going to do this. But if I have to carve them myself all night by hand, you'll have 'em. Call me Thursday – and Dan, good luck, mate. Don't let 'em get you down.'

I put down the phone with immense relief, because our plastic oars had been worrying me for some time. In the back of my mind I always mistrusted them over the long distance of the Tideway race. I did not think these inexperienced boys could handle them under pressure. And I had a sixth sense that conditions would be horrendous on the day. It had been blustery, with rain squalls ever since Friday, and all my instincts were telling me to gamble on a very rough Boat Race.

It's a strange thing, but in heavy water, a wooden oar seems to have a life of its own, swinging back after the end of each stroke with what seems like a light flicking action. Probably because there is more weight out-board. As the boat runs underneath you, the oar seems to fly back and you always seem much more secure at the catch (the start of the new stroke).

I have used plastic oars myself in headwind conditions on the Tideway rowing for London Rowing Club and Tideway Scullers, and

I remember the aching which developed across my shoulders and upper arms after only about half-a-mile of racing. Holding those oars steady on the feather, with the wind blowing right at you is very tiring. There is something ungiving about plastic against plastic – and these days we race in plastic boats. But the combination of oars and boat made of the same synthetic material produces a harshness, a rigidity which is not there when either the boat or the oars are made of wood. All plastic is fine for an explosive power sprint over 2000 metres in good conditions but not so great over four turbulent miles.

I remember watching Cambridge racing against the Thames Eight two weeks before the 1986 Boat Race in rough water and a strong headwind. They could not get away from Thames and I could see then they were having difficulty controlling those plastic oars. They were working just as hard on the way back to the catch as they were through the water on the stroke. In my view those oars could easily be a liability to us, and I resolved not to use them for this Boat Race. Cambridge, though, were using them again this year.

The following day, Wednesday, the weather took a turn for the worse. The wind had swung around to the south-west and was blowing in fierce squalls down Putney Reach. The water was rough, enough to make novice oarsmen pale in fright and today we were going to race Imperial College. They had beaten us by five seconds at Reading, and their coach, the world silver medallist Bill Mason, had them really geed up for this race with us.

We buffeted our way to the start for our first four-minute piece. I noticed that Imperial College did not have splash boards fitted, and I thought they might find difficulty in the conditions. But they did not seem bothered, and both crews shot away to a good start. They raced line abreast hard for about fifteen strokes and then Imperial began to slip behind, their boat taking on water at every stroke. After thirty more strokes they began to founder, grinding to a halt, and the crew began to panic. But they struggled safely to the bank and dragged their waterlogged boat ashore.

I called over to Bill, 'Let's both go in and empty out and maybe we can get back out here in twenty-five minutes and give it another shot.' Bill signalled his agreement, and I called out to Oxford: 'Okay, paddle back, and we'll come out and race again as soon as Imperial are ready.'

At this point I received a howl of protest. Stewart shouted: 'No we're not going back – we've just beaten them!'

'What do you mean?' I yelled. 'You haven't beaten anybody. They nearly sunk.'

'Yeah, but we still beat them.'

'Don't be bloody ridiculous,' I called back. 'These fixtures are to help us beat Cambridge. We're here to train, to work. Not score silly points against crews which have filled up with water. Head back in, and be ready to row again in half-an-hour.'

There was much resentment. Stewart, the chief protester, was joined by Hull, Ward and Gleeson. They just did not want to go out again and race. I told them if Bill Mason had his boys dried out and were ready to race again it would be a complete disgrace if we were not prepared to face them. Finally they agreed.

We paddled back out to the start, and Imperial College thrashed us comprehensively. They took two-thirds of a length off us over two minutes, which infuriated me. Then they had two-and-a-half lengths off us over five minutes. Then we held them to a half-length. And finally they just tore us apart, taking two full lengths off us in a three-minute set piece. Again we showed little resistance. It was so depressing I could have wept.

The next day we were scheduled to race one of the best crews on the Thames, the experienced Tideway Scullers, with their crew of former internationals. I spoke after dinner that night to Donald about the total lack of fight in our Oxford Eight. 'It might help if I hit that big sullen Gavin Stewart squarely in the mouth – and I don't care how big he is,' said the President. 'He's like a monstrous rain-cloud hanging over this crew.'

It occurred to me how odd it was that throughout this whole business no one had actually resorted to fisticuffs out of sheer frustration. Athletes were, after all, pretty highly-strung creatures.

But we both had to face the fact that they did not seem prepared to have a go with another crew racing alongside them. I could not remember when we had last won a race against anybody with real authority, and I told Donald that something had to be done. We should consider throwing a couple of them out in favour of some of the Isis boys. 'Whatever we do cannot possibly be worse than it was today,' I said. How wrong I was. Because the next day would be a disaster of even more grotesque proportions.

We paddled out to the start to join the Scullers, who were stroked by Sverre Løken, the Norwegian world gold medallist, just the kind of opponent we did not need. The race was to be our last long trial piece before the big event, twelve minutes up to Chiswick Steps, and I did everything I could to fire them up, make them realize how important this two-thirds course was.

In return for my urgent exhortations they piddled off at half-cock. They had no desire to race. No fight, no guts.

The Scullers powered away off the start, completing their first stroke before Gleeson had moved. They were striking forty-four, and had a length before Donald and his boys knew what had hit them. We were on the Surrey station, in the best of the stream, but the Scullers just annihilated us, going four lengths in front as they shot Hammersmith Bridge, and finishing more than five lengths up when they eased at the Steps.

It was one of the worst defeats suffered by an Oxford Boat Race crew in my charge at this stage of their training. And what made it even more humiliating was the presence in the Scullers Eight of Matt Thomas at 2, and Mark Evans at 7, both former Oxford Blues. Bert just shook his head. At that moment something inside me snapped. I could no longer find it within myself to coddle them for a moment longer. I turned my head sideways to the wind and I bellowed at the top of my lungs: '*Wankers! You're a bunch of useless, gutless, wankers.*'

Their heads went down. And with my voice shaking with fury I said through the megaphone, 'That was pathetic, horrible. You had no acceleration. You showed no fight through the first mile, and before the Bridge I reckon you jacked it. Now we're going to row back from here right back to Putney and this time you're going to do some work. Because you have not done any f - - - ing work so far.'

All the way home I made them row a series of thirty-second and one-minute sprint pieces at ratings of forty and over. And it was remarkably good work. In the rough water they were really flying, which made me even angrier, because they could clearly do it if they wanted to. They were furious with me, furious with themselves, with life and with the Boat Race they now resented. They had been well and truly shafted and for once they took all their fury and frustration out on the oar handle and the blade in the water. When we finally docked at Putney they were dead on their feet.

The difference between this evening, and any other evening was that now I did not care one way or another what they felt. I did not give a damn what they wanted. As from this moment I was going to play it completely my way. If they didn't like it they could get out.

'Now listen to me . . .' I began.

'Oh, come on Dan, we're wet. Can we go and change?'

'*Sit down*' I roared.

They sat, and I proceeded to read them the kind of riot act I rarely inflict on my crews. I told them that we were not going to go on like this. There was evidence of far greater speed in the boat but their current sullenness was making it impossible for us to progress I said I still wanted to beat Cambridge whether they wanted to or not, and I told them I was going to make some big changes. They knew of course that two of the Isis boys, both Old Blues from recent Boat Race crews, Gavin Screaton and Rob Clay, were currently rowing very well in the reserve boat and that they both represented a possible threat to any one of the first boat incumbents. There was always the prospect that I could send a couple of them home, with no rowing Blue, after all. That would always shock a crew into line.

They sat before me, completely cowed by what had happened out on the river that afternoon. Their minds were racing – 'I hate Topolski. I hate Macdonald. I want my Blue, but do I want it this much?'

I said that I was prepared to keep faith with this line-up if there was a sea-change in their attitude. I told them I did not want to hear any one of them moaning ever again. I told them my changes would mean unfamiliar places in the boat for some but that each one of them was going to row precisely where he was told to row, not where he felt he ought to row. I told them I had had enough sulking from them to last me a lifetime. 'Where I tell you to sit does not matter. Every position in this boat is crucial. Some of you may feel demoted, but don't bother to mention it, because I am not interested in your personal pride. Judging by your performance out there today, not many of you have any.'

Tomorrow, I said, we are going to disappear. We are going upriver to get away from this pressure-cooker atmosphere here on the Tideway with all the Press watching our every move. 'I'll tell you where and when tomorrow. But the changes I propose are going to be made in private. You are to tell no-one of our plans. Not even our boatman.'

I finished by informing them that they were nothing like as bad as they thought they were, and that the sprints on the way home had been fast. They just did not show any spirit when there was another crew alongside and their mental attitude was causing that condition to become acute. I had previously coached crews that were not good enough to race, and I had even coached crews that didn't know how to race. I had actually rowed in crews that were too unfit to race. But I had never met one like this one, which simply lacked the heart to race.

CHAPTER THIRTEEN

THE FINAL DAYS

It was an extraordinary moment. Stewart did not want to answer. He did not want to admit the truth, and he had to fight the words out. I glanced at Donald and his hands gripped the oar tightly as he waited for the verdict of the strokeman who wanted him out of the crew.

On that bleak, rainswept Thursday night, with just nine days left before the race and with no semblance of morale left in the Oxford crew, I began to draw up the plan I hoped would win us the Boat Race. First I called the rowing master at St George's College, Weybridge, and asked him if he could keep a secret. Then I asked him if he would mind being host to the Oxford Blue Boat for a couple of days and help us avoid the Press. He loved it, and swore to tell nobody.

I called Jerry Sutton again and told him I needed the wooden oars as life itself on the following morning outside the St George's boathouse. Jerry promised they would be there, even though he would have to stay up all night painting and finishing them.

Then I phoned another old friend, Len Neville, an ex-club rower who makes riggers at Staines, and asked him to check over the light, three-stay aerofoil riggers he had constructed for our boat. They were very rigid, and made of alloy and had originally been designed by 'Jumbo' Edwards to cut through rough Tideway water. We had refined them and I would never dare to race a Boat Race without them. The usual five-stay round riggers tended to catch rough water and funnel it into the boat, but these were ideal for our specific purposes. They looked a bit odd and unwieldy and had been ridiculed as yet another Topolski eccentricity. But I had lost my first Boat Race as a coach because I had not used them and I always keep a photograph of that struggling waterlogged 1973 crew on my wall to remind me never to go out improperly dressed again. The Boat Race had never been postponed because of unrowable conditions so I had to be prepared for any eventuality. We would use those riggers nine days from now.

I was now operating on instinct. I was going back to what I knew, what I had confidence in: the oars, the riggers, the equipment I knew would work in the tough conditions I was sure we were going to meet on 28 March. I was also going to return to the tactics and the refinements that had served me so well in the early years but which had recently come under criticism from the 2000-metre merchants.

I was answering to no one, and all of my decisions were being made on the run as it were, instantly, instead of going through hours and sometimes days of agonizing that I usually did before making any changes. Also no more committee meetings to make sure everyone 'felt comfortable' about the decisions. At this moment it was me against the world, and I knew exactly what I was doing. I had endured enough bullshit this past six months to sink the *QEII*.

My next problem was human. And its name was Gavin Stewart. Somehow I had to force him to put his regrets aside. Since he was by far the biggest man in the boat, if he was not rowing at full pressure, he was also the biggest anchor. The key to him rested in the triumph of Isis last year. In that crew he had moved down at the last moment to stroke the boat, and with Andy Lobbenberg coxing he had led the Oxford reserves to a famous victory over Goldie. He had made his name in that crew, and I decided to try to get him to rekindle his glory of 1986. He did not yet know it, but Gavin Stewart was going to stroke the Blue Boat against Cambridge the following Saturday.

Jeff Jacobs, his former coach with Isis, had always told me that he thought Gavin found it very difficult to follow anyone else, but that he could blossom as a leader at stroke. In the torrent of thoughts rushing through my mind I also flashed back to a day in the winter, when we raced those Fours after our Sculling Championship on the Isis before Christmas. I remember Gavin stroking a boat of real second-raters. He was striking around forty-two, grinning all over his face and leading a Four which contained Chris Clark.

He was such a huge man and still relatively inexperienced that it was hard for him to move to someone else's rhythm. In any crew he moved to his own beat, but it was the beat of a different drum, and it had to be followed. Otherwise it just did not fit in with the rest of them. That, I concluded, was part of our problem: this enormous powerhouse in the middle of the boat, slightly out of step.

This meant that Gleeson had to move back. His lack of racing experience was killing him, and us. He was good and tough, but he was not strong enough. I would change him with Gavin and put him at 6.

Now, although usually the biggest and most powerful men in any Eight sit in the engine room at 6, 5, 4 and 3, and give good backing to a weaker stern pair, I desperately needed some real strength and experience in the stern to follow Gavin. This meant moving Tom Cadoux-Hudson down from 5 to 7, for this is a critical position in the boat, some say THE critical position, for 7 is essentially the bowside stroke. But he must also mirror exactly the stroke's movements, for if he's wrong, they're all wrong. In this seat you must have a man with knowledge of the Tideway, vision and the instincts of a racer.

Tom had every one of these. Also he would realize the historic honour of rowing for the Dark Blues in the 7 seat – the seat of Gully Nickalls, of J. C. Cherry, of John Clay who rowed behind Davidge, of Rod Carnegie, of Mark Evans, Bill Lang, Duncan Spencer, Nick Tee, John Wiggins and Mark Andrews. Not, of course, to mention D. Topolski (1967). The great Steve Fairbairn rowed at 7 for Cambridge and reckoned it the most important seat in the boat.

It's a strange thing in a boat crew but although they are all working just as hard, the stroke is always under tremendous pressure, and always out of breath. It is often the 7 man acting as tactician, who makes the keen observations, and calls the shots. It is a vital place in the Dark Blue boat, and one which requires the utmost respect. Cadoux-Hudson's promotion meant that Hull would move to 5. Ward would move back to 3. With Donald at 4, Gish at 2, and Pelham in the bow.

That was the order in which they would row. No ifs or buts. Now there were some technicalities left to take care of, two of which were crucial; and it was conceivable that neither of them would be very popular. But I wasn't going to worry about that at this stage.

Since 1983 I had been consistently outvoted by men such as Mike Spracklen, the Evans twins, and Graham Jones in terms of the gearing of the boat. This means the adjustment of the pin which holds the gate – the fulcrum of the oar – and the positioning of the restraining collar around the oar shaft – the button. The easiest way for me to explain this is to ask you to imagine the gate fixed to the narrow side of the boat right by the oarsman's hand. It would obviously mean the oar could describe a huge arc, and be almost impossible to pull. The further out that gate is positioned over the water, the smaller the arc becomes. Thus if it was somehow slung out ten feet only a foot from the end of the oar, the arc of the blade would clearly be tiny.

Now when you get to the most effective area of adjustment with the pin, a couple of feet out from the side, every centimetre is critical. Because a centimetre there is greatly multiplied by the time it gets to the end of the oar. This is known as gearing, and the further out that gate is positioned, the easier it is to row. But you have less power, because the arc is smaller, and I now proposed to move that gate further in towards the boat, for a bigger arc and a tougher stroke.

For four years now the international class 2,000-metres men had argued in favour of going for best speed over the whole distance and with longer oars rather than taking the effect of tactics into more consideration. All my 1970s crews had rowed with my harder gearing, and they all reaped the benefit of that extra power and that wider arc off the start. They all flew from the stake boat with big, potent strokes. Damn nearly killed some of them, but that's what they were in the Oxford Boat for: victory or death.

So now I was doing it my way, because in 1983 and '84, although we had won, I was always a bit disappointed that we did not annihilate Cambridge, and in my mind I always blamed it on that easier gearing. In 1986 we lost using the wider span, and right now I thought again: 'The hell with it. I'm going for high-risk tactics.'

This 1987 crew was going to row in the tradition of those earlier Oxford rigs, like Andy Baird and the boys used in 1976 when we smashed the course record and beat Cambridge by six lengths; like Ag Michelmore and Shealy used in 1977 when we crushed them by seven, and again in 1978 when Cambridge sank trying to stay with us.

On each occasion we powered to a one-length lead in the first ninety seconds. That's what I call domination. And that gives a rookie crew an irresistable burst of confidence. And that's what we were now going for. I knew the dangers involved in giving them a stiffer gearing and the risk that they might falter over the second half but we had no choice. We had to go for the jugular right from the word 'go'.

I wanted Oxford in the lead. Early. And if they could show themselves to be tough enough I knew how to get them there.

The other change I made was to drop the height of each gate by a quarter-of-an-inch – to six-and-a-quarter inches above the level of the seat. This would allow them to pull more horizontally, keeping the blade tips better buried in the water right through the stroke.

This sudden flurry of activity had a fantastic effect on me. I suddenly felt liberated for the first time in ages, as I flung off the constraints, and went to work in the way I understood best. My mood was beginning to bubble, though I could not imagine why, since the Oxford crew had thus far lurched from disaster to disaster culminating in that afternoon's humiliation against the Scullers. But now I felt in control. Deep down I felt that old stirring of aggression as I began to plot and to plan the downfall of Cambridge. I knew it was not possible but I felt it all the same. My head told me it was simply not feasible with this crew, but my heart kept reminding me that it's never over, 'till it's over.

I went back to the house for dinner and I think my own mood had an effect on them. I told them I was feeling very optimistic about the following morning, and to be up early, with a light breakfast. And I added, as I left for home, 'This is going to be the turning point. Big things are going to be happening for us. And all of them good.'

The following morning, Friday, we left the house immediately after a seven o'clock breakfast. We arrived at the boathouse in Putney before anyone was around, and went into action like a professional hit squad. We loaded the boat onto a trailer, tied it down, packed up a set of oars, hoisted aboard the rubber dinghy with its engine and told Albert the boatman we were leaving and would see him on Monday.

Donald revved the engine to life, and with Albert asking blankly what he was supposed to tell the Press when they arrived to watch us training, the Oxford camp roared off in convoy, heading west.

The evacuation had taken nine minutes. Oxford were gone without trace. And no one, not even Albert, knew our destination. The reason for this exercise was that I badly needed some peace, some time to think and I wanted the crew to be able to work for a couple of days without being watched. Basically we needed privacy and there was no chance of this at Putney.

I led the way in my car, with Donald at the wheel of the van and all the boys packed into the back. We arrived at the deserted St George's College boathouse which looked out over a quiet, lonely stretch of water, on which not a boat stirred. And set along the wall next to the big main doors was the most welcome sight. A beautiful set of Sutton oars with the blades painted Oxford Blue.

The St George's coach had left everything for us as planned. The boys unloaded the boat, and armed with my set of spanners I reset the gearing of the boat to that used by Michelmore, Rankov and Shealy ten years ago. I adjusted the height and the pitch of the oars and then I called the boys around for a meeting before we went afloat. I told them about the changes for the first time.

'Gavin,' I said, 'I am moving you from 6 to stroke.' For a brief moment he just stared at me with his customary gloomy look, and then his entire face lit up with an enormous grin. It was literally the first time I had seen him smile since we left Spain three months before; I knew he was remembering his previous year with Isis and the joy of that heroic victory.

I told Gleeson he would swap back into the important 6 seat. Tom Cadoux-Hudson would go 7, Ward to 3 and Hull into Tom's old place at 5. The rest would stay where they were.

We pumped up the dinghy, put the boats in the water and set off, with Gavin slipping into a long easy paddling rhythm and clearly savouring every second of it. The first twenty strokes told me all I wanted to know. It looked right. The Oxford boat was knifing through the water, covering more distance between the strokes with the stiffer gearing, and the crew suddenly looked much more comfortable behind their big powerful new stroke.

I shouted out that we would paddle on up to the weir and see how it felt; but I knew how it felt, because I could see Gavin rowing easily, with a half-smile still on his face. After a couple of miles, I called out to them: 'Looks good to me. Let's try some bursts.'

'Yeah,' said Gavin instantly, 'Let's go for it.'

It was a long time since I'd heard him react like that, and when I sent them away the boat really began to surge and sing across the water. When we arrived back at the boathouse the mood was transformed. I felt on a high because I no longer needed to ask any of them how they felt. There was no back-chat, no argument and I had no doubts. All the changes I was now making I knew would have been impossible before with the Americans. Now I couldn't give a damn for any doubting Thomases. There was a curious sense of optimism creeping in, even a little bit of positive input for the first time in months.

I told them I was pleased with the short sprints, and that now they should get a cup of tea and then stand by for a hard 2,000-metre row in an hour's time. No one batted an eyelid, no one griped, moaned or complained. Gavin actually said 'Great, Dan.'

We paddled up to the starting point putting in some good warm-up bursts on the way. The 2,000-metres stretch lay before us.

'Okay, guys,' I shouted. 'I want you off at a sharp forty-three and then stride down to thirty-six and hold it at that to half-way. Then squeeze on from there over the second half.'

What followed was the best piece of work the Oxford Eight had done all year. From behind, the blade heights and the lengths were good and the boat was running true. I moved the little launch up alongside them, checking out the puddles left by the gleaming new blades. Gavin's was big and solid, so were those of Cadoux-Hudson, and Donald. And for a while it seemed that at last I had this combination in the right order and in some sort of shape. But as we raced along into the second half of the work I began to notice a weakness. One of the oars on the strokeside was beginning to get washy and to ride out, as the pressure began to tell on the man pulling on the handle end. The spacing between the puddles was no longer even. It was the puddle right behind Gavin's, the puddle left by Paul Gleeson, and it was a weakness being highlighted, because that particular whirlpool fell between the big tight puddles of Stewart and Macdonald.

I said nothing until we docked. And I told them how pleased I was, but that I was making one more change. Would Paul Gleeson move back to 4, and would Donald move down the boat to 6 behind

Tom. There was a moment's hesitation. All the old antagonisms began to bubble. The idea that the man they had for so long maligned should be tried in the critical 6 seat was almost too much for them to take. But I was only interested in finding the fastest line-up and I hoped they would have the grace to acknowledge that.

Most of them did not know that Donald had rowed at 6 for London and for Isis in '85. And none of us knew the reverence in which he held that position. I was to discover much later that, for him, the number 6 seat, with its high degree of control over the boat, represented one of the biggest challenges in rowing. It is why he was so privately critical of Clark's performance in that seat the previous year.

Donald has a very strong sense of destiny and it nearly killed him keeping quiet while Gleeson occupied the place he regards as something close to holy in the Dark Blue Boat. In the past thirty years some of the biggest names in rowing had taken the 6 seat. The giant Yalies – Reed Rubin. Harry Howell, and John Bockstoce – the world champions Ken Brown and Al Shealy, the Olympic gold medallist Mike Evans, Graham Jones and Olympic silver medallist Chris Mahoney. Graham Cooper, the Olympic oarsman of 1960, collapsed in that seat in the following year's Boat Race.

And now I was offering it to Donald, the hungriest man in the boat, and he was going to seize that chance. When that boat went out for the second 2000-metre row, we saw an outstanding exhibition of power rowing from Donald. He rowed like a man who had waited for this moment for a very, very long time; and now that boat was really motoring. There was little doubt about the difference he made.

His enemies did not of course want the experiment to be a success, and Ward and Gleeson in particular were rather peeved at what they considered to be their demotion. But there was really only one man's opinion which mattered now. So when we got back to the boathouse, I disembarked from the launch, and walked right up to the man who resented Donald the most – Gavin Stewart. I stood right over him, looked him squarely in the eye and said: 'Okay Gavin. Which was better?'

It was an extraordinary moment. Stewart did not want to answer. He did not want to admit the truth, and he had to fight the words out. I glanced at Donald, and his hands gripped the oar handle tightly as he waited for the verdict of the strokeman who wanted him out of the crew.

Then Gavin looked up at me, and he said firmly: 'It was better with Donald at 6.' He had finally acknowledged publicly that Donald was a key man in this crew, a member of the critical stern three. And the beauty of it was, *they* had picked him, not me.

It was important to maintain this momentum and that the more negative members of the crew should not slip back into their old sullenness because they felt they had somehow been tricked. But there was no need to worry because Gavin, whose mood was critical, was revelling in his new leadership role; he felt that he was now in the very front line of our challenge. Having pulled it off with Isis a year earlier, why should we not be able to do it again? For the first time, a real desire to win was replacing the innate bitterness of this crew.

Gavin's cheerful mood alone had changed the entire atmosphere. As we headed home to Putney, I began to feel positively aggressive. Although I knew it could not be done, my Dark Blue heart refused to stay quiet. Maybe, somehow we could still have a shot. When I caught up with the infuriated Press corps, which had been waiting for news of us for most of the day, I greeted them with a flippant breeziness I had not felt in a long time.

Where had we been? Sorry, gentlemen. Can't say a word. State secret.

The next day we did our vanishing trick again, hurtling down to our special hideaway on the outskirts of Walton-on-Thames for another excellent work-out. We now had the two most experienced Tideway match-racers together in the critical stern of the boat, Donald and Tom at 6 and 7, a pair of fiercely competitive athletes. Most of the crew did not know that Donald had won twenty-two finals for London Rowing Club, which constituted nearly eighty races, most of them on the Tideway. Tom had done more, and in one far distant event they had raced against each other in a London RC v. Radley College fixture. If you ever ask them who won, they chorus in unison: 'We did, who d'you think?'

When we broke for the weekend I was at last beginning to see a faint glimmer at the end of the tunnel. If we could just win a race against someone, any bloody race would do, I might even dare to hope that we could stop Cambridge from getting completely away and humiliating us.

Back at Putney I finally told the Press what we had been up to; I was also in time to see Cambridge being taken apart by the National Squad Eight which included the Olympic gold medallists Holmes and Redgrave. Cambridge lost by six lengths; but a little while before they had rowed much better, holding the National crew to just half-a-length.

I had begun by now to notice a performance pattern developing in the Light Blues. A week earlier in their races with Reading University, Cambridge had thumped them by nineteen seconds on the first row, but in the second they had won by only three-quarters of a length.

When they had raced the University of London it was in the last piece again that they were badly beaten, earlier they had been much better. This all suggested to me that Cambridge might be demonstrating a vulnerability. I have coached crews like that before. It is a very subtle psychological weakness which shows itself after they have proved themselves with one good race. The result is reversed on the second piece. The culprit is 'complacency'. An attitude creeps in which says: 'We have done it. We've killed off Reading University', or 'We've just held the National Squad to half-a-length' or 'We're as good as London University who clobbered Oxford'. Ask them to go right out and do it again, and they fail to psych themselves up properly again for another go.

I thought this weakness had also manifested itself the day the Scullers wiped us out and the Cambridge Blue boat had gone out to race their reserves, Goldie. They were confident, very pleased with themselves, and not quite into what American football coaches call the 'down and dirty' – or as Ronnie Rowe had said at the dinner last year, 'the dig and hoik'. What happened? Goldie beat them, that's what happened.

I put this down to a lack of mental toughness, or more to the point the hard professionalism of experienced competitors who know you have to hit the opposition when they're hurt. I wondered too whether their bout of illness a couple of months earlier might have conceivably left a mark. With these snippets of intelligence I scented blood, which is the natural reaction of the match-racer. It is an instinct, like that of a predator. As I stood there watching Cambridge trailing home behind the National Squad, I knew that next Saturday we would have to put those guys under instant pressure. We would have to try and break their spirit, shock them right off the start line, by going for the Achilles' heel they did not even know they had – that susceptibility that could make them falter if things suddenly stopped going precisely to plan.

Every experienced athlete knows that if you win the first encounter of a series, your opponent, if he's any good, will come back at you harder. The mark of the true competitor is that when he's ahead, he sticks the knife in deeper, and then twists it. The taste of first-blood inflames his instincts and there are few sports in which this is more true than in major rowing encounters between two crews on the river. Only inexperienced competitors relax, and I had seen Cambridge do it on several occasions. They had to be vulnerable to a guerilla attack by us if we could just force ourselves into a position to exploit what we knew. We had to force them into making mistakes.

The other thing I suspected was that they wanted the Middlesex station, the right-hand side of the river looking down the course towards Hammersmith. This would give them the advantage of the first shallow bend, worth about a third-of-a-length. I had seen them consistently select this side against pacing crews, and they always seemed very aggressive at the start, steering over towards their opponents, intimidating and threatening a clash.

The Cambridge coach Alan Inns is a former international coxswain, who knows the Tideway well, and these are real cox's tactics – unnerving your opponents by moving in close towards them and then steering back upon the umpire's command, before doing it again. It is as well to remember that no one has ever been disqualified in the Boat Race.

Three times, on three different days I had seen Cambridge go through these manoeuvres against other crews, and I guessed they thought we would pick the Surrey station, in the hope we could hold on for the first mile and then try to claim the inside of the big Hammersmith bend. Alan Inns, who had been my cox in the past when we were both at Scullers, was probably aware that this had invariably been the Oxford choice throughout my years as coach. He also knew I had a boatful of rookies, and that such barging aggression from Cambridge might throw us off our stride at the start. Well, we would see about that – and we would also take Middlesex if we won the toss, which would put them on the side of the river to which they were least accustomed.

Meanwhile I would continue to take Oxford into bad water, in the worst possible weather conditions, because I still had an overwhelming feeling that it would be that sort of day, and if my hunch was correct then we would want the Middlesex station anyway.

On that Sunday afternoon some of us drove up to Henley to watch the Women's and Lightweight Boat Races between Oxford and Cambridge, and as usual, the Light Blues were dominant. As I strolled back along the tow-path, a figure hurried towards me with his hand held out in greeting: 'Hi, Dan. No hard feelings I hope.' It was Chris Huntington. I shook his hand warily. Then I said, 'No hard feelings? How can you say that? Of course there are hard feelings. And they'll probably last for the rest of our lives. You simply don't realize the damage you caused.'

He said he would like to talk sometime and I said I would too but not until after the race. We would get together and really thrash it out one day. He wished us luck, and said he would not be in England for the race; then he walked off. I have not seen him since, but as he went I felt very sad. If he had not fallen in with the others he could have been a great Oxford oarsman, probably stroked the boat for us. To this day I have no idea why Hunt ever got mixed up in the mutiny. And I have a sneaking suspicion that he doesn't either.

Monday morning and just five days to go. We were due to race a crew of Old Blues, a traditional fixture, which would take place after the Weigh-In. This little ceremony confirmed that Gavin Stewart would be the biggest and tallest man, and Donald would be the oldest man, ever to row in the Boat Race. We would also outweigh Cambridge by seven pounds per man.

I was rowing myself in this series of short races with other half-fit Old Blues like John Wiggins, Mike Diserens, Richard Yonge and Lynton Richmond. At their best they could give most crews a hard race for half-a-mile. Thereafter their progress chart would start to take a dive.

It is worth bearing in mind that not one member of the 1987 Oxford crew had won a race since they beat London University with Hunt, Penny and Lyons in the boat back in January. In fact this crew had never beaten anybody. So I did everything I could to charge them up and I impressed upon them the necessity to race and to fight, right from the first stroke against the Old Blues.

Oxford took to the water for what I fervently hoped would be a morale-boosting session against a crew which sported their poor old coach pulling away in the bow. At the command '*Go*' Oxford moved off quickly, not like lightning but fast enough. I could feel them pulling inexorably away from us, and when I glanced to my left I found myself eyeball-to-eyeball with the cox Andy Lobbenberg, a sight that would normally have inflamed me into action. But on this day it brought only a grim smile of pleasure. Donald and his boys were murdering us in rough, difficult windswept water.

Gavin had taken off at a brisk forty-three and they settled to thirty-six finishing two lengths up in two minutes. Then we had another race for three minutes, and they took four lengths off us, striking thirty-four strokes a minute. I heard a yell of triumph and looked round to see some of the boys punching the air and clapping each other on the backs in celebration of their first victory together.

It was only a minor victory – none of the Old Blues were super fit – but it meant everything to that Oxford crew. And after the boats were put away I could hear excited voices in the dressing room: 'That was great! We knocked the hell out of them!' That sounded very much like that elusive factor, team spirit. I felt a great surge of relief.

Just to hear them starting to weld together, to focus on the defeat of Cambridge was so gratifying after the past months. But there was a danger that this new-found optimism could be short-lived because the next day we were due for our last sparring session before the race against a local club crew – the Thames Rowing Club Eight. God help us if we should lose for it would be impossible to restore self-confidence in the short time remaining.

We had a talk that night and I told them I had *never* seen a Boat Race crew deal with rough water as well as they did. I also told them that in my view this windy, squally south-wester would hold through the weekend, and that if it did, they would have a real chance of beating Cambridge. Because rough water is a great equalizer. It could take the speed-edge off a greyhound crew like Cambridge even with their five internationals. And it could turn the race into a real slogging match, a contest of courage and watermanship. That could be our chance. In flat, calm conditions this very fast Cambridge Eight would probably leave us standing at the start before we even had a chance of getting in a blow.

The little speech I gave them was, to say the least, a bit of an exaggeration since I had of course seen and been in plenty of crews which had gone through rough water as well, if not better. But we were now into the final four days of our build-up to the race and *nothing* could be allowed to disturb their belief in themselves. I had to build their morale a little higher each day, so that by Saturday morning they would be like tigers, nine men ready to eat raw meat, and hungry to go out and destroy Cambridge.

Our last encounter against Thames Rowing Club had to be a major psychological boost, and I prayed our opponents would prove to be only as modestly talented as I believed them to be. I could not imagine what I would do or say if the boys were beaten.

Before we faced Thames I went out to take a careful look at Cambridge racing Kingston Rowing Club. Again they chose the Middlesex station and at the start they once more swerved over, clashing after forty strokes. The clash upset Kingston a bit and they immediately dropped a quarter-of-a-length. At the end the Light Blues had opened up an advantage of nearly two lengths. The tactic worked well.

A short while later we set off against Thames from the race start just above Putney Bridge. Gavin wound the rate up to thirty-nine strokes in the first minute for a solid half-length lead, and then began to draw away powerfully, settling into a good striding rate of thirty-five as Thames sprinted along at forty. It was mature stuff and the boat was running smoothly without check. They were two lengths up when they stopped and eased. I could see one or two fists go up in triumph and I noticed Tom turn round and shake hands with Donald. After all of our troubles I found the gesture strangely moving. I have to admit that I had never been quite so relieved to beat an average club crew.

But the boys had been good and I told them that for the first time I thought they had a real chance of springing a big surprise. That evening we invited all the local boatmen who are involved with the Boat Race crews for a drink at the boathouse as we did every year. Len Neville, who made our riggers, Jerry Sutton, Bert and all the other watermen were as always friendly but you could tell, with the best will in the world, they didn't hold out much hope for us. Only Bert knew of our improving speed and we were not telling anyone, not even our closest friends.

At dinner that night I noticed none of the usual divisions which had characterized this crew for so long. Afterwards none of them left to go to the pub. Donald and Tom were talking to Gavin, which was a new and encouraging sign. Pelham and Hull were chuckling irreverently about an invitation we had issued to Cambridge for tea the next day. It was an unusual thing to do, but I wanted them to see that the Cambridge lot, far from being an invincible squad of supermen, were in fact a crew of anxious students like themselves trying to build confidence for the biggest day of their lives. The boys wanted to play practical jokes on them but I told them it would be far more effective if we behaved politely like perfect hosts.

They came with Alan Inns and their Canadian Olympic gold medal-winning coach Neil Campbell. They stayed an hour and they left metaphorically feeling for their wallets, wondering what we had managed to take off them during the short meeting. In fact the boys had discovered that our rivals the 'Tabs' were having to pay full price for their partners' entrance tickets to the Boat Race Ball after the race. We had negotiated great reductions and the crew were delighted. Trivial triumphs, maybe, but every little bit helped to improve morale.

Wednesday was busy: both Oxford coxes Lobbenberg, and Stubbs of Isis, went over the course in the launch with Bert early in the morning. Then they steered their two crews in practise starts alongside each other. Donald spent lunchtime on the phone trying to get hold of some of the special low-friction hull tape from America which Dennis Conner had used on the bottom of *Stars and Stripes* when they regained the America's Cup in Perth.

This was real space-age kit, but the makers, Minnesota Mining and Manufacturing, were not at all sure it would help. Its design was so specific to hull-shape they even thought it might make us go slower. I called the US National coach Kris Korzienowski for guidance since their Olympic Four had used it when they won the silver medal behind the British in Los Angeles. He was non-committal, saying that they had run tests and had found it made no significant difference to boat speed and that they no longer used it. But at this stage we were prepared to gamble on anything. 3–M arranged to send their technicians over with a supply that evening for a secret boathouse rendezvous with Donald.

Dinner that night was like a Feydeau farce because we had our team of coaches for dinner and Donald, Hugh and Paul Gleeson had to keep disappearing in turn to the boathouse to help with the taping of the hull. We wanted no one, not even our closest friends, to know of our secret operation.

Thursday was rehearsal day with the umpire the Rt. Honourable Colin Moynihan, former Oxford cox and car-driver during the season of Shealy's British all-comers 'mooning' record on the M4. Now Minister of Sport, Mr Moynihan wanted us on the water at 10.30 a.m. He took the crew out to the stake boats to practise the procedure for the race start and then he took Lobbenberg and the Cambridge cox for a run over the full course in launches. On the way back he sat them both down and told them he expected them to react to his instructions at all times. 'If you stray off your station, I will raise my white flag to signal you to get back to your own water,' he said, 'and I will warn you three times. If you ignore the order, I shall have no hesitation in becoming the first Boat Race umpire in 133 years to disqualify you.

'My launch will be in the centre of the stream and I want you on either side of that line. If there is any breakage due to something beyond the control of the crews during the first two minutes along the Fulham Wall, I will restart the race. This also applies to a sinking. Once you have cleared the end of the Fulham Wall, however, you will abide by any accidents and the race will proceed to its end.

'I expect you both to steer sensibly and with caution, and to obey the normal rules of this race. I will see you on the stake boats five minutes before the start at ten minutes past twelve on Saturday. And may the best crew win. Good luck to you both.'

Afterwards Cambridge went out for a final sparring session against a world-class Italian Eight, Campania. It was stuffed full of international oarsmen, including four times world and Olympic champions the Abbagnale brothers. They were in town to take part in the Tideway Head of the River Race, which would involve 420 Eights racing over the same four-and-a-quarter mile course in reverse, three hours after the Boat Race on Saturday. Cambridge raced brilliantly, holding the Italians to under half-a-length in three two-minute high-rating sprints. the *Daily Telegraph* said flatly: 'This could prove too much for Oxford.'

It was an observation I could not argue with for every shred of logic pointed that way. And yet I still felt we had a chance.

On Thursday night we ate our pasta and chicken and I began to touch upon the tactics we would employ against Cambridge on Saturday. 'For a start,' I said, 'we want the Middlesex station and that initial little bend advantage. I suspect that Cambridge are expecting to get it because we usually choose Surrey if we win the toss. But this year is different. As far as you are concerned this is going to be a straight fight for three minutes. I don't want you to even think beyond that. Our plan is simple. Nothing matters after the Mile Post. I don't care what happens after that, because if you are not with them there we might as well go home. The only way we are going to beat the buggers is to devastate them at the start, throw them off their stride. So we're going to fight them tooth and nail for those first strokes. They expect us to be much slower away than them, and we are going to give them the shock of their lives. When they glance across expecting to see us slipping back, they are going to be stunned. Because we're going to be right there, matching them, blow for blow right through those first three minutes. After that our tactics will be largely a matter of constant pressure. Because I'm counting on them to falter with those light oars of theirs, and for our surprise attack to crack 'em before we reach the Mile Post. Your aerofoil riggers, stiffer gearing and cleverness in the rough will see to it.'

The boys listened in deadly silence. Gavin, upon whose shoulders so much depended, was beginning to look very tense, so I took him aside to sit down with Tom, Donald and Andy, the stern committee so to speak, to get down to the nitty-gritty of the race. We thrashed out questions of when to schedule our attacking bursts, where the critical corners were, and what to do in an emergency, should someone catch a crab and bring the boat to a shuddering halt; what to do in a clash if we made a mistake at the start and lost ground. 'Don't panic, don't rush to get it back; just take off for ten and settle again. Peg them back stroke-by-stroke, long and steady.'

Tonight some of them would have trouble sleeping, because by now they were realizing at last the enormity of this occasion which each one of them would be helping to shape. Each man was becoming inevitably haunted by his own role in the forthcoming struggle which, if past races were anything to go by, would surely be discussed long after they had hung up their oars for good.

I left them discussing tactics together, all friends now, but only, I suspected, for as long as it would take to deal with Cambridge. I had seen this happen before during the final forty-eight hours before the race. With the enemy in sight, something almost mystical takes over and binds the crew together. Old quarrels evaporate and a heady feeling of comradeship prevails as if none of them had ever had any past, as if only those forty-eight hours would ever count for anything in their lives.

I, too, found it difficult to sleep. In my mind I turned over the evidence again and again. On all known form, personnel, credentials, racing records and experience, we had to lose. On that very afternoon I had watched Cambridge going head to head with a crack Olympic-class crew from Italy. Against that we had done nothing but beat a very moderate Thames Club crew. Our training had been interrupted. There had been nothing but dissension in our squad for months on end.

Our boat had people in it like Peter Gish, whose experience was negligible, Paul Gleeson who had even less, Richard Hull who had been rejected by the Cambridge University Boat Club during his time there and three men and the cox from last year's second boat. I had to face the fact that I was fielding a crew of reserves for this race, which was why some bookmakers were making Cambridge probably the hottest favourites in the history of the race – 6–1 on.

And yet . . . was it possible that we might still somehow pull it off? If we could just hang on to them at the start. If Gavin, Tom and Donald, with their enormous strength, could haul us off that stake boat level with Cambridge . . . well . . . maybe, perhaps we might have a squeak of a chance, if someone in the Cambridge boat collapsed.

I got out of bed and went over to the window. The wind was howling and the rain beat against the black window panes. Memories tumbled about inside my brain, and tugged at my sleeve. How many times had a classy crew like Cambridge come to grief on the turbulent Tideway? The Oxford crew of 1935 for example, hot favourites for once, were so unimpressed by Cambridge they decided that they needed a real challenge. Their cox taped the intermediate fastest times to his thigh so that he could monitor their attempt on the course record. Throughout the race they bettered the times at every stage, ignoring the Light Blue crew hammering along beside them. They did indeed break the record, but they lost the Boat Race. Now I believed Cambridge had chosen to use the wrong oars and the wrong riggers, and possibly the wrong gearing for this supreme tactical contest, this unrivalled endurance test. And I also believed that they were mentally vulnerable. There *had* to be a chance for us, however remote. And if there was, we would be there to grab it.

On Friday morning we were all on parade early, with a gale-force south-wester howling down the Tideway. 'This is *your* weather,' I told the crew, 'and out there it's *your* water – no one can cope with those waves like you guys can, least of all Cambridge. You have the weight and the technique for rough water – and better still, you have the nerve for it. And I don't think Cambridge have that nerve. If it stays like this I really think you could pull it off tomorrow.'

They looked pretty confident as they paddled the boat out into the buffeting river, rowing straight and hard into the chop. We tried three or four good starts off the stake boat, and I particularly noticed Gavin Stewart's big powerful blade whacking through the water as they got into their stride, the strokeside oars picking up the catch in perfect unison. There was a sharpness and an eagerness to their stroke that we had not had even in the days before the mutiny.

We went home for a light brunch and a rest and then took a further short outing to coincide with the time of the race next day. The wind was still blowing hard, and I saw that our foul weather equipment was all working well. The special riggers were slicing through the water, the oars were ideal and the big rubber inner-tubes we had inflated and crammed beneath the seats were helping with buoyancy and occupying space that would otherwise be filled with overflowing river water. The big breakwater behind Hugh was deflecting the waves which broke over the bow canvas. Then we went off for our traditional private film show in the West End of London. Pre-release films like *Chariots of Fire, Dirty Harry* and *Defense of the Realm* had inspired their predecessors. This time *Personal Services*, the story of Cynthia Payne the Streatham luncheon voucher Madame, was the film chosen to put them in the mood.

We got home shortly before six o'clock for the last dinner we would have together at Ranelagh Avenue. After we had eaten I asked Louise to bring in the decanter of vintage port and each member of the crew poured himself a glass. This is an old Oxford tradition on the eve of the race, because it not only steadies tightly-stretched nerves, it also helps them to sleep the night before the battle.

I took the telephone off the hook, shut all the doors, and began the final briefing. It was now that I would confirm our tactics and tell them how I thought the race would go. 'Tomorrow I think the weather is going to be rough and I hope it is because, as I have told you before, you are much better than Cambridge in that kind of water. Broadly our plan is as I outlined it last night. We have to shock them in the first three minutes. You are going to have to row like bastards to do that – row as if your lives depended on it, row until you think you can't take any more. Because this race is not just about speed. It's even more about *hunger – courage* and *will power*. And I don't honestly know how hungry you guys really are. That's up to you.

'We know a lot about Cambridge. And one of the things that we know, and that's good for us, is that a few days ago they moved their 6 man Paddy Broughton down to stroke the boat. Now I remember watching them, three weeks before the race last year, racing Thames in very nasty conditions, using their plastic oars. That club crew hung onto them all the way to Harrods, and however hard Cambridge tried, they just could not get away. They got more and more pedestrian, their blade work disintegrated and their rating dropped lower and lower. When Thames dropped out, they were picked up by Goldie, who walked all over them up to Chiswick Steps.

'Next day they very sensibly swapped Paddy with John Pritchard, which greatly improved them, and if you remember they went on to beat us for the first time in eleven years. But now, this week, they've made the same mistake again. Broughton is back in the stroke seat, and although I think he's a good hard-working guy in the middle of the boat when everything is going right, he is not the man to lift a crew when the pressure is really on. I am also convinced they are using the wrong oars and their five-stay riggers will pick up all the rough water and chuck it straight into the boat.

'The other thing going for us is that Cambridge expect to win. And however much their coach tells them to take nothing for granted, that they have a real race on their hands, deep down they know we don't have a prayer. *That's why we must kill them in the first three minutes.*

'I want you nice and loose and relaxed before the start, so don't hold anything back during the warm-up. We want the blood pumping round your body. There will be lots going on, a helicopter above you, people shouting from the bank and from the bridge, so it's easy to get distracted. You have to concentrate, keep your minds on your job. You'll be in a bit of a daze and everything could just wash over you. It's a very normal reaction to high pressure and this is something you have to fight. You must stay alert, slap each other on the shoulders, keep passing on instructions and reminding each other. "Are you there Paul?" – "Everything okay Tony?" "Come on Richard wake up, this is getting serious."

'Don't feel shy, while you're waiting for the start, to put your hand out and touch the man in front of you, ruffle his hair or something, just so that each man knows he's not alone out there. We're all in it together, ready to fight together, remember that.

'Remember too at the start, to square up and take the pressure on your blade on the words "Are You Ready?" Don't get pulled out past your strong position. Once you square your blade in the water you are committed. And on the "G" of "Go" squeeze out that first stroke and *wait for it* – wait for your mates at the finish, in case someone is a bit slow. It is critical that you do not rush away from that first finish. Hold out the first three strokes, and make sure they come out together and high off the water.

'Don't forget to breathe because it's very easy in the anxiety of the start to forget, and to hold your breath; then you take time to recover and start gasping for breath around the twentieth stroke. Whatever you do, keep your eyes in your own boat. Do not look at them because it cannot help you to go any faster. It will only distract you and mess up your rhythm.

'Your first strokes must be clean. Sit back on the finishes. Hands well down and away. Get the blades clear of the water and your hands down the length of your thighs. Remember to touch the woodwork of the gunwhales with the oar handle on each recovery.

'Then you start to build up your length on the slide, two extra inches with each stroke. On six you'll hear Andy shout: "Full length!" *Then you wind her up*, building the power and stretching for length between six and fifteen. After that, establish the stride. The next five strokes have to be spot on and hard drawn because if they're good they'll set you up for the whole race. If they're bad you will be fighting to find a rhythm all the way. So keep drawing and striding till Andy calls out at twenty. We consolidate the rating after one minute, at which point we should be striking thirty-six to thirty-seven. It will come down naturally another pip or so to your racing pace but make sure you keep drawing out those finishes. Through the second minute it has got to be flat out, so go for it as hard as you can. If the strike rate is too low Andy will call for an immediate power-twenty. And you must react instantly.

'Remember there may be only about another minute of the race to go for you, because I don't care if you die at the Mile Post. As far as you are concerned you have just one task in this life, and that is to smash Cambridge in the first mile. If they get past you after that I don't even mind, because I know you will have given your all. But please, just beat them to the Mile Post.'

Of course I knew that if this crew was able to get to the Mile Post ahead, Cambridge would be suffering, and *we* would be so surprised we would hardly notice how tired we were from the efforts of the first mile. It would act for us a little like an aphrodisiac. What I did not want was some bright sparks coming up with something pseudo-scientific like saving their strength for the second half of the race. If anyone did anything so idiotic, there simply would not be a second half of the race for us. We'd be rowing on our own, a distant speck on Cambridge's horizon.

'Now,' I said, 'no matter which side of the river we are on, we must have a power-twenty on that first bend at two-and-a-half minutes, just past the wall by the Fulham football ground. That is what this race is about – fighting to defend your water, attacking on the bends, whether to get away from your opponent on the inside or to hold position on the outside. Either way you are fighting for water. It is a concept you must always have in your mind so it is important you all know exactly where you are on the river; that way you can anticipate Andy's calls.

'I don't want to talk to you for very long, nor do I want to talk about the race much beyond the Mile. Because for you, there is no race beyond the Mile. That is all you have to do. And it could hardly be more straightforward.

'If you listen to that wind outside I am sure each of you can imagine what it's going to be like out there tomorrow. And I want you all to go to bed visualizing it. You may not sleep tonight, but don't worry, you are all well rested. On your own think hard how you will behave in the race and be sure that you will not let yourself or your crewmates down. Remember, when you are mentally right for the battle you *never* imagine defeat. Only victory.'

We talked a little more about how to deal with unexpected incidents and discussed individual worries that needed answers. Then I wished them good night and told them to get to bed early. 'Tomorrow you're going to go out there and shatter that dream of victory which Cambridge have been naïvely nursing for such a long time.'

We all got up from the table. They were in good spirits and I noticed that Gavin had been sitting across from Donald, and they were both talking very seriously with Tony Ward. The only obvious sign of the mutiny that still persisted was between the President and Richard Hull. They did not speak much to each other, although they were not in any way hostile.

I left the house in pouring rain and set off for home. For some reason I stopped the car just before Hammersmith and got out. I wore no jacket, but I walked to the middle of the bridge. The wind was still blasting out of the west and I stood there for a few minutes gazing down the course across the black threatening water below me. The rain beat down, soaking me through, but I did not feel it. Would big Gavin pull something special out of the bag tomorrow and drive the Oxford crew into the lead beneath where I was now standing? And where were all those American stars now, on the eve of the big race? Gone, most of them. Half-a-world away. And the six college captains, where were they in these final nerve-tearing hours before the combat? What could they offer? There was no place here now for anyone except the real warriors.

I noticed one or two cars slowing down as they passed, probably imagining me to be a potential suicide case. They were not to know that my destiny would be decided down there in those heaving waters, not tonight, but tomorrow, just after midday; then my lonely place on this rainswept bridge would be taken by five police cars, and a dozen television cameras.

Many weeks earlier, I had been on a launch down there trying to get Chris Clark to do a seat race. That's when all the trouble had begun; from that time when they would not race in conditions much like these but in broad daylight. If I could turn the clock back and do it all over again, would I change my mind and select Clark for the same number 6 seat he had occupied rather inauspiciously the year before?

Hardly. Because this year I had a man who clung to a belief that he could win, a tenacious man, with a deep almost insane craving for victory, who relished more than anything his key role in the 6-seat of the Oxford crew. He was a man who believed, in spite of everything, that the Dark Blues would somehow fight their way home in front. His name, of course, was Donald Macdonald.

I walked back to my car, now a rather bedraggled figure, wearing a slightly manic grin. Because I too suddenly felt we might win, as long as the water stayed rough. I felt unexpectedly calm and relaxed. Tonight my dreams of triumph would be borne on the great west wind.

CHAPTER FOURTEEN

A MIRACLE ON THE THAMES

And now Cambridge call for a power-ten, and they battle their way forward, still on an angle, heading right at us. Suddenly they are level, but too close. The umpire shouts a warning. And Donald shouts in desperation: 'Here they come!' Tom roars: 'Well push! For Christ's sake push!'

Saturday, 28 March. Boat Race Day – the only day of the year when Britain divides itself into two dogmatic, idealistic factions – the supporters of the Dark Blues, and the supporters of the Light Blues. People the length and breadth of the country, many of whom only just managed to fight their way out of comprehensive schools with an 'O' level to their name, suddenly become impassioned devotees of the universities of Oxford and Cambridge.

It was just after 7 a.m. when I set off for Putney, driving fast through the quiet London streets, wondering in what frame of mind I would find the Oxford crew. At the first traffic light I reached on the approach to Hammersmith, a taxi driver, with a light blue rosette on his jacket, leaned out of his window and shouted: 'The hell with you Topolski. I don't want you bloody beatin' us again.' For all I know he possessed a double first in English and History from Trinity, but more likely he was from one of those East End families which for generations have trooped down to the river on this day each year to roar home the student oarsmen from the

University of Cambridge, or in their Latin idiom, the Cantabs, or to us, 'The Tabs', or in the Oxford colloquial, 'The Filth'.

The Light Blues have always had a large and vociferous group of supporters from the cockney boroughs of Whitechapel, Stepney and Bow, and further east from Mile End, Leyton, West Ham and Hackney. I had always thought that this traced back to when the mile-stones and signposts pointing out of the East End said Newmarket and Cambridge. They still do of course, but in bigger lettering.

Conversely, on the west side of London the main trunk roads out are signposted: 'Oxford' and 'South Wales'. And before midday today sports fans from the capital would be on the march to the Tideway all the way upstream to Chiswick Bridge to roar home the gladiators of the river in the most brutal rowing contest on earth.

Boat Race Day belongs to everyone, as does the Derby, and the Grand National Steeplechase. But it remains a peculiarly British anachronism, that a private challenge between the Boat Club Presidents of Oxford and Cambridge – perhaps the most rarified bastions in all of sport – should suddenly climax in a battle that is joined by everyone throughout the land.

It is a battle in which East London cab drivers feel perfectly free to bawl abuse at Oxford graduates, and where groups of hard-drinking labourers consider it eminently acceptable to pour scorn and derision upon any man wearing a rosette of a different colour. It is of course all part of the fun, and the tradition of this strange little corner of England's heritage. And whereas horseracing men are often apt to quote the old adage that 'all men are equal above and below the turf', it is certainly no more applicable on their Derby Day, than it is on our Boat Race Day. 'Sorry, m'Lord, you're gonna be right out of luck this afternoon. Cambridge will have 'em by the short 'airs.'

Of course, whatever you forecast in advance of this race, you stand an even money chance of being correct, since there are only two runners in it. I may have been the only person in England still uncertain about Oxford's chances. The rest of the country was pretty well agreed on the hopelessness of our position, especially the newspapers: they *all* confidently tipped Cambridge. There had also been a worrying development since last night which greatly concerned me. The west wind had dropped, the water was still choppy, but much calmer than it had been all week. It was a blow.

Naturally the boys were nervous. Breakfast was rather quiet, each of them pensive and withdrawn for once. Appetites and witticisms were more subdued. Some of them had a bit of toast or a little cereal, but the usual bulldozing rush to the trough was non-operational this morning. They sat quietly in their Dark Blue tracksuits, each nursing very private thoughts. We were probably one of the biggest underdog crews on record, and that produces a very special kind of pressure – cold determination allied to a fear of revealing that everyone else was right after all.

I thought that Paul Gleeson and Richard Hull looked very highly strung that morning, which was worrying, because much was expected of them. Donald was quiet, but self-contained and Tom likewise. But I could tell that Gavin had a lot on his mind.

Just before eight o'clock we went down to the river, and embarked immediately for a short outing. The tide was still running out and the wind still seemed to be dropping, but since I could not change any of those things, I concentrated on what I *must* do, and that was to begin psyching them up. I sent them off on a long, loose paddle up to Harrods, letting the boat move ahead nice and free, with lots of run between the strokes. My aim was to get rid of tension, and to warm muscles. I asked for two short sprint bursts on the way back, to let them feel their harnessed power and remember it, to feel their great strength and to concentrate their minds. I had to try and distract them, at this stage, from any of that paralyzing worry, so I wanted their minds usefully occupied. This brief work-out was as much psychological as physical.

We swung away to starboard just before Putney Bridge, round the line of boats and pulled into the wind as we eased and glided to a stop outside the boathouse. Their faces were tight. No smiles. The only chat came from Hugh Pelham, who seemed extra bullish, spoiling for a fight, full of pent-up tension. He simply could not wait to get at Cambridge. A great guy to have in the boat.

I noticed that Donald looked fuller in the face again, that drawn hunted look gone, and he seemed fully recovered from the ordeal of the mutiny. But he appeared older now, less innocent and his face was set in a grim expression. He at least would give nothing away today. Not a single yard, while he was still alive to pull the oar.

I told the boys to leave the boat the right way up, and while they headed home for brunch, I took my bag of spanners into the boathouse and proceeded to go over the hull and the riggers with a fine-tooth comb. I always do this before a race as a sort of ritual, partly because I don't trust anyone else to do it as thoroughly as I do – too many races are lost through neglect on this score – and partly because it is therapeutic and gives me something useful to do. I checked every nut and every bolt attached to the yellow plastic hull. I checked each splash board, and I had a brief chat with Len Neville who was once more satisfying himself that all was well with those rough-water riggers of ours. Jerry Sutton popped in to look over the oars, which Albert the boatman was scrubbing carefully with hot water and disinfectant until the handles were spotless. Overnight he had touched them up with a final coat of Dark Blue paint.

It took me forty-five minutes to satisfy myself that every joint was tight, and that my trusty wrench had us all in fail-safe condition for the race. I am usually accused of being finicky about this but all the while I coached Oxford we never had a gear failure. I concluded my checks, making particularly sure that the rudder attachments were sound. Someone had tampered with our boat in Amersterdam a few years back just before the final of the world championships which we won, and I had spotted it moments before we went afloat.

The final task was to fit our big number two aluminium break-water behind the bowman's seat to deflect those Tideway rollers. I had them specially made in three sizes and Albert bolted the one we would use today firmly onto the boat.

As I left, carefully locking the big doors behind me, I could see the crowds beginning to arrive. The police were already sealing the area off to traffic with 'No Entry' signs; the umpire was there talking to Duncan Clegg; there were the rosette-sellers, programme sellers, souvenir sellers, and many old Boat Race regulars who usually had a cheerful word for me as I went about Oxford's final preparations. This year there was not much confidence. I heard a few shouts of 'Never mind Dan, there's always next year', and a few 'Poor old Oxfords', as I picked my way through the mass of BBC technicians, with their miles of cables and towers and huge vans, microphones and cameras.

I had a short interview to do for television together with the Cambridge coach Alan Inns, whom I thought seemed very anxious. I, the complete underdog, found myself rather chirpy, and in fact in my own mind I am always the underdog, because it keeps me sharp and hungry.

I drove back to the house where the boys were having brunch –

just poached eggs, toast, and a few potatoes if anyone wanted them. There was nothing I could do now to ease the pressure on them. They had to cope with it on their own; no one was able to fully prepare them for the enormity of the occasion, and the realization dawned on them slowly.

At 9.30 a.m. I told them to get down on their beds for an hour for a final reflective rest. I took Andy Lobbenberg down to the river for a run over the course to Hammersmith in the launch. The river was unusually crowded with crews because the Head of the River was being rowed later in the afternoon and many of them were out practising, making use of the last ninety minutes before the Thames would be completely cleared for the Boat Race.

As we got on board I paused briefly, and my heartbeat increased. The wind was definitely coming up. I could feel it on my left cheek, gusting down the Putney reach. So could Bert, and we set off in the Oxford launch to give Andy his final instructions. We huddled beside the driving seat as the wind picked up even more around the Fulham bend. 'She's gone due west, Dan,' said Bert. 'And I'd say she'll build up for another two or three hours.'

The wind was still nothing like as strong as it had been yesterday, but it was significant. And I told Andy: 'Now look ahead to the corner, past the Black Buoy – look how the water changes, just as you come around this bend. This is where you call for your first power-twenty, right on this curve. You will be two and three-quarter minutes into the race, and the water gets just a fraction better here; that's where you push the accelerator flat down to the boards. The moment you hit the better water.'

We chugged on a bit more, Bert saying nothing, Andy making mental notes. Suddenly as we approached the Mile Post, Bert spoke up urgently now. 'Look, Dan. Look at that.' I peered forward, and then I spotted it, a wind shadow stretching ahead. The water was flatter where the huge shadow of Harrods' Depository shielded it from the westerly breeze.

'That bugger'll stay there too for a while,' said Bert. 'But it's flatter there. No doubt.'

I turned to Andy and showed him the changing pattern on the water, until he too was absolutely clear in his mind where it was. 'Right', I said. 'I want you to steer a very delicate line off the corner right after your power-twenty. You've got to aim your bows right into that wind shadow. It will be there waiting for you and the moment you hit it shout for the boys to give it everything they have, the power-twenty to end all power-twenties. O.K., that's all we need to know; let's get back.'

By the time we docked, the big red and blue coach bearing the Oxford crew, with a full siren-wailing police escort in close attendance, had edged its way through the packed crowds and deposited the boys outside the boathouse. They looked resplendent in their white shirts and trousers and their dark blue ties, blazers and initialled sweaters. There was no blasé attitude about dress anymore. The sheer big-time atmosphere of this event had pulled them all into line.

I bounded up the steps to the dressing room and collected Donald for the traditional coin-tossing ceremony. 'Middlesex still Dan?' he asked, checking. 'That's the one,' I said. 'We really want that station.'

'I've talked to the boys,' he said. 'We're agreed on the call.'

'Good. But don't tell me. It's bad luck.'

I led him to the gathered throng of television men and officials, and then backed away, out of camera range, not out of discretion, but because I could hardly bear the tension. Christ, I wanted the far side today. And so did Cambridge. I glanced across at Steve Peel, the Light Blues President, and he looked ashen with nerves, swallowing repeatedly to moisten his dry mouth.

I listened for Donald's voice, because I knew that, as the challenger, he would call. Colin Moynihan flicked the old golden sovereign high in the air and Donald said firmly, 'tails'. I turned away as the crowd murmured with anticipation. Then I heard Donald say clearly: 'Middlesex', and I punched my fist into my right hand with delight.

An interviewer asked rather pointlessly, 'Why did you pick that station, Donald?' (as if in our wildest dreams we would disclose that) and the Oxford President replied archly, 'because my coach told me to.'

As we walked back up towards the changing room I could feel the wind hardening still more. The boys were waiting anxiously for the news: 'We've got Middlesex,' I told them, 'and I have a feeling things are going our way. Even the wind is blowing up stronger for us.' They all sat round totally united. We were a thousand light years away from those acrimonious days of committee room blood-baths which had threatened to destroy us all.

'Okay, settle down,' I said, 'and let's go over this again very quickly now that we know which side we're on. You know this is a three-minute race, that's all. Forget the rest. Andy is going to lean on Cambridge right from the start. We're going to stay close to them without any clashing, but edging them onto the outside of the bend, trying to keep them stranded there. Then we slam them with a legs-twenty as we come onto the corner, where the water will flatten out a bit for us just before three minutes. That's where we've got to make full use of the advantage of the inside of that bend.

'But for Andy to be able to do that you are going to have to pull as you have never pulled before. Because he cannot do it if he's down. He can only do it if you put him there, right up level with the Tabs. Remember everybody is responsible for every bit of this effort. We've got to be locked tight together as a fighting unit. Every stroke has to be *hard* in the water, with a *hard* finish, no matter how rough it is. I want you *vicious*, like bloody executioners; and I want you to remember that every hard stroke is another nail in Cambridge's coffin.

'Now, we've just been out on the course and there's a wind-shadow from Harrods around the area of the Mile Post. The water will be a little better there. It is likely that Andy will call for another push at that point, because I doubt if Cambridge have noticed it.

'If you count the toss, and the wind-shadow, there have been two big breaks this morning. And they're both ours.'

I saw Gavin's fist clench tight. Pelham's hit the bench beside him. And Donald and Tom nodded to each other, terse, unsmiling.

This crew really wants to race, I thought. I could feel their eagerness, sense the aggression and anticipation. A week ago they would have been sitting here terrified, with defeat written all over their faces. But now somehow they were different. Why? God knows. I supposed dryly that it was because we'd beaten Thames. But the truth was that every move we had made this past week had been correct. The gearing and the oar changes, putting Gavin and Tom in the stern, with Donald's blade behind them at 6, all had worked well; and it was all paying off. The mood in here was good, so utterly different to that sceptical deadness of 1986. This room already bore the smell of warfare; and I could feel it rising, that old match racer's instinct, the one that knows no doubt, no fear, only the determination to destroy the enemy. I felt a rush of adrenalin, because like them I was becoming blinded to the realities of the task ahead.

Our dressing room was a capsule, divorcing us all from the facts. I could hear myself telling them we were going to *win* – and I wasn't kidding them. I believed it. I thought for a brief idle moment that I was becoming schizophrenic. The sheer impossibility of it all was washing away from me as if it did not exist. And I was willing the boys to reach through the pain to row as they had never rowed before.

'You know you are the best in these conditions,' I said. 'So just throw aside feelings of tension, because it will only slow you down and inhibit you. Just stay loose in the rough water. You all know what to do. Hands well down and away, get the blades over the tops of the waves. But when the oars are in the water – no hesitation, no uncertainty. Give it *everything*. Hang on to those finishes. And lean into the headwind.'

Nothing I said must be allowed to daunt them now. They had to be inspired for the fight. 'You have the right equipment for this race,' I said, 'the right oars, and the boat is ideally rigged. The question is: *How hungry are you? Do you really want it? Because that's what it's going to come down to – who wants it most?*'

They were on their own now, for twenty minutes, to stretch, to do some warm-up exercises – squat jumps and a few press-ups. But they were all pumped up. I told them I would keep the door shut, and that they should prepare mentally as they exercised. They were due on the stake boat in forty-five minutes. As I walked out through the crowded club room, I came face to face with reality once again. Away from the fantasy cocoon of the dressing room, I saw friendly faces shaking their heads in sympathy as if for a condemned man. But back inside Donald says the difference with the previous year was extraordinary. Stewart was on top of the world and Pelham was grinning all over his face. Tom was lying on his back, gazing at the ceiling, psyching himself into his most aggressive frame of mind.

Donald went to a quiet corner of the dressing room for a moment and prayed, not that Oxford should just go out and win, but that everyone should reach their full potential and row as well as they ever could. He said how grateful he was that we were all here on this day, and that he hoped we would all come through our troubles stronger and better people. In his hand he clutched two postcards – one from Ruth which read: 'I love you my darling – whatever happens'. The other read: 'Be filled with the will to win. Take what belongs to you. Do not be denied. All best wishes and prayers. Michael Suarez.' Donald ended his few moments of contemplation with the whispered words: 'Please, please God, let me row the race of my life today.'

He sat there, with his heart pounding, ready to take the strain, ready to follow Gavin and Tom into hell.

Outside it began to rain, but the wind continued to build and the sky was overcast. The Cambridge camp supporters were a few yards away, laughing in the next boathouse heartily, fully confident of their inevitable victory. I had a quick word with Albert, checked the boat again and went upstairs to get the boys. Inside the dressing room I called: 'Okay lads, let's go down and watch Isis start against Goldie, then we'll go straight out on the water.'

As each man came out, I wished him a personal 'Good luck', although I doubt if they were aware of my words by now. And when the President stepped out I shook his hand and said: 'This is it. Go get 'em Donald.'

We stood outside in the rain and gave a rousing cheer as Isis powered bravely by in the reserve crews' Boat Race; but since we had taken half their rightful men it was not surprising they were on their way to defeat, albeit a narrow one.

We carried the Oxford Boat down to the water and Albert held her steady as the boys went back for their oars. Each man took his place, screwed his gate down tight, and I went quietly along the crew giving them a final word of encouragement, the last time I could speak to them before the start. 'Give 'em hell, Hugh.' 'You're a key man here Tom. Make it a good one.' A side-fist punch on the arm for Donald. 'Make that 6 seat work!' 'Have a great race Gavin. Keep 'em at it'. 'Stay sharp, Paul,' 'Okay Andy? Remember the plan. Lean on Cambridge early, and *use* the corners.'

By now there are thousands of people on both banks of the river, which has been sealed off to traffic. An enormous cheer goes up as Oxford pull out into the stream. The television cameras are whirring. The eyes of the world are upon us now. Can the Oxford no-hopers possibly pull this off?

The launch *Bosporus* eases into the bank to pick me up. Against all my old superstitions – since I reckon we don't have a chance anyway – I smuggle Ruth, Suzy and our baby on board together with Chris Davidge, the famous iron man of the stroke seat. Only twelve passengers are officially allowed. As I climb aboard I can hear shouts of 'Tough luck Dan, old son. Maybe next year.'

Someone yells, 'You might as well have stayed in the boathouse, Topolski.'

I join the other coaches in the bow of the Oxford launch, a space in the front reserved among Hugh Matheson, Steve Royle, John Pilgrim-Morris and Michael Barry. I give the thumbs-up sign and a wry smile to Bert. And someone asks: 'How are they, Dan?' I grin and shrug: 'As well as can be expected. But this could turn out to be horrible!'

Dr Barry comments: 'Well, at least we have a crew on the water, which at one point looked extremely doubtful. From where we came from that is an achievement in itself.'

Cambridge are also on the water and they look good as they come past us on their way to the start. I watch their cracking sharp stroke, an Old Blue Paddy Broughton, from last year's Great Britain Eight. 6 foot 5 inches, he's a big tough guy, with an outgoing personality. Behind him at 7 sits Jim Garman, 6ft 5ins, also a senior international and a member of the British coxed Four. At 6 is the 6ft 7ins Jim Pew, a US oarsman weighing over 210lbs. Also a Blue from last year's victorious Eight, he is the lynch-pin of the crew. At 5 is the 6ft 6ins President Steve Peel, the best man in the boat, also a British international from the same British national Eight. He would shortly become one of the country's star oarsmen, and an Olympian.

At 4, is Matt Brittin, a 6ft 4ins freshman, but one of the best junior oarsman ever produced in Great Britain; an eighteen-year-old tiger. At 3, Nick Grundy, a former school crewmate of Hugh Pelham's and due to join the British Lightweight Eight for the world championships; one of the toughest men in either boat. At 2 is the 6ft 3ins Richard Spink, one of the best college oarsmen at Cambridge. And in the bow sits Ian Clarke, a really hard nut, also from Cambridge's winning crew the year before and an immaculate bowman. I'd always fear him in a race. Their freshman cox, Julian Wolfson is the least experienced man in the boat.

By any standards it is a bloody good crew, which on its day would run any national Eight extremely close. How can we possibly beat them? We have three virtual novices, two rather awkward, not very successful junior internationals, one failed Cambridge oarsman, an international past his prime, and the oldest man ever to row in the Boat Race. It is impossible to quarrel with the odds of 6–1 on Cambridge. Out here, away from the insular fury and determination of our own dressing room, and with the reality of Cambridge right in front of our eyes, the result of the race has to be a foregone conclusion.

By now the wind is beginning to howl, and the rain is sheeting at an angle down Putney Reach. As our launch moves out towards the stake boats, the dark clouds begin to thicken, and the water is growing rougher by the second. There are sheer walls on either bank of the wide river here and the waves hit the sides and bounce back just as hard, particularly when the tide is building as it is now.

Oxford head down towards Wandsworth and then turn, rowing a good hard thirty-stroke racing start on the way back. Our launch moors alongside a tug and we sit there in the slashing rain, on this heaving water, waiting for the boys to re-appear. There is thunder in the distance and it's heading our way. Then Andy brings the boat through the bridge and Donald sends me a big grin. I give him the thumbs up, and behind him, I can see Cambridge coming on to their stake boat.

Conditions are terrible, virtually unrowable, with the waves tossing the little Boat Race armada all over the river. Suddenly there is a gigantic flash of lighting, which hits a BBC television tower, followed immediately by a deafening clap of thunder, the mystical Hammer of Thor. To me it booms: 'O-X-F-O-R-D!'

These waves simply must blunt the speed of Cambridge, and must surely render their light plastic oars a horrendous liability in this wind. 'Start it now! Start the race now!' I mutter.

The crews are taking off their sweaters and passing them down the boats. I look over at Cambridge and they seem to have a round-shouldered, almost cowering look to them, as they peer over their shoulders at the raging Tideway which lies ahead.

'I don't believe it,' I say to Hugh. 'Look, they don't want to race.' We can see their reluctance very clearly. Cambridge do not want to tackle that water. They are momentarily more concerned with the danger, with how unfair it is, than they are about beating us. The favourites realize the odds are no longer quite so overwhelming and the new guys in the middle of their boat are looking desperately anxious.

'*Start it!*' I say again. For a moment I have a flashing image of the rebel Yanks in just this sort of water. I can hear their reaction: 'shit guys, there's no way they're going to race us in this stuff. They're crazy. Hell man! No f---ing way.' It is fortunate that none of them are out there to dampen the spirit of this new Oxford crew.

I look back to Oxford. Their heads are up, and they are grinning expectantly, talking urgently to each other as they get ready. Both coxes have their boats in line on the stake boats now, but each of them has his arm in the air signifying he is not ready. Then I see an unexpected movement in the middle of the Oxford boat. Richard Hull and Donald Macdonald, lifelong enemies, are, very quietly, shaking hands. They acknowledge the bond that will tie them together as brothers for the next twenty minutes.

The rain continues to pour down and it is becoming hard to hold the two crews on the stake boats. I think to myself, 'Christ, I hope he doesn't stop it. He mustn't.' Just then the umpire's launch pulls alongside and Colin Moynihan shouts out: 'Dan, what do you think? It's terrible. What should we do?'

Now I know that Colin is a Member of Parliament and is obviously mindful of the safety of the contestants, he does not want to be the MP who becomes infamous for presiding over the drowning of eighteen Boat Race oarsmen. What he needs is reassurance from his former coach, and I shout back: 'It's fine; it's getting better. Let's get on with it!'

'I'll have to ask Cambridge,' he yells and he chugs off. As he does so, I notice that Oxford are already three-quarters of a length up. The incoming tide is causing the stake boat to drag its anchor. Cambridge are now looking round in panic, pointing to the fast increasing disparity between the two crews. Someone shouts: 'Oxford are a length up!' The boys are roaring with laughter. Our stake boat men are valiantly pulling on the anchor rope which has finally found a grip, and are dragging themselves and the entire crew back into line. Now I notice that the driver of the umpire's launch is in trouble.

His reverse gear has gone and I think the umpire is going to postpone the race for sure. 'Get him over here,' I bellow to the driver. Somehow we haul Colin and his white flag on board our launch.

At this point I can see we need to change tactics. If we head straight upriver now, staying close to Cambridge with the water so turbulent and the stream relatively slack, we will forsake our Middlesex advantage. Oxford *must* head for the relative cover of the Fulham Wall over to Andy's right. Sitting where I am, behind the umpire, I begin waving my right arm up and down like a madman, pointing towards the Wall, and after a couple of minutes, Donald finally spots me. 'Look Tom, Dan's signalling.' Cadoux-Hudson passes the message to Lobbenberg: 'Dan wants us to head over to the cover of the Wall, and by the look of it he really means it. Get your bows over.' I see Andy look round and give a thumbs up as he swings the boat over, calling to the bowside to dig their oars in. 'Too far,' I groan, but it's too late. They're under starter's orders.

The squall is passing, but it is still incredibly rough. We're drifting rapidly forward in our launch now and Colin has got to start them.

Someone shouts, 'We're nearly level with them. Quick we'll run over the oars.'

Instantly Colin calls out: 'Get ready please'.

The oarsmen in the two boats tense and settle into position; still the launch drifts forward. Over in the Oxford boat, Donald says grimly, 'Good luck boys.'

And then the umpire bellows: '*Are you ready? . . . Go!*'

A massive roar goes up from the crowds packed twelve deep on our side of the river. The Oxford blades dig deep into the water, the first three drawn out strokes throwing the boat forward, to the right, across the wind towards the Fulham shore. Cambridge takes off a fraction faster, but they go straight up the middle of the river in a cloud of spray, ploughing into the waves which break over their bow and against their five-stay riggers.

The two crews are heading off at a tangent to each other which no one has ever seen before. Within seconds the Cambridge cox realizes his mistake but hesitates. He's too late. Oxford are now getting into their stride and have taken a lead of a couple of seats – maybe three or four feet – and they are getting into slightly better water. '*F-u-l-l length!*' bawls Lobbenberg on the sixth stroke. '*Now build it!*'

Cambridge, insufficiently briefed and indecisive, angle back towards Oxford, slewing round about 45 degrees off their original course. They come crashing diagonally across the waves, with the spray flying above them, and water cascading off their riggers. I notice for the first time that they have an electric pump which is working overtime to bail out. 'I'd rather stop the water coming in than try to get it out,' I think to myself with a degree of satisfaction.

Oxford are now going like the clappers, Gavin hauling on his oar with monstrous power and Tom matching him blow for blow. But the water is not a lot better for us and on the eighth stroke we hit a massive wave. Richard Hull, sitting right behind Donald, sees his blade bury dangerously on the backswing.

They recover quickly and with each mighty stroke they build up to their racing rate of forty-two in the first half minute. Gavin hits maximum revs on the fifteenth stroke, and right after that Andy yells '*S-i-i-i-t back!*', and Gavin throttles them down to thirty-eight. Oxford are by now close up against the wall and the roar of the crowd is almost intimidating as they fight their way along the edge of the river, with Cambridge thundering across to join them.

Oxford now have nearly a third-of-a-length, and Gavin is going like a train, with Donald's blade right behind him backing him up on every stroke. In the bow Hugh Pelham is pulling like a lunatic, as if each and every stroke he makes will be his last.

Cambridge call for a power-ten, and they battle their way over, still at an angle, heading right for us. Suddenly they are level – but they're too close. The umpire shouts a warning. Donald shouts in desperation: '*Here they come!*' Tom roars: '*Well push, for Christ's sake, push*'. Gavin prepares for a major effort and on Andy's command, his huge head rolls back with the strain as he increases the rate, tugging his oar out at the finish with a volcano of a puddle on the end. Tom and Donald are right with him. Their faces are both contorted, their lips dragged back from their teeth as they pull with every ounce of strength in their bodies. Behind them Richard Hull is cracking on to his catches and the bow four of Gleeson, Ward, Gish and Pelham are taking the brunt of the rough water.

In a screen of spray Cambridge fight their way alongside Oxford, but I can see their light oars are being caught and thrown about by the wind, and the tops of the waves are breaking over their riggers. That short Oxford burst has put them narrowly back in front once again and at the two-minute mark Andy calls out: 'a third-of-a-length, guys. I've got two men on them.'

Now we are right on the bend, and the boys are getting their second wind as they hang on grimly to their tiny lead. Andy can see they are beginning to feel the murderous pace through this strength-sapping water, but he keeps them striding at thirty-six, with the slightly flatter water now within his grasp. But almost immediately he has to call for the legs-twenty we have planned.

Once more the crews plough into a series of big waves, which crash against their riggers and the Cambridge cox calls to his men to steady the boat. That is all Andy Lobbenberg needs to hear. With the anxious yells of the Light Blue cox ringing in his ears, he roars at Oxford: 'Okay boys, here we go, let me have it right now – *in–three, in–two, in–one, go!!'*

Again Gavin gathers himself forward and wrenches the oar through the stroke with brute power, every muscle stretched to its limit. The rest of the crew follow his lead with tremendous courage for Andy has already demanded an awful lot of them so early in the race. Almost immediately he snaps: *'I'm level with Peel, their 5 man. We're moving on them.'*

But Cambridge are not done yet. They too call for a twenty push, responding to Oxford with all of their strength. But it's not enough, and Oxford keep going heroically, inching in front with every stroke. Off Fulham football ground they squeeze a few more feet, increasing their lead to three-quarters-of-a-length. Lobbenberg shouts: *'I've got their bowman!'* And he throttles Oxford down again off the power-twenty to their racing rate of thirty-five.

We are beside ourselves with excitement in the launch. We cannot believe what is happening right there in front of us, for we all knew in our hearts that the race would be over and done with in the first minute. Now Michael is saying we've got them on the run, and I'm saying, it's crazy and it can't last, and Cambridge will change gear at any second and charge right through us. 'Our bend will run out in a moment, you'll see, and the station advantage will begin to swing their way. It's been fun though – far better than we could have dared hope.' But they aren't coming past us yet, and the further we go the more a mood of hysterical optimism rushes round our launch.

We do not have clear water yet and Andy is reluctant to start his move across towards the centre of the river, the course he must take if he is to claim the inside of the Hammersmith bend. He hangs on, hangs on in the relative shelter of the Wall, as the boys strive for the extra inches to give us the magic clear water we need between their bow and our stern post.

But Tom Cadoux-Hudson can't stand it for a moment longer because he knows that on this side of the river, on our station, we have the right of way and Cambridge have to stay clear of us wherever we go. *'Cross now!'* he bellows. *'Steer the bastard over!'* Andy obeys instantly, converging on Cambridge and Gavin steps the rate up a fraction. Cambridge right behind us, overlapping but nevertheless still in our water, are again warned by the umpire, who points his flag to the left, towards the Surrey station.

Then disaster strikes. Gavin catches a massive crab. His blade hits a big wave on the way back for the catch, which drives the oar deep into the water. The handle smashes into his stomach with enormous force and the boat shudders, slewing round towards Cambridge, its speed instantly and dramatically cut. The Oxford rhythm is shot to pieces.

Gavin, with an outrageous display of strength, rips the blade out of the water and rams it back in, without missing a stroke. That crab could have thrown a lesser man straight into the Thames, but all it does is cost us a part of our lead. Cambridge grab back a third-of-a-length.

Vainly the boys try to regain their magnificent fighting rhythm, but four strokes later Ward clips his finish on the top of another big breaking wave. Pelham then catches a worse one on the very next stroke. But he shrugs it off bravely, forcing his blade clear, struggling to keep in time with a desperation I can actually see from the launch.

Two strokes after that, with the boat rolling, Hull catches his knees with the handle of the oar which ploughs in deep and sticks. Cadoux-Hudson's blade slams back, missing Hull's by a fraction as it hangs limply over the side. Hull misses that stroke altogether, which sets us back another quarter-of-a-length. '*For f---'s sake!*' I scream, '*What's he doing!!*' He recovers at last and gets going again.

Somehow Oxford are holding Cambridge at bay, racing through this windswept rough water with a kind of unflinching desperation, but the Light Blues hit back with a vengeance matching us stroke for stroke as we head up towards the Mile Post. We're back in exposed water again here, and once more both crews are slamming into the waves. Hugh Pelham, up in the bow, is getting soaked to the skin with water pouring into his eyes; but nothing puts him off his stroke; he never misses a beat.

The two boats are still locked together, but Oxford are now miraculously ahead by over half-a-length.

Up ahead Andy can see the wind-shadow he knows awaits us, and he continues to drive Cambridge back across the river even though they have an overlap. Moynihan cannot put up with this for long because we are now in neutral water, he grabs his white flag, and for the first time issues a warning to the Dark Blues. '*Oxford return to your water*', and pointing his flag towards Middlesex he shouts again: '*Move over Oxford!*'

We coaches are delirious at this dreamlike race, some laughing in disbelief. 'Well, our three minutes is up,' I say. 'That was what we came for. They've done everything I asked.' We are all still resigned to eventual defeat but nevertheless enjoying the present experience hugely. However, out on the water, the crew have anything but defeat on their minds.

Lobbenberg steers over a fraction, but right then Cambridge launch their biggest attack. Paddy Broughton forces the rate up to thirty-six in a desperate bid to defend his Surrey water. If they can only hit Oxford, caught over here on their side of the river, they could force a disqualification. Wolfson, the Light Blue cox is urging his tiring men to yet another effort, driving them up inside the battling Oxford crew. They gain a foot, then another, and another. Now they have a four-foot overlap, and Andy glances over his left shoulder, sees Cambridge are on him and gaining with every stroke.

Very calmly he says: 'Okay boys, this is it. The big Oxford push to Harrods.' And once more he calls in time to the rhythm of Gavin's powerful strokes: '*In–three!.. in–two!.. in–one!... Now go!*' And eight pairs of white Oxford rowing socks slam into the stretcher boards.

With a superhuman effort, Gavin, Tom, Donald and the crew, their oars bending almost to breaking point, virtually pick up the boat, and fling it forward like a missile. As they do so the Cambridge effort begins to disintegrate, their stroke growing shorter and more laboured as they fight to keep those light plastic oars under control, forcing them back into the wind for every catch. On the seventeenth stroke of the Oxford push we have nearly two-thirds of a length of clear water, and I swing round to the others in the Oxford launch. 'It's the oars!' I bellow, 'It's those bloody plastic oars. They're killing Cambridge off.'

Cambridge seem to falter on the sixth stroke of their effort and imperceptibly Broughton's challenge begins to fade as their rating drops, first to thirty-four and then to thirty-two. This proud and talented crew are, for the moment, rendered impotent by the harsh, rough conditions, and the equipment with which they have chosen to do battle.

Incredulously I glance across at Gavin. His head is leaning to one side at every stroke, but he still has Oxford firing along at thirty-five, and behind him the boys are following in fine form, their cohesion getting better the further they go, as they fight their way towards Hammersmith Bridge. Hell, I've never seen them rowing so well. They are opening up a lead of nearly two lengths and for the first time I'm thinking they might actually get away with it. They are all very tired now, but Andy is holding them together well: '*Keep those finishes buried and sit back. Hands down and away! Coming up to the bridge and it's rough again up ahead.*'

Always cautious, I still think Cambridge have the strength and the brilliance to launch another attack, and I am by no means certain that we can repel it if they do. I can see how weary Oxford are, only a third of the way through this battle for supremacy, and it is with mounting horror that I see the Light Blues begin to harden their stroke as Oxford drive towards the left-hand side of the centre arch.

A great cheer goes up from the crowd as the Dark Blues shoot the bridge seven seconds ahead. As they burst through with a good punchy racing stride of thirty-four, the crowds on the other side can't believe their eyes. It is as if mass hallucination has conjured up a ghost: the rank underdogs come powering underneath them holding a lead of nearly two lengths.

'*It's Oxford!*' A yell of disbelief erupts when they catch sight of Pelham's Dark Blue blade. Lobbenberg steers hard left for the Surrey side close to the crowds and Donald is startled to hear people clearly shouting '*Come on Donald, you can do it,*' from the bank. They are calling out his name, cheering and chanting: '*Mac–Donald, Mac–Donald, Mac–Donald, Mac–Donald.*' A brand new, rather shy British hero is being born.

Now Cambridge are attacking again, blazing through the bridge with all guns firing. With tremendous courage and resilience they quickly slice half-a-length off our lead, driving a line for the Surrey bank, on our inside. Suddenly they are within a length of the overlap which will allow them to push us back out across the river. They are matching our rating, and with every stroke they seem to be gaining a bit more. Haven't Oxford seen them? They're going to get caught!

Donald shouts first: '*They're coming back!*' Cadoux-Hudson, realizing the danger, roars: '*Go – go – go!*' In front of him Gavin reaches out once more, beyond the agony of his aching arms, and accelerates the oar through the water. They are all hurting now, but somehow they match Gavin's long deep action. The pain in their thighs and backs is excruciating as they dig deep for something extra. This is what all that endurance training through the winter was for. This is why everyone in the squad had to give 110 per cent, why no one could shirk. This race is indeed unlike any other in the world.

The whole crew looks agonized, their mouths flying open as they lean back into the stroke. Their hair lies matted, flattened by sweat and rain and river spray. They are not yet halfway and Cambridge are closing fast. The lactic acid is throbbing into their joints. Shoulder muscles are crying 'No more!' But now Lobbenberg is calling for another effort.

'Come on, Oxford! Answer them ... give me ten ... right now ... in one! ... go!' Cadoux-Hudson's head jerks back as he follows Gavin into the stroke. I can see Donald's oar bending into an arc as he follows the two giants in front of him. And now Gavin's head tucks down onto his right shoulder – the position he always adopts when he's digging deep for the will to ignore the pain.

On my stopwatch they are at thirty-five, and at this pace I am not sure how much longer they can take it. Because this is not a boat race any longer. This is a prizefight on the river, and it has come down to raw courage. Who has the hunger? Who wants it most? And although there is always a special private nobility about such a contest, what finally decides it is when one crew finds suddenly that it has nothing more to give.

Cambridge's last desperate push beyond Hammersmith was full of valour, in a race where valour is a common virtue. But the first mile had hurt them badly, and when Oxford hit back, when they answered that final urgent demand from Lobbenberg, that was just too much for the Light Blues. They caved in, the fight draining away from their tired bodies.

And now we seemed to be floating out from the shadow of Hammersmith Bridge into brighter weather. I looked back down the racecourse to the black clouds which still hung over Putney, the scene of so much of my despair during the past months. For me they were symbolic of the black mood which had hung over the Boat Club for so long. The light beyond the bridge now promised that we would break through into paradise, and all I could see was Oxford rowing strongly away along Chiswick Reach, well clear of a Cambridge crew that could not find it in themselves to come back at them again. At least not today, they wouldn't. And I was suddenly free.

Perhaps I would return to coach Oxford again in a few years time, but not until the rebels were all finally gone. For now I was resolved to sit back and enjoy one of the greatest Dark Blue triumphs in history, and to put the blackness and the gloom far behind me.

Up along the island they rowed, past Chiswick Steps and round the corner. Stewart still had the rate up at thirty-four although they were a good three lengths ahead. And they looked good; damned good, better than they had ever looked before. At Barnes Bridge they stepped it up for a grandstand finish and all along the river people were shouting, '*Oxford!*' and '*Well done, Donald.*' '*Terrific row, Donald!*'

They went past the four-mile mark with three-and-a-half lengths to spare and came through the last 374 yards at a fierce finishing pace, storming over the line four lengths clear of the favourites, a bare second inside a marathon twenty minutes. Cambridge, hanging on as they had done throughout the race, dragged themselves home ragged and exhausted. For the losers this race is always a never-ending nightmare.

As the Dark Blue boat drifted under the bridge, I saw a sight I have never before witnessed after a Boat Race. A lone figure was standing up in the Oxford Boat, balancing like a statue on the two wooden stays which run just beneath the saxboards inside the boat. His mighty arms were raised upwards to the sky, and his face stared in ecstasy into the heavens beyond. It might have been a demonstration of brute strength, or even a display of massive triumph – the bold stance of the victor. But for a few brief shining moments, Donald Macdonald was alone with his God.

The sight of him standing like that is the image most people will always treasure in their minds about the 1987 Boat Race. It was photographed a hundred times during the twelve seconds in which he remained there. As he sat down again, he let out a primeval roar of joy which echoed under the bridge and out to the crowd. And all the crew were cheering and shouting, and shaking their fists in jubilant celebration. I just stood there and watched, laughing with relief at the sheer exhilarating fantasy of it, tears uncontrollably streaming down my face. The tensions and heartbreak of the last weeks were draining away, but the relief was tinged with sadness. In spite of everything, I wished somehow that the Americans could have been there.

It took for ever for Bert to dock the boat in the general

pandemonium of a Boat Race finish, and I was about the last to disembark. By this time the television interviews with the crew were over, and the bottles of champagne had been opened and drunk, and sprayed; and up in the dressing room the celebration was in full swing.

But as I stepped ashore there was one person on his own to greet me, the only man who really knew that I had rowed every stroke with them, all the way from Putney to Mortlake. And he said quietly, 'We could have been disqualified out there, Dan.'

'How do you mean?' I asked.

And Donald flung his arms around me in a great bear hug and his words will live with me for ever.

'Because we had ten men in our boat, and they only had nine.'

EPILOGUE

DONALD MACDONALD elected to conclude his career in competitive rowing in the comparative peace of the sunlit 1987 Henley Royal Regatta in late June. He selected a partner and entered as a Pair for the fabled Silver Goblets, rowed along the same course in fine summer weather, where once he had done battle in sub-zero temperatures.

For a man in search of rest and recuperation he made the mistake of choosing Hugh Pelham for his partner. No sooner were they on the water than the Oxford bowman was spoiling for a fight. Over the horizon came the Oxford Coxed Four who were seeking British selection for the world championships. Unfortunately for Tom Cadoux-Hudson he had teamed up with Stewart, Hull, Ward and Lobbenberg, to race in the Prince Philip Cup. For Pelham this was like a scarlet muleta to a fighting bull, and he formally challenged them to a duel.

All the old animosities had by now returned (Stewart had written a letter to the *Daily Telegraph* immediately after the Boat Race in which he sought to attack Macdonald all over again) – and suddenly the two factions were once more at daggers drawn. Hull, Ward and Stewart had maintained to the bitter end that Macdonald was marginal and could not move boats, while Stewart had always claimed that the Eight had better 'swing' with Ward than with Pelham.

It should of course have been 'no contest'. A Four ought to have a good two lengths to spare over a quarter-of-a-mile. But in a brilliant flat-out sprint, with Macdonald at stroke, the Pair flashed past the mark a third-of-a-length up. The Oxford Four were dumbfounded.

They demanded a re-match. Demanded to swap stations. Pelham, with a manic grin, agreed and immediately said: 'This is a private challenge now, from you to us. And I accept.' Macdonald braced himself for another battle. Once more they flew up Temple Island. The Four didn't stand a chance. Seven months of pent-up emotion fuelled their opponents, and this time the Pair finished half-a-length ahead. There could scarcely have been a more evocative statement from the President they had sought to destroy. The Four lost in the first round of their event and abandoned their selection ambitions.

In the Silver Goblets event the Pair reached the semi-final where they faced the Russian world champions, the Pimenov brothers. Pelham was determined to beat them. Again the Oxford Pair charged out of the blocks and took a narrow lead. Pelham, beside himself with excitement, roared '*Christ! We're winning*' as they matched the finest Pair in the world. After a quarter-of-a-mile they were still level, but then the Russians eased out to a two-length lead where they sat coolly all the way to the enclosures. 'It was like my old Beetle against a Ferrari,' smiles Donald now, in retrospect.

But nonetheless the grittiness of the two Dark Blues brought the entire grandstand to its feet with a thunderous roar of applause. '*Wind her up, wind her up!!*' yelled Hugh. '*I've wound her up you silly bugger,*' gasped Donald. At which point the Russians sprinted for the line and won by five lengths. 'Another couple of days practice, and we'd have got 'em,' said Hugh.

Spurred on by this performance, they entered the National Championships and took second place. They were the last competitive strokes Donald Macdonald ever rowed. He declined an invitation to compete for England, because, he said, 'I could never put Ruth through it all over again.' My own view is that he never intended to row seriously after the 1987 Boat Race. But somehow, he had needed just one final act of defiance against those who had once doubted him. He had had to establish his credentials beyond dispute.

He proved himself, irrevocably, undeniably, at the highest level of British rowing. Satiated at last, he went home to Lime Road where he hung the big Dark Blue oar he had pulled so valiantly in the 1987 Boat Race, above the dining room table.

His final act as President of the OUBC was to nominate his successor, and he named the big winning number 7 man Dr Tom Cadoux-Hudson, Oxford's most experienced racer and the obvious man for the job. However, the old American lobby returned to overthrow his recommendation in a secret ballot, and Christopher Penny was elected President for 1987–88.

Donald took his degree in English Language and Literature and left the university at the end of the 1988 summer term. He began work at Lloyds of London on 4 July 1988, American Independence Day.

CHRISTOPHER CLARK, on hearing that Oxford had won the Boat Race, remarked 'just another slap in the face.' He obtained his Diploma in Social Studies after two years at Oxford. He rowed for his college in his second year and returned to the USA where he failed to make the National Team, now being regarded by the coaches there as 'only a recreational rower'. In 1988 he failed again to make the United States Olympic team. In that year he returned on a short visit to Oxford, with his father, and spent some time coaching the Oriel Eight for the Henley Regatta. It was Oxford's top college crew containing the three Blues, Gish, Ward and Hull. They were defeated in Henley's Junior Restricted event, The Thames Cup, in the first round.

DAN LYONS went home to the United States without taking his Special Diploma. He and his Four failed to defend their world title, but finished third in the world championships in Copenhagen. In 1988 Dan Lyons failed to retain his four place, but went to the Olympics in the Coxed Pair, finishing last.

CHRISTOPHER HUNTINGTON took his Diploma in Social Studies and returned to the United States for trials. He failed to make the National team which went to Copenhagen, but regained his place in the Olympic team the following year.

JONATHON FISH did not remain at Oxford to uphold his statement to the *Sunday Times* in which he said of the American group: 'We're not talking guys who have just been to welding school. We're talking pretty solid academic backgrounds'. He never took his Diploma at Oxford, and returned to the United States with no further solid academic qualifications. He did, however, retain his place in the US Coxed Four which had won a bronze medal in 1986. In Copenhagen they finished last and were eliminated, having collided with the lane buoys. He joined Penny's coaching team for 1988, and was selected as cox of the US Olympic Pair with Lyons.

CHRISTOPHER PENNY, as the new Oxford President, decided not to return to the USA to pursue his international rowing career. He won the election partly by promising to revise the constitution of the OUBC, to make the President more accountable, and to 'return the Boat Club to its constituents'. He also decided to create a Freshmen's Eight to supersede Isis and the usual University third crew. The Freshmen's Eight was intended to serve as a nursery for the Blue Boat, hitherto Isis's traditional role. Penny saw his task as 'teaching English guys to row well.'

In the event his Freshmen's Eight drew new talent away from the Isis crew and seriously weakened it. Isis lost the reserve Boat Race against Goldie by six lengths and the Freshmen's Eight was later disbanded.

Penny's Presidency was, however, distinguished in that he had the luxury, for the first time in the history of the OUBC, of a full-time professional director of rowing, Steve Royle, who took over all the administrative and logistical work at the club. This left the new President free to concentrate solely on his rowing, something not possible for his 133 predecessors. Together with new head coach, Mike Spracklen, they reinstituted all the traditional Boat Race training schedules – running, circuits, pyramids, ladders, staircases, morning workouts and double outings on the weekends – which had been the source of all the discontent the previous year. The idea of core-time was discarded. Spracklen insisted upon longer sessions on the water. Five hours a day became the norm. Penny seemed assailed by nostalgia for the old days, and upon his election he telephoned me with the following enquiry: 'I haven't decided on my coaches yet, but I just want to know that if I decide to use you, will you be around?'

I told him: 'Not available.'

In the end he selected six Old Blues from my 1987 crew. The missing three were of course Macdonald (retired), Gish (withdrew after the first month) and Ward (suspended from college for a year). Their replacements were a British Junior World gold medallist, an American from the Naval Academy and Penny himself. Of the oarsmen and players from the year before, Oriel's Peter Baird resigned, like Gish, a month into training, as did the St Benet's captain Robin Geffen, chosen by Penny for the job of College secretary; and Julian Richards, the antagonistic reporter on the university paper *Cherwell* which attacked Macdonald throughout the crisis, was quickly marginalized in Pairs trials and quit.

Isis men, Chinn and Race, loyalists to Macdonald, although the fastest pair in the 'B' group, were dropped on the grounds that they had 'reached their full potential.'

Despite losing to the University of London and to Leander in the Reading Head by twenty-four seconds in early fixtures, Oxford won the 1988 Boat Race by four lengths.

GAVIN STEWART was 6 in Penny's 1988 crew and later went on to row at 4 in the British Olympic crew which won the Grand Challenge Cup at Henley in 1988. (It is deeply ironic that he won his place despite having finished bottom in the seat racing tests. Mike Spracklen just put him in regardless because he thought he would pull harder than others).

TOM CADOUX-HUDSON rowed at 5 for Penny and then retired from competitive racing to pursue his medical career.

MICHAEL SUAREZ made his final appearance in the world of the Oxford–Cambridge Boat Race when he attended the captains' meeting which elected Christopher Penny. At one stage late in the evening, he was joined, in the seat next to him, by Dan Lyons.

'Hi,' said the Philadelphian. 'I'm Dan Lyons. You've probably heard of me. I won a gold medal in the world championships.' But his smile melted when he heard the name 'Suarez'.

'You spoke for Macdonald against us at the captains' meeting,' he said. 'And you should be ashamed of yourself as an American.'

'Why do you say that?'

'Because I thought you of all people would stand for fair play.'

'I do, Mr Lyons,' replied the Jesuit poet. 'That I most definitely do.'

GLOSSARY

BLADE: Portion at the end of the oar or scull which enters the water during the rowing stroke.

BOW: Forward part of the boat and the name given to the rower who sits in the bows.

BOWSIDE: (Starboard). Left-hand side of the boat from the rower's point of view.

BURST: Tactical increase of speed.

CANVAS: Covering which encloses the bow and stern sections of the boat and is a term used to describe a leading margin by one crew over another – representing approximately 5 to 6 feet.

CATCH: Moment of entry of the blade into the water at the beginning of the rowing stroke.

CIRCUITS: Intensive gym exercises done in repetition to improve muscle endurance and heart and lung function.

COX: (coxswain) The steersman who sits facing the strokeman and who issues instructions through a microphone/speaker system. In some cases, the cox may lie full-length in the bows of the boat facing forward behind the bowman to improve the weight distribution, particularly in the smaller class racing boats.

CRAB: Occurs when blade enters the water at under square position, goes too deep and gets stuck at finish. This can sometimes stop the boat.

CREW: The rowers who make up the team in an Eight, Four, Pair, Double or Quad.

DOUBLE: (double scull) Boat with two men sculling (using two sculls each).

EIGHT: Eight-oared racing boat with eight rowers and a cox.

ENGINE ROOM: Term used to describe the four big, powerful men in the middle of an Eight at 6, 5, 4 and 3.

ERGOMETER: Land-based rowing machine for testing.

FEATHER: Position of the blade being swung forward parallel to the water as the rower prepares to take a stroke.

FIN: Attached to bottom (hull) of boat for stability.

FINISH: Moment of blade extraction from the water at the end of the stroke.

FOUR: Four-oared racing boat with four rowers. There are two classes of Four – coxless and coxed – the former being steered by one of the oarsmen using a device attached to his foot stretcher.

GATE: (rowlock or oarlock) U-shaped attachment at outer end of the rigger to hold the oar or scull in place at the pivot point.

HEIGHT: Distance of gate position above the seat; this measurement is adjustable for best efficiency and comfort according to athlete's size.

LEGS/ or POWER TEN/TWENTY: Cox's call for maximum tactical effort.

PADDLE: Easy rowing at low rating and minimum pressure.

PAIR: Two-oared racing boat; two classes of boat – with or without cox, and the two oarsmen holding one oar each.

PITCH: Angle at which the blade enters the water, fine adjustments are made by tilting the gate forward or backward, in or out.

PUDDLE: Swirl left in the water after the blade has been extracted at the end of the stroke.

PUSH: Tactical increase of speed.

OAR: Finely carved length of timber (or carbon/plastic/glass fibre) which the rower uses to row the boat along. Usually 381 to 386 cm long or 12 feet 5 inches to 12 feet 7½ inches.

QUAD: (quadruple scull) Four-man racing boat in which the rowers have a pair of sculls each.

RATING: Number of strokes rowed per minute – used to advise crew of their working rate. The word 'pip' is used by rowers in this connection, e.g. take the rate up two pips – from 34 to 36.

RECOVERY: Rest phase during stroke cycle when rower is swinging forward to take the next catch.

RIG: Includes riggers, oars, height, pitch etc. – i.e. all adjustable elements involved in the fine-tuning preparation of a boat for racing.

RIGGER: Adjustable metal frame projecting from side of the boat to support the gate which holds the oar or scull at the pivot point.

RUDDER: Steering device in the stern operated by the cox using connecting strings or wires.

SCULL: Single-scull racing boat for one man using two sculls (similar to oars but smaller). The name applies to the boat and to the oar type.

SCULLER: Rower racing in a quad, double or single-sculling boat.

SHELL: Racing rowing boat.

SLIDE: Runners on which the sliding seat rolls back and forward to enable the rower to use the strongest muscles in the body, the thigh quadruceps, and achieve the longest effective stroke.

SPAN: (T.D.) Distance from the 'pin' or pivot point of the gate to the centre or keel of the boat.

SQUARE: Position of the blade at right angles or perpendicular to the water just before and as it enters for the catch, through the stroke and at the point of extraction before being rolled onto the feather for the recovery phase.

STRETCHER: Adjustable support for feet to which are attached flexible shoes.

STERN: Back end of the boat where the cox sits – or further back to the stern post.

STROKE: The rower who sits in the stern of the boat facing the cox and who sets the rhythm for his crewmates sitting behind him. In an Eight the rest of the crew are numbered from stroke – 7, 6, 5, 4, 3, 2 and bow. In a Four it is stroke, 3, 2 and bow. Rowers on the continent of Europe number their positions in reverse order. Also the term given to the rowing action – as in 'taking a stroke' or 'the stroke cycle'.

STROKESIDE: (port) Right-hand side of the boat seen from the rower's point of view.

THE BOAT RACE COURSE

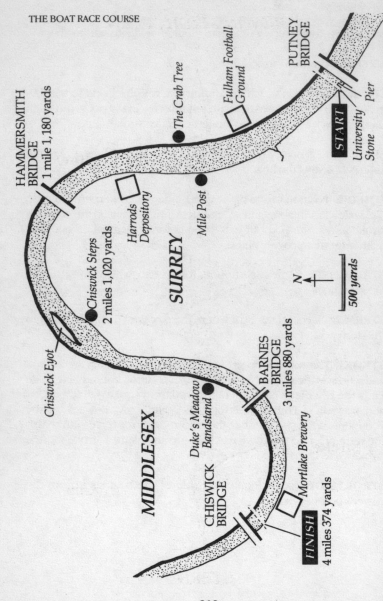

PUTNEY BRIDGE

University Stone

Pier

START

Fulham Football Ground

The Crab Tree

Mile Post

HAMMERSMITH BRIDGE
1 mile 1,180 yards

Harrods Depository

Chiswick Steps
2 miles 1,020 yards

SURREY

Chiswick Eyot

N

500 yards

Duke's Meadow Bandstand

BARNES BRIDGE
3 miles 880 yards

MIDDLESEX

CHISWICK BRIDGE

Mortlake Brewery

FINISH
4 miles 374 yards

ROWING EIGHT PLAN

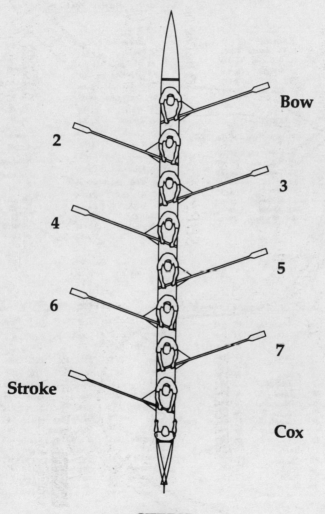

Bow

2

3

4

5

6

7

Stroke

Cox

STERN

Appendix III   Oxford Squad Test Result Notes

_1_

WALLINGFORD

1. Diserens 15.42 (open.)
11. Macdonald 16.22
12. Pelham 16.24
21. Topolski 16.44
36. C-Hudson 17.05
57. Leach 17.52

READING

1. Hamilton 14.12 (open.)
9. Macdonald. 14.46
27. Pelham 15.07
36. Topolski 15.15
38. Hull 15.19
54. Leach 15.35
73. Ridgwell 15.52
108. Ward 16.35
125. Stewart 17.02

MARLOW

1. Redgrave 20.10
8. Jones 21.46
12. Pelham 21.57
18. Topolski 22.16
20. Macdonald 22.20
21. C-Hudson 22.32
24. Hull 22.39
25. Lyons 22.40
31. Clark 22.52
38. Leach 23.08
63. Huntington 24.08
81. Penney 25.04
88. Ridgwell 25.36
99. Gleeson 26.20
100. Gish 26.22
110. Kent 27.21
115. Machin 28.21
129. Cheatle 34.27

HENLEY

1. Diserens 11.58
5. Pelham 12.12
12. Macdonald 12.20
22. Lyons 12.29
28. Ward 12.33
   Topolski 12.43
   Hull 12.58
   Leach 13.05
   Clark 13.20
   Huntington 13.57
   Ridgwell 14.05
   Baird 14.11
   Penney 14.41
   Gish 15.14
   Cheatle 16.12

Concept II: 5,000 metre Ergometer (Nov.)

1. Stewart 15.48
2. Huntington 16.03
3. Penney 16.08
4. Ward 16.28
5. Hull 16.29
6. Leach 16.36
7. Ridgwell 16.41
8. Baird 16.42
9. C-Hudson 16.50
10. Pelham 16.59
11 = Cheatle 17.04
11 = Macdonald 17.04
13. Gish 17.14
14. Clark 17.23 (Jan.)
15. Gleeson 17.27
16. Kent 17.32
17. Race 17.39
18. Chinn 18.04
(Lyons absent)

Maximum weights (Nov.) ($\frac{1}{2}$) = half squat   LP = Leg Press

	Clean	Squat	Pull	Press	Total
Penney	245	300($\frac{1}{2}$) 275	220	155	898
Huntington	245	–	–	–	–
Pelham	215	330($\frac{1}{2}$) 298	186	186	885
Stewart	205	585($\frac{1}{2}$) 315	198	160	878
Leach	215	286($\frac{1}{2}$) 258	198	190	861
Macdonald	220	260	200	175	855
Clark (1986)	195	212	202	215	824
Gish	175	335($\frac{1}{2}$) 307	162	182	822
Hull	170	520(LP) 280	174	180	804
C-Hudson	215	470(LP) 253	165	165	798
Ward	205	286($\frac{1}{2}$) 258	170	160	793
Cheatle	182	383(LP) 206	175	160	723
Gleeson	166	395(LP) 213	175	154	708
Ridgwell	163	405(LP) 219	162	150	694
Baird	163	320(LP) 173	170	140	646
Lyons	175	310(LP) 167	162	110	614

OXFORD

1. Macdonald 8·11
2. Pelham (bank) 8·13
3. Ward 8·26
4. C-Hudson 8·32
5. Hull 8·32·5
6 Clark 8·34
7 Leach 8·46
8 Ridgewell 8·58
9. Chinn 9·14
10 Baird 9·16
11 Penney 9·27
12 Gleason 9·27
13 Huntington 9·31
  (Chin - lost 3/4 min)
14 Cheatle 9·38
15 Stewart 9·44
16 Race 9·50
No race: Lyons, Gish, Kent

PAIRS HEAD

1. Bedford   13·22 (2-)
5. T.S.S.   13·33 (2+)
14 Macdonald } 13·47 (2-)
   & Ward
18 Pelham }   13·47 (2-)
   Gleason
30 Mochin }   14·08 (2-)
   Giles
31 C-Hudson } 14·09 (2+)
   Stewart

FOURS HEAD

1. Nott'm 13·42 (Q)
7 Reading 14·17 (4-)
14 Cambridge 14·27 (4+)
15 Cambridge 14·29 (4-)
18 Oxford 14·32 (4-)
(Hull, Macdonald, Hudson
  Huntington.)
20 Cambridge 14·33 (4-)
28 Oxford 14·43 (4+)
(Leach, Clark, Lyons, Penny)
44 Oxford 14·55 (4+)
(Stewart, Pelham, Gish,
  Baird)
63. Oxford 15·03 (4+)
86 Oxford 15·17 (4+)
114 Oxford 15·27 (4+)

Bench Test (R = restricted compression)
12·1·87

1. Huntington   102
2. Roberts (R)   101
3= Lyons (R)   100
3= Hull (R)   100
5 Pelham (R)   99
6 Ridgewell (R) 96
7= Stewart   95
7= Macdonald   95
9 Kent   86
10= Cheatle   85
10= C-Hudson   85
12 = Clark   84
12 = Chinn   84
14= Gleason (R) 81
14= Ward (R)   81
16 Race   80
17 Hill (R)   79
Gish, Baird, Penney ill.

Circuit Test - 2 x 20 reps. 12·87 - 7ex's.

1. Macdonald   6·45
2. Hull   6·47
3= Ward   7·21
3= Lyons   7·21
5 Cheatle   7·40
6 Huntington   7·45
7 C-Hudson   7·49
8. Pelham   7·52
9. Gish   8·13
10. Kent   8·22
11 Hill   8·26
12 Stewart   8·45
13 Roberts   8·56
14 Baird   9·27
15 Chinn   9·39
16 Clark   9·51
17 Race   9·52
18 Ridgewell   10·17
19 Gleason   10·22

2 x 20 reps.
RUN - 4·1·86

1. Ridgewell 20·04
2. Pelham   20·14
3. Kent   20·29
4. Cheatle   20·39
5. C-Hudson   20·43
6. Huntington 20·56
7. Ward   21·24
8. Race   21·24
9. Stewart   21·36
10. Hull   22·08
11 Chinn   22·09
12 Macdonald 23·21
13 Roberts   23·26
14 Hill   23·54
15 Gleason   24·55
Lyons, Penney, Gish, Clark
Baird - absent.

2.

LONDON ERGOMETER - Jan.

		metres	seconds	strokes	Av. metres per min	Av Power per min	Av str. length	Energy	Average Rating
A/	1. Penney	418.1	120	248	59.73	3.48	1.69	207.9	35.4 S
	2. Stewart	396.9	120	233	56.7	3.31	1.7	187.7	33.3 S
	3. Macdonald	399.6	126	225	57.1	3.17	1.78	181	32.1 S
	4. Cheatle (est)	426.1	140	235	59.1	2.96	1.76	174.9	33.5 S
	5. Lyons	391.6	129	229	55.9	3.04	1.71	169.9	32.7 B
	6. Pelham	386.7	126	236	55.2	3.07	1.65	169.5	33.7 B
	7. Huntington	400.9	136	225	57.27	2.95	1.78	168.95	32 S
	8. Gleason	406.4	140	236	58.1	2.9	1.72	168.49	33.7 S
	9. Gish	410.5	145	238	58.6	2.53	1.72	165.8	34 S
	10. Hull	385.2	128	229	55	3.01	1.68	165.5	32.7 B
	11. Ward	383	127	216	54.7	3.02	1.77	165	30.9 B
	12. C. Hudson	416	153	249	59	2.72	1.67	161.6	35.6 B
	13. Clark (est)	380(343.8)	131	225	54.2	2.9	1.69	157(163.5)	32 S
	14. Race	365	127	222	52.14	2.87	1.64	149.9	31.7 B
	15. Kent	371.9	142	211	53.13	2.62	1.76	1.39.14	30 S
	16. Ridgewell(x)	361.3	137	234	51.6	2.64	1.54	136.19	33.4 B
	17. Chinn	359.7	142	224	51.39	2.53	1.61	130.17	32 S
B/	1. Macdonald	419.6	130	238	59.9	3.22	1.76	193.5	34 S
	2. Huntington(x)(est)	406(412)	125	227	58(50.8)	3.25	1.79	188.5	32.4 S
	3. Cheatle	398.6	123	226	56.9	3.24	1.76	184.4	32.3 S
	4. Stewart	398.4	126	244	56.9	3.16	1.63	179.95	34.9 S
	5. Ward	395.9	127	226	56.6	3.12	1.75	176.6	32.3 B
	6. Ridgewell	401.3	133	250	57.3	3.02	1.61	173.1	36.7 B
	7. Clark	394.7	136	233	56.4	2.9	1.69	163.6	33.3 B
	8. Kent	401.8	141	240	57.4	2.85	1.68	163.6	34.3 S
	9. Race	379.2	126	224	54.2	3.01	1.69	163.14	32 B
	10. Roberts (est)	380.3(395)	127	234	54.55	2.99	1.65	162.5	34 B
	11. Gleason	374.6	124	236	53.5	3.	1.59	161.6	33.7 S
	12. Hull	388.9	135	243	55.6	2.88	1.6	160.1	34.7 B
	13. Gish	402.4	148	234	57.49	2.72	1.72	154.4	33.4 S
	14. Pelham	377.7	130	235	53.9	2.9	1.62	154.3	33.6 B
	15. Lyons	376.2	130	229	53.8	2.89	1.62	152.3	33.6 B
	16. C. Hudson	392	144	229	56	2.72	1.71	152.3	32.7 B
	17. Chinn	376.7	134	228	53.8	2.81	1.65	151.2	32.6 S
	18. Baird (1st go)	379.8	137	229	54.3	2.77	1.66	150.4	32.6 B.

Penney ill. est = metres slipped upwards. Result extrapolated from metre readings per minute.
x = pressure slid up 2 points
NB = bow side readings show higher resistance than stroke side, so rankings only applicable to candidates on same side.

Seat Racing - Thorpe Dec 13-15 : 4½ min

Hull bt Leach 3L
Gleason bt Gish 2½L
Pelham bt Ward 1¼L (-¼ crab)

Gleason bt Gish ½L
Hull bt Pelham ¾L
Ward bt Leach 3L.

Stewart bt Gleason 1¼L
C-Hudson bt Pelham 1L
Ward bt Baird 1¾L

Huntington bt Stewart 1½L
Ward bt Baird 1¼L.

Stewart bt Macdonald ⅔L
Pelham bt Ward 7/12L

Penney d/heat Stewart
C-Hudson bt Hull 1/12 (level)

(conditions good.)

Seat Racing - Putney & Henley
Jan. 1987

Putney to Hammersmith 8½ min
(ratings varied 1-2 pips. Water rough)
C-Hudson bt Lyons 1½L (4 secs)

Henley : 7mins

Ward bt Pelham 2L.
(Pelham stretcher loose + ill)

Clark bt Macdonald - CVS (½L)
(Penney crew 1 pip higher until
last min - Gleason then 4 pips
higher). At 6mins - ½L.

Clark & Ward swap sides.

C-Hudson bt Clark 1½L.
(NB. Two oarsmen changed
sides in same boat. Unsatisfactory)

Isis seat Racing.

Chinn bt Roberts - 3⅓L
Roca bt Hill 3½L
Ridgewell bt Baird ¾L

Roca d/heat Baird
Cheatle bt Kent ½L.

Chinn bt Kent 1¼L.

315

Appendix IV
President's summary of test results for Captains' meeting

PRESIDENT'S SUMMARY OF TEST RESULTS

The following numbers refer to places taken in team tests. The first numbers
listed refer to the places taken in tests of the entire squad. The numbers
given in parentheses refer to the relative places taken within the Blue Boat
plus Chris Clarke.

Name	Sculling	Weights	Concept Erg	Electronic Erg	Circuits	Bench Row	Average of Places Finished[a]
Hunting-	8 (6)			7(5)			
ton	8 (6)	2(2)	2(2)	2(2)	6(5)	1(1)	5.4(4)
	13(7)						
	4(3)			10(6)			
Hull	5(4)	9(6)	5(5)	12(6)	2(2)	3(3)	6.1(4.3)
	5(4)						
	9(7)			1(1)			
Penney	11(7)	1(1)	3(3)	Absent	Absent	Absent	6(4.2)
	11(6)						
	5(4)			5(4)			
Lyons	3(2)	16(9)	Absent	15(7)	3(3)	3(2)	7.1(4.4)
	Absent						
	Absent			2(2)			
Stewart	Absent	4(3)	1(1)	4(3)	12(7)	7(5)	6.4(4.1)
	15(8)						
	3(2)			12(8)			
Hudson	Absent	10(7)	9(6)	16(8)	7(6)	10(6)	8.9(5.8)
	4(3)						
Mac-	2(1)			3(3)			
donald	2(1)	6(4)	12(7)	1(1)	1(1)	7(4)	3.9(2.6)
	1(1)						
	Absent			11(7)			
Ward	4(3)	11(8)	4(4)	5(4)	3(3)	14(8)	6.9(4.9)
	3(2)						
	6(5)			13[6],			9.8[9].[d]
Clarke	7(5)	7(5)	14(8)[b]	(9[5])[c]	16(8)	12(7)	(6.3[5.9])
	6(5)	(1975/6)		7(5)			

[a]These averages are obviously skewed by multiple trials and the absences of
rowers in some tests. They are included only as a rough indicator of overall
performance in these tests.

[b]Team tested on 9 December, Clarke tested in January.

[c]Two different scores for first trial due to problems with meter.

[d]Two different scores due to problem with Electronic Erg in first trial.

INDEX

For reference to individual races, see under 'Boat Race'

Index